National Dance

Margaret Allenby-Jaffé

THE CROWOOD PRESS

First published in 2006 by
The Crowood Press Ltd
Ramsbury, Marlborough
Wiltshire SN8 2HR

www.crowood.com

British Library Cataloguing-in-Publication Data
A catalogue record for this book is available from the British Library.

ISBN 1 86126 781 9
EAN 978 1 86126 781 8

Dedication
To my husband, without whose unfailing support none of this could have come to fruition.

Acknowledgements
 With grateful thanks for knowledge so generously shared over the years: Håkan Andersson, Egil Bakka of Trondheim University, Dr Jan Petter Blom of Bergen University, Maria Matilde Ferraz Péreira Viana Côrte-Real, Donna Isabel Maria Calejo, Hans Deibel, Daniel Dost, Jean and Danielle Duc-Martin, Femke Van Doorn-Las, the Universities of Amsterdam and Groningen, the directors of Het-Nederlands Openlucht Museum, the directors of the National Museum Copenhagen, Bjørn and May Engebretsen, Lief Epel, Jean-François Gueganno, Roberto Diez Gutiérrez, Bo Godsk, Carmen and Miguel Ramos Garćia, Nicole Houillion, Dr Ben and Gena Hartman, Jaap and Maryella Van Der Hout, Johani and Sari Heinkila, Cliff Jones, Jens Skjold Jensen, Claus Jorgensen, Thomas and Lotta Karlson, Kemdalch Elsche Korf-Schroder, Raymond-Ives Martinez, Kathy Mitchell, Jan and Wouda Minet, Esther Nielsen, Theo and Elly Olderaan, Rómulo Do Patrocinio, Gunnar and Siv Persson, Svend and Lisbeth Sandkvist, Verenice Strumia, Agnes Svenningsen, Henry Sjöberg of Dansmuseet, Stockholme, Flemming and Henny Thomsen, Hemming Urup of the University of Copenhagen, Ove and Else Viberfeldt, Jan Visser, Otto Zaagsma and, in particular, to Robert Harrold for unceasing support and advice. To Heather Rees for technical assistance, photographic work by Nigel Allenby Jaffé, Lucy Kaupe, Robert Harrold, Richard Dixon Phillip, Dorothy Marchall and Amy Addison. To Amy Addison for proof reading and especially to Stephanie and Richard Dixon Phillip for undertaking the entire typescript.

Typefaces used: Photina MT (main text); ITC Cheltenham Bold Condensed (headings).

Typeset and designed by
D & N Publishing, Lambourn Woodlands, Berkshire.

Printed and bound in Malaysia by Alden Press.

CONTENTS

INTRODUCTION

WHAT DO WE MEAN BY NATIONAL DANCE?

The publishers, in their wisdom, have selected the name *National Dance* for this book. This is a title that can mean many things to many people, but most importantly, something to everyone. So what exactly do we mean by national dance, and what explanation can we offer to those outside the dance fraternity who may never have heard of it? The name, to most people, is evocative of countries as we see them in the twenty-first century, with political boundaries already firmly drawn, regardless of earlier ethnic and tribal groupings. It is the name most commonly used by dance teachers and students when referring to dances in which the music and costume are representative of a specific country as seen today, and the steps are drawn from a vocabulary associated with that country. It is used to name the classes that offer this type of work in dance competitions and, because of this rather ambiguous title, it could open the door to a steady dilution of genuine material – after all, the overall title 'French Dancing' can hardly apply to every aspect of the dance of the largest country in Europe – approximately 550,000km², about twice the size of the UK and with a population of some 57.6 million people who, even today, between them speak several different languages. It would pose a more truthful title for a book with many different chapters, and now with the national curriculum introducing dance into educational schools, national dance is the term used to describe the dances from different countries about which the children may be learning. It is, however, very gratifying to note that in many cases the dance is being taught in conjunction with cross-curricular activities and so is taking its place as a truly educational subject. The English

Folk Dance and Song Society are already producing some excellent project books that help the children to set the dance in its true perspective and to learn from it so much of what it can tell us about the culture of so many different countries. But what of the other titles that come readily to mind, such as traditional dance, folk dance, ritual, character? How do they relate to this form of dance and in what way do they offer a valid comment and lay their claim to correct description? Traditional dance and folk dance seem to be saying the same thing, but we can perhaps propose one vital difference. If a child grows up in a typical village community, unaffected by modern influences, especially the inroads of tourism, and where ancient lifestyles and custom are still the norm, he or she will learn the local dances from their parents and grandparents by the simple method of joining in the communal dances – copying and following. In many a remote Balkan village, one can still see the dance, led by the elderly men, followed in order of seniority by the men of the village and finally the boys, with the same pattern followed by the women and girl-children. This surely is traditional dance unadulterated by input from the world outside their community. If, however, we learn those same dances from someone who, however accurately, has collected them through careful and genuine research, the dilution has already begun. We would probably learn them at a folk dance class and this is what we should now truthfully call them. They now belong to the world of folk dance – that constantly growing area of classes, workshops, courses and festivals where aficionados quite rightly enjoy the wonderful world of folk dance. But, however genuinely we try, we cannot expect to dance through a varied programme of dances from several different countries with the same emotions as those of the village dancer in his or her own closed community. We have brought traditional dance into the international arena where it has a legitimate role to play but, in doing so, we must now surely refer to it as international folk dance.

When amongst folk dances one is found that suggests some specific theme, it is often loosely labelled 'ritual dance'. In fact, one would be hard-pressed indeed to find a ritual dance in present-day Europe, which in any way reflected its true origins, for the simple reason that twenty-first century people can have no conception of what these dances originally meant to their primitive ancestors. We may know the 'story behind the dance', and there is plenty of evidence as to why they were done but, even in our deepest memory, we cannot possibly feel the primitive emotions of those early dancers and understand their basic needs. In our modern world we have completely lost touch with the early dependence of human beings on nature and we have forgotten those primitive beliefs that enabled them to take their first steps towards an understanding of their place in the world. Ritual dance came hand in hand with the first glimmerings of religion. It was perhaps humankind's first experience of prayer, for if there were beings, spirits, and eventually gods to honour and placate, what better way to do it than in dance, which could join together a community in a common bond. We have many records of how, with the growth of human awareness, the ritual dance grew with them – Ancient Egyptians, Romans, Hebrews, Greeks, all developed the ritual into an important act of devotion. Perhaps one can truthfully say that, originally, there was no ritual without dance, which could reflect all emotions, from fearful humility to joyous gratitude. Keeping in step with human early progress, primitive superstition gradually gave birth to more formal religion. The advent of prayer cut out the need for the former rituals, and the dances that had been a part of them now slipped quietly into the people's social lives.

Keeping in step with progress, however, it is not surprising that, with the advent of Christianity, St John is quoted as having said that after the last supper, Our Lord directed the apostles to join hands and dance round Him while they sang a hymn. There are certainly records of the first Christian bishops leading a sacred dance around the altars,

and this is reflected even today in the Orthodox Greek tradition when, after the marriage ceremony, the priest leads the newly married couple round the altar. In early times on saints' days, people sang and danced in the churchyards and, recognizing that psychologically to forbid people something that had been an integral part of their former rituals could only alienate them, Pope Gregory I advised the English bishops to allow dance in the church. So the old rituals were adapted and incorporated into the new Christian calendar and as far as the people were concerned, it was safer to 'hedge one's bets' and not chance offending the old gods while worshipping the new. The custom spread throughout Europe and there are many records of the practice both in France and Germany. These early dances in the church were reverent and dignified in style but, unfortunately, they degenerated as other elements crept in, and sadly we know most about their development from the edicts enacted against them, until in AD692, dancing was forbidden. It is a historically proven fact that these 'edicts', however powerful their source, were never really 100 per cent successful. It was certainly impossible to control all of the people all of the time, and we have evidence that dancing in the church continued in many places and was quietly condoned.

There exists a book written in France in 1683 by Pére Lienestrier describing choir boys dancing in a circle while singing hymns, which points to a quiet continuation of the old custom. One of the few remnants of our early ritual heritage that can still be seen today, takes part annually in Spain, where in Seville at Corpus Christi and the Feast of the Immaculate Conception, twelve choir boys dancing in two sets of six dance before the holy sacrament in front of the high altar. They still wear medieval dress – blue for the festival of the Virgin and red for Corpus Christi. The dance is named Los Seises (the sixes). During the dance the clergy kneels and the congregation watch with deep reverence. This is surely the nearest connection we now have with the final flourishing of the ritual dance in Europe.

There are a few threads that we can pick up in Europe's overseas colonies, where local pagan dance rites were incorporated into Christian ceremonies rather than attempt the futility of banning them. Several examples can be found today in Mexico, an inheritance from Spanish colonization. In Africa there is a striking example in the sacred dances of today's Abyssinian (Ethiopian) church. These dances, which are a part of the church service, are strongly reminiscent of the choral worship of Dionysus, the ancient fertility god, who was probably the most popular deity ever worshipped, and whose influence can be clearly seen even today in the primitive village drama of Eastern Europe. With the advent of Islam there are also threads to be picked up. Egypt today retains some mystical dances; for example, the dancing dervishes, who turn ceaselessly as did their founder Mevelava, who is said to have turned ceaselessly for four days and nights in honour of Muhammad. So we must leave ritual dance to take its place in the social calendar when the ritualistic need for it ceased to exist and leisure and even pleasure, became a possibility.

Turning to our last remaining title, character dance, we can say that the name speaks for itself. It is the product of a gigantic step forward, namely people dancing in character – not for any primitive belief that in acting out what they most desired the gods might be persuaded to grant it, but in the realization that, out of the vast reservoir of dance, we can take an unending supply of material and use it to create an exciting and vastly entertaining theatrical performance. Here we have now come to a generation of dancers who are trained in basic techniques and who are drawing on the overall vocabulary of traditional dance and using the material choreographically. So – character speaks for itself, whether in childrens' competition dances or on the august stages of the world, where the great classical ballets each present their own selection of character dances, in which music and costume have become easily recognizable to us. It would be a brave and even somewhat foolish person who would try to create one name to describe all the different facets of this wonderful heritage of dance. Sufficient that each to his own – we select the material relevant to our needs and name it as we see it, perhaps remembering that dance can open up for us the great encyclopaedia of the history of humankind. So now let us look from whence it came and how it grew into the national dance of today.

PART ONE

1 HISTORY AND DEVELOPMENT

At the end of the last Ice Age, 12,000 years ago, northern and central Europe was more or less a blank space waiting for future colonists to fill in the map. With the gradual improvement in the climate, it did not take long for the first exploratory expeditions to be followed by waves of settlers, and the foundations were laid upon which the Europe we know today began to take shape. Who were these first inhabitants and from whence did they come? How do we recognize them through the mists of time and, least of all, attach labels to them? As modern archaeology gathers momentum, it gradually becomes easier for us to peel back the wrappers. Identification is not too difficult as human beings never pass by without leaving some evidence of their presence. The foundations of early habitations, discarded artefacts,

graves and even rubbish tips, all provide clues to former inhabitants. In fact the contents of the latter can provide evidence as to what the people ate and from this we can see if they were hunter-gatherers or agriculturists who possessed domesticated animals. This in turn can point to possible origins.

Hunter-gatherers have always travelled far searching for supplies and moving on when local possibilities are exhausted. Their route into Europe would have traversed green valleys and grasslands where food would be more readily available. In particular, the Danube delta provided an easy entry into the heart of Europe from the east. We must remember that at this time the continent was not easily habitable, and for a long period these early arrivals would literally have lived off the land and, although they left a trail of evidence regarding their presence, it would

Wall painting from the church at Ørslev, Denmark (c. 1320), showing the dance leader carrying his wand of office and followed by a chain of dancers.

be a very long time before we could even begin to speculate on their cultural background.

The ice cap had never of course covered the whole of Europe so there was already the vanguard of a future population living along the fringe and ready to move north as the ice receded. If we draw a line from the Danube delta on the Black Sea roughly through the centre of the Balkans, across northern Italy and through Spain and Portugal, we can safely say that south of this line people were already living and waiting to move into the new territories becoming available to them. Their long-established presence can be evidenced by the primitive figurines and cave paintings found in southern Europe and the Balkans. So already the story begins to unfold, as some of these cave paintings depict people dancing, and figures wearing animal heads give evidence of rituals already established. So the colonization moved slowly forward and by 7000BC the Neolithic revolution saw the gradual change from the hunter-gatherer culture to animal husbandry and crop growing, probably fuelled by colonists from the grasslands of the east moving into central Europe. This required a totally different way of life. People were now dependent upon one another. Not everyone could be conversant with rearing animals, knowledgeable regarding agriculture or the production of the artefacts necessary to a settled way of life, so people banded together in communities where specialization gradually became the norm. Hunters still followed their game, but now not all animals would be killed, some would be captured alive and brought back to the settlement where those skilled in animal husbandry would domesticate and care for them. In the same way others began to develop the planting and harvesting of crops and the manufacture of the work implements and pottery vital to the welfare of the community. There is of course safety in numbers and this new, more secure lifestyle led to a massive expansion in the population and with it pressure on the land. With the need to feed a growing population, methods of bringing more land into use were improved but, in spite of this, people would move on and take over new territories.

So the colonization continued and as people lived a more settled way of life, the ancient primitive

OPPOSITE PAGE:
TOP: Greece, Ionian Islands, dancers from Gastouri, Corfu. The dance leader carrying his handkerchief leads the girls' chain.

BOTTOM: England, Cotswold morris. Team of six men in white, dancing Lads a Buncham.

rituals would also settle down, become codified and part of the community's growing cultural background. While a great deal of Europe was by now populated by settled communities, in the far north there were people who pursued a nomadic way of life, following the vast reindeer herds, a lifestyle that can be found even today in Lapland, and which had its own specific rituals and beliefs. So the slow movement towards what we see as modern civilization continued through 9,000 years of continual development. The metal age arose in Egypt, travelled north through Crete and on into Europe, and stone age cultures gave way to bronze and iron ages, each in turn adding to knowledge and experience, and each creating new needs in the sphere of ritual, as different materials were required for the new technology. Always there was the ongoing awareness of the need to propitiate Mother Earth from whom these things were taken – in fact some of the people most heavily involved in ritual were the early miners. The darkness and danger surrounding their work and the fact that they were literally invading the body of Mother Earth laid them open to constant fear and superstition. According to the research of Violet Alford, their rituals would give rise to future sword dances. Another addition to the increasing depth of ritual was the necessity to show gratitude to the new gods from whom the advancing technology came. Humankind was only too aware of the importance of giving humble thanks for their very existence in ever increasingly complex rituals.

We have already considered ritual in some depth amongst the types of dance available under our overall title, and having looked at our roots and development, I would propose that all dance grew out of ritual. At a primitive level, humans would

LEFT: Georgian dancers. Typical male dancers from Georgia carrying swords and shields. (Formerly part of the Soviet Union now an independent country.)

OPPOSITE PAGE: Typical boy's dance step in Ibiza. The boy 'shows off' while the girl follows very demurely. (There is no physical contact between the dancers.)

have little place in their life for anything else, and the concept of relaxation and amusement was as yet in the distant future. If we could see the world through their eyes, it would be a world in which every situation was fraught with potential danger, and every step forward would initially be hesitant. So dance in any form now recognizable to us, was not an option for them. Their fragile grip upon survival, left them no time or inclination for anything other than ensuring that survival and this, of course, is where dance quietly opens the door and makes a tentative entrance upon the world stage in the guise of humankind's first method of self-protection, more akin to superstition than to any form of religion or dance as we now know it. Certain rituals ensured protection against what must have seemed to be a very hostile environment, and somewhere, quietly, the concept of the circle as a symbol of security and unity was born. Rituals could ensure a successful hunt – perhaps a primitive enactment of the drama of the chase appeared to procure the desired result, and then there must be more rituals to placate the spirit of the slaughtered animal, because who could tell what powers they might wield even in death, and a vengeful spirit might be mollified by offerings made by humans, walking, stamping and even leaping in a manner that gradually, through repetition, became the accepted format. Even today, the true Native North

Americans who have such a strong affinity with nature, temper their hunting with an infinite respect for the creatures that they hunt. Forgiveness is asked, and thanks given. Killing is never undertaken wantonly. It is significant that after many millennia, the dance repertoire of the Native North Americans contains many animal dances, both realistic and ritualistic in concept, and always performed in a deeply reverential manner. People gradually became aware that there were many unknown forces, which must be respectfully approached to ensure the basic necessities of life; for example, water spirits would be amongst the earliest and most important, and as the spirits took on a more tangible form in their imagination, they were transformed into the first gods and goddesses, named and recognizable figures. As human awareness grew, these first primitive deities expanded into a vast pantheon of gods and goddesses, many of them still known to us today. Each had their own attributes, and all demanded special treatment, so that ritual was expanded and codified, and dance moved alongside with people ever more aware of what they were doing and why.

The development of agriculture brought with it a realization of the effects of weather upon the crops, and this in turn gave rise to a whole range of propitiatory acts, some of which are still with us. For example, the French harvesters' dance, Danse

LEFT: Young Irish dancers in a ceilidh dance – very different from the formal step dancing.

BELOW: Norway, dancers from Setesdal, performing the star quadrille.

des Moissons, in which the dancers sing and mime the sowing and harvesting of the oats. The same theme is found in our own Oats and Beans and Barley Grow, a classic example of ritual and dance now a children's game – a very understandable progression as each in turn loses its essential element, is discarded and takes its next place as usage demands. The sun and the moon have long been recognized as all-powerful deities upon whose actions the welfare of Mother Earth and our very existence depended. Sun and moon symbolism still exists in dance today – the wheel of the sun is a popular figure in many German and Austrian dances. In this the boys, with feet extended to the centre of the circle and hands firmly grasping shoulders, support the girls who sit on the joined arms of the boys as the wheel slowly turns. This figure is always immensely popular with audiences at folk festivals and is guaranteed a round of applause. Unfortunately for purity of tradition, this fact has been noted by groups from other countries, and it has now been added to dances that owe nothing to ancient sun worship! In certain Portuguese dances the *media luna* pattern traces the crescent moon, and this crescent shape can also be seen in some Russian dances when skirts are made to swing in the crescent pattern.

When eventually the component parts of Europe had settled into some sort of order, we must not imagine that they each decided to create their own dance – rather the dance was already with them, always an integral part of their development historically and socially. The strength of this bond between human and dance shows that, while so many things have disappeared over the centuries – customs, religions, even languages (for example, our own ancient Cornish language, which 200 years ago was commonly spoken in Cornwall but has now completely vanished) – dance is made of sterner stuff and refuses to go away or be left behind. Rather it firmly 'hangs on', always preserving small clues as to its origins long after people have forgotten from whence it came. For instance, in the north of England, in some of the local dances certain holds and movements specific to the area remind us that they are also very typical of Danish dance and could possibly have arrived with the Danish Vikings who settled in this particular region. So when we look at

our evolving map of Europe, there are many clues to be found in dance indicating the movement of peoples. The ancient chains still weave their way through Europe, and people circle as they have always done, except that gradually the meaning has changed and what was once vital to existence has now, mirroring humankind's social development, become a part of that social life – a pleasant occupation for people who no longer feel threatened and have time on their hands to indulge in recreation.

The circle must surely have been the first form of dance. Dancing round a sacred tree, a vital source of water, a symbolic stone or altar – all these things were relevant to people's lives. Perhaps even earlier, the feeling of security engendered by people joining hands in a closed circle was an important factor in ensuring its continued appearance in every form of ritual and early dance. Throughout history the circle dance predominates. As the main social dance of medieval times it appeared as the chorale – the dignified circle dance of the higher echelons of society, with people singing as they danced. At this time, the concept of instrumental accompaniment had not yet appeared. The steps were very simple – never travelling too fast or too far, and often with a backward step inserted. The circle has always been a magic symbol. Safe within its confines, people are protected from evil and it was believed that both sick people and animals could be cured by placing them within the circle while prayers or charms were recited over them. Today in some of the primitive dances that remain with us, the shaman (medicine man) of the community still presides over the circles. Examples can be found in northern Siberia, and while modern eyebrows may be raised at some of these proceedings, to actually be included in these ceremonies is a truly moving experience and one that easily banishes scepticism. Similarly in Romania the *calusari* (medicine men) still work their magic as they dance round the sick people brought to them. The instinctive need to dance round something is still with us, and nowadays people dance around their maypoles, and in the Scandinavian midsummer celebrations people circle their bonfires. In the same way, early Christians circled their churches, and in Islam today, pilgrims to the holy city of Mecca circle the sacred stone, the *kabba*, seven times. (Seven has always

Balkan folk dancers, performing at a festival in Agrigento, Sicily.

been regarded as a magical number.) In Ireland people still hold their Puck Fairs where they dance around a decorated goat, which is tethered on a raised platform. In Catalonia the shepherds dance round a goat, while in France the dance is round a cockerel at midsummer. This circling of animals and birds must originally have had sacrificial connotations – fortunately today the custom continues without the bloodshed.

By the time the circle had become the social norm it had already developed some complexity. Apart from its basic form, it could have a sung or danced theme – with those who were acting out the words of the song standing in the middle, while the rest danced around them. There even exists a record of the text of one these pantomime ballades dating back to AD1200 (by which time the pattern was probably already 1,000 years old). The words in the existing example describe the movements of the dance: hopping, stepping, turning – all done in strict time with the rhythm of the words. This development of rhythm from the spoken word is found in

Greece today. Originally the women would chant the stories of gods and myths while they trod the threshing floor. Eventually the spoken words developed into song, while still maintaining the original metre. When the singing circles and chains were absorbed into the social dance and instrumental accompaniment appeared, it still followed the ancient rhythmic patterns, which have remained unchanged over the centuries. It is an interesting fact that, when all levels of society have tired of a custom and discarded it, it is often taken up by the younger generation and appears in children's games. Many long-forgotten dances have been adapted into the children's store of amusements – especially those that had any mimetic actions, and the theme of someone inside the circle while others circle around them appears in several children's games. In the same way, ancient lyrics become garbled over the generations, until they now only exist as nonsense rhymes to accompany children's skipping and hopping games. (Another theory related to this is the possibility that if the words originally had some

mystic or sacred meaning, they would be deliberately distorted so that only the medicine men and priests were aware of the true meaning.)

Considering the physical limitations imposed when people are linked together in a circle or chain, it is remarkable what a tremendous range of steps have evolved. After all, a human has only got two legs and balance is always a consideration, but the intricacy of the footwork, for example, in the Breton dance of north-west Europe, in contrast to the different but equally complex steps found in the Balkans, between them offer a range of footwork and rhythms that are truly breathtaking, both in their choreographic complexity and the demands made upon the dancer's energy. In complete contrast, the branles, danced by medieval society, were basically simple, almost to the point of walking or gliding to a sung accompaniment. With the opening of the circle into a chain, the development of pattern could commence and the farandole, the early chain dance, was a step in that direction. Led by their leaders, the chains would travel in serpentine patterns round the dancing space, until when meeting another chain, the dancers would release hands and the chains would thread through each other to reform again at the other end. Paintings of these early circles and chains show us that they belonged to all levels of society, the difference being that the peasant version obviously had more energy and less dignity that that of high society. Some of these peasant circles and chains are beautifully illustrated in the paintings of Bruegel, in which their energetic and rumbustious quality is very obvious. Following the chain dance today we can marvel at the complexity of today's Provençal farandole,

*ABOVE: **Turkish children in a chain dance formation.***

*BELOW: **Boy and girl dancers from the Ukraine.***

while remembering its origins in the simple chain with the basic steps and actions first danced 2,500 years ago. It tells the story of Theseus, son of the Athenian King Aegeus, leading the Athenian boys and girls to safety out of the Cretan labyrinth, where they were to be sacrificed to the bull-headed Minotaur. Aided by Ariadne, daughter of the Cretan King, they escaped and sailing homewards,

15

Hungarian folk dancers, performing at a folk festival in Sicily.

landed on the sacred Isle of Delos, where, in thanks to the gods for their delivery, they acted out the story of their escape from the labyrinth. This first simple winding farandole still exists in Greece today and it was with the ancient Greek colonization of southern France that it found its way into Western Europe. It has become such an important part of today's Provençal folk dance that there are farandole schools throughout the province, where the dance, with all its vast repertoire of variations, is studied and the farandole competitions are an important part of local festivals. One wonders whether Theseus would have recognized any shadow of his simple act of worship in the intricate balletic steps practised by the boys and girls of today – particularly looking at the latter in their 'cheer leader' type costume of white blouse and red kilt. Enough to say, that given fertile soil, dance will put down firm roots and flourish happily.

In looking at the story of Theseus it is interesting to note a very similar myth from China at the same period (500BC). In this story, the daughter of the King of Wa took her own life. Her distraught father ordered the construction of a vast underground sepulchre for her. When she was buried, he commanded that everyone should dance the ancient crane dance in her honour, and as soon as the young people joined in the dancing in the tomb, it was promptly sealed up. On this occasion, sadly there was no Chinese Theseus waiting to rescue them, and no release for the hapless youngsters, but in the theme of young people dancing in labyrinthine chains and circles the implication of human sacrifice is very obvious. Despite very widely separated regions of the world, humankind was treading the same path wherever they lived and in both instances the dances belonged to the ancient rituals, designed to ensure the regeneration of life by the sacrifice of youth.

Portuguese folk group. The covered basket on the floor will be carried on the lady's head when the dancing commences.

This eternal theme of death and resurrection was certainly a vital part of many early dance rituals, and it has come down to us today in the sword dances with their ritualistic beheading of the leader who always returns to life. In the funeral rites of some African tribes, the nearest male relative of the dead man would take his place in the coffin, so that at the right moment in the ceremony he could spring to life – again death and resurrection. Although this theme seems to have disappeared from western dance, there are two dances in which, although the theme does not occur in the action of the dance, it is there in the words of the accompanying song. *Lott is Dead* is found in Germany, Scandinavia and the Netherlands. It varies from one country to another, all with the same tune but with different words. The basic story is that the 'dead' man was only feigning death so that he could see who was truly mourning him and who had only come to take his goods. There is also a Polish folk song with a similar theme. This time it is about a man called Matthew, who loves dancing so much that when music is played at his funeral, he leaps out of his coffin and starts to dance. The theme still exists, however, in the folk customs of many countries, when at the turn of the year it is acted out in the street plays of many villages, where it has been handed down from father to son for generations. The fact that the people no longer know why they do it, except that 'it is the custom', is irrelevant, as who, even in these sceptical modern times, really likes to push their luck and dare to be scathing in declaring their disbelief. Better to keep the customs going – fun for the whole community, if for no other reason, and providing a vast reservoir of possibilities for the serious researcher.

So the processional dance weaves its way throughout Europe today, and still firmly flourishes in many places. A living example is our own Helston furry dance, a processional morris dance performed each year at Helston in Cornwall in early May. It is danced by couples in procession – firstly by school children, starting early in the morning, continued by the élite members of the community led by the Lord Mayor in the afternoon, and finally carried on into the evening by any who wish to join in. Steeped in local mythology it has many stories to tell, the most popular being that of St Michael, the archangel, rescuing the town from a fiery dragon intent on devouring everyone. The dragon has also been identified with the devil, who threw the large stone that sealed the gates of hell into the town, where it landed in the inn yard. A large stone did in fact lie in the yard of the Angel Inn for several centuries, but unfortunately, in the eighteenth century, it was broken up and carted away. It would have been interesting for the modern researcher to identify the composition of the stone and consider whether it might originally have been a fiery meteorite from outer space. Enough conjecture however, the resulting celebration, after the intervention of St Michael, was a procession of dancing townspeople carrying flowers and green branches. Another rescue, another procession, flowers and green branches – perhaps originally another Spring fertility ritual of regeneration and rebirth. We may lose the original meaning, but folk memories persist, and even today the school children wear spring flowers as they dance – bluebells, forget-me-nots and lily of the valley for those who attend the town's oldest school. Incidentally, the town's name is derived from the devil's weapon – hell's stone, and St Michael slaying the dragon is depicted in the stained glass window of the church. And the labyrinth (until recent times the procession wound in and out of the houses, literally in at the front door and out at the back),

Portugal, folk dance in Cidacos.

symbolizing the sweeping out of winter by the green branches of spring.

The winding processional dance is also reminiscent of early snake worship, and the snake-like lines of single people in procession can be found in many cultures from Egypt through the Middle East and Greece. There is constant evidence in illustrations on vases, plates, friezes, temple ruins and tombs of the motif of the procession and, nearer to our own time, it appears in paintings; for example, the early medieval *Farandole of Four Angels* by Fra Angelico, and the fourteenth-century fresco in the Danish church at Ørslev, which shows dancers in line led by a leader carrying his wand of office. Another living example of the chain dance can be found in the ballade of the Faeroe Isles, where people sing and dance in a closely knit chain, following their leader who sings the opening bars of each refrain. This is then taken up by the group who sing as they move slowly forward, with an unchanging six-beat step of side close, twice to the left and once to the right. Originally the song told of ancient myths – stories of gods, giants and warriors, and many of these old ballades still exist. This was of course an important way of recalling and imprinting historical facts at a time when people could not read or write and there were no written records. Nowadays the leader is not averse to slipping in some local gossip when the community's conscience needs a nudge.

The fact remains that the ancient rhythmic pattern of the dance has never changed, and the basic footwork, rhythmically stepped out by a large number of people, and repeated for several hours, produces an hypnotic effect, and to be allowed to join in and feel the electricity that runs through the group, is a very moving experience. The Faroese themselves say that they never allow anyone who is not 'in tune' with them to join in, as it would weaken the flow of energy that pulses through the chain.

The circle and chain are still the main dances of the Balkans, and vary little from those of ancient times, except where folk dance groups, performing at folk festivals abroad, deliberately embroider their dances in order to make them more exciting for the audience. This approach was regrettably the norm under Communist rule, as the impression of happy dancing peasants was a view that the Communists

Basque couple from the Pyrenees.

were anxious to promote. Also, with the more exciting offering of choreographed dances led by professionally trained leaders, the folk groups were able to tour Western theatres and earn much needed hard currency. In spite of this, however, the people in the villages away from the tourist routes continue to dance their basic chains and circles. The dance leader may be the poorest man in the village and low on the social scale, but when he leads the dance he is king, respected by all and questioned by no one. In Serbia, the *kolo* (wheel) is the accepted form. In Greece, the *kalamatianos* is the most popular dance, and at village weddings it is often led by the priest, and the chain is made up of alternate members of the two families. Its compulsive long-short, short rhythm (often translated by dance teachers as 7/8 time, a term unknown to Greek villagers), forms the basis upon which the dance leader shows off his improvisations. In the countryside it is danced on every occasion, weddings, funerals and village *panaghyri* (saints' days) unadulterated by modern innovations, although in hotels and tavernas it can appear amongst the young townspeople in a more lively form. In Romania, the *hora* (circle) still holding pride of place, as it has done over the centuries, includes in its circle those who

England, Lancashire mill girls. A clog dance carrying garlands.

are socially acceptable in the village community. The worst public disgrace possible is for the sinner to be barred from joining the dance – and in a village community everyone would know the reason.

One very important question, which must be foremost in our minds, must surely be to ask at what stage did men and women first dance together as couples. It is of course, impossible to answer this with any degree of certainty, but as soon as references to couples dancing appears one can be sure that it did not happen suddenly and for no apparent reason. As in every aspect of dance development, somewhere in the mists of ancient ritual, the couple dance evolved in answer to some specific need, and once in the repertoire it would proceed forward in line with every other aspect of dance. The earliest written reference to the couple dance dates back to AD1000 and by AD1023 we can quote the following, written by Roudlieb (*Folk Dance of Europe –* Nigel Allenby-Jaffé, p.146):

> The young man jumps up, and towards him moves the girl. He is like a falcon and she is like a swallow. No sooner are they near to each other than they are already parted. He tries to grasp her lovingly, but

she flies away. And no one who watches this couple is able, in dance, springing and gestures, to better it.

This description would not be out of place if applied to many of the *ländlers* danced today in the more rural areas of Germany and Austria. Although the description does not give us a specific formula for the choreography of the dance, it does suggest lively movement, interplay between the couple and possibly a difference in step between the man and woman. The hawk suggests strength and attack, while the swallow is more evocative of beauty and flight. It is also obvious by the depth of feeling in the quotation that it is the result of a process of evolution – it could not have appeared suddenly without a gradual, natural development. Regarding its origins, we must remember that the first main focus of human worship was Mother Earth who provided all things necessary to sustain life, and therefore she must be persuaded, by acts of sympathetic magic, to be benevolent and fruitful. The acting out of courtship rituals in dance and the early ceremonial wedding dances were all performed with this end in view, and the need to encourage people themselves to produce a constant supply of children was of paramount importance to the community in an age when the high rate of infant mortality was such that only one out of every ten children survived the first year of life.

It is interesting to see in the courtship dances of today's folk dance, with their constant theme of boy pursuing girl and her initial rejection before they eventually dance together, the unbroken link between the eleventh century and what is preserved in the folk dance in the twenty-first century. There was a great flowering of the couple motif in the thirteenth-century Provençal courts, where the courtiers had time to indulge in personal pleasure. It now became the fashion for the gentleman to lead out his lady and show her off, presenting her to the assembly, and introducing themselves as a couple. At this point there was no suggestion of a real dance, but just a dignified presentation by each couple in turn. It was laying the foundations for a recognized code of courtly, chivalrous behaviour. However, we can conclude that the spectators were gradually drawn in, and with several groups of people moving together in a society where manners and deportment were carefully prescribed, it would not be long before the dancing master would be waiting in the wings.

Meanwhile, the old couple-dance continued as before, and thus, to the accompaniment of singing, it continued until well into the seventeenth century, and in the same form appears even today in some countries. The custom of singing the accompaniment is still very much alive in Portugal, where, although there are now musical instruments, the dancers do not move until the singing starts. This is usually sung by a man and a woman, and their 'question and answer' type of lyrics very much reflects the interplay of the old couple dances. Portugal, in fact, has one of the most unadulterated folk-dance cultures in Europe. It has never been choreographed or customized to suit an audience and, fortunately, it is in the hands of a very strong organization to which all folk groups in the country are affiliated, and which ensures that every folkloric detail is meticulously guarded. It is interesting to note that their integrity and simplicity of performance often wins first place for Portuguese groups on the World Folk Festival scene, in spite of the

England, Britannia Coconut Dancers in action on Easter Saturday in Bacup.

Denmark, folk dancers in action.

21

exotic choreographies and over-stated costumes of some of the competitors from other countries.

As it entered the realms of social dance, the couple dance became popular at all levels of society, and while the upper classes imbued the dance with dignity and a strict code of manners, the peasants danced it very much for fun and gradually divested it of any remaining vestiges of propriety, to the extent that the authorities became alarmed at its boisterous nature. So we read that in 1404 in the town of Ulm in Germany, a ban was imposed, which compelled the couples to dance in single file, to prevent them coming into such intimate contact. Both civic and church leaders railed against the kissing and unseemly behaviour indulged in by the peasants in their dancing. The gulf between the classes was already marked, by the early thirteenth century, and the two opposing approaches to the same basic dance would continue for some considerable time, with the upper classes and refined court circles pursuing their highly mannered interpretation. While they despised and disliked the unseemly behaviour that went hand-in-hand with the dancing of the lower classes, feelings were reciprocated, and the peasants scorned and made fun of the aristocratic way of dancing. There is a reference from Magdeburg in Germany in 1235 to the dance of the aristocrats; telling us that they:

> ...danced with sliding step with dainty holding of hands, the ladies in their long trains with their fluttering eye-lashes and hovering smiles on their lips.

It was all too much for the rough-and-ready peasants. They much preferred their own rollicking and uninhibited dancing.

Soon, however, there was to appear a third interpretation, a middle way that eventually would become the strongest and most widely followed. By the beginning of the fifteenth century, a burgher middle class began to assert itself on the social order, beginning in Italy and Flanders and

Girls from northern Cyprus dancing at Billingham International Folk Festival.

gradually spreading throughout Europe. It absorbed into its ranks members of both classes, above and below, and with the new blood, a new form of dance appeared, which took into it the qualities of both of the former opposing styles, uniting the dignified processional of the court with the lively rustic dance of the peasants. So the new middle-class dance had two parts: the fore dance, based on the old dignified dance of the aristocracy with its

deference to social standing in its processions; and the after dance, which had all the elements of the peasants' dance, with lively turning and springing steps. Firm evidence of the dignified gliding procession followed by an energetic leaping dance can be found in an early quotation, which tells us, 'Lightly the dancers did the glide, and afterwards the leap'. And the pattern of a calm, slow, preliminary dance, followed by a lively and much quicker, second part, is followed by many European countries up to the present day. By the fifteenth century, it had grown in popularity with both middle and upper classes, and its chief and unusual characteristic was its lack of any particular choreography or even basic arrangement of steps. The fore or basse dance consisted of very simple steps and bows with the accent on a calm and dignified presentation, and relied entirely upon the inventive skills of the master of ceremonies. The after dance was given over to the more exuberant efforts of the younger dancers and over the centuries would see the emergence of many dance forms still with us today. One of the earliest forms of the after dance was the *saltarello* – a gay, leaping dance, with a strong flirtation motif, which was the basis of the tarantella which is still danced in Italy today and, indeed, is now accepted as the national dance of Italy. There is also the *sardana*, which is very much alive in Catalonia. The step throughout the dance never varies, but after a lengthy and dignified beginning, the rhythm doubles in speed and the basic step becomes more energetic and is danced with more

ABOVE: Romania, couple from the region of Transylvania.

RIGHT: Procession at a Central European folk festival.

23

elevation. A classic example of the fore and after dance is found in Hungary, where the slow *lasser* is followed by the lively *frisse*. This last example has been perpetuated in the music of Brahms, who followed this form in his Hungarian dances composed for piano in the nineteenth century.

Dances and particularly rhythms are seldom permanently static. Each generation brings change with usage and the predominating fashion. So by the end of the sixteenth century, the fore dance with its basic gliding/walking rhythm, had developed a triple rhythm, and as the polonaise has retained this in the dancing schools and ballrooms up to the present day. Synonymous with Poland, the polonaise became the grand opening for balls and important functions, again stressing the social status of the participants, as they followed in order of importance. It was immensely popular in Tsarist Russia and in Austro-Hungarian society, and memories

of it linger today in Denmark, where it often opens the folk dance evenings. Its final flowering came when, as a character dance, it passed into the great classical ballets. The basse dance and after dance became generally known on the continent as the 'deutscher tanz' (German Dance), and through trade links with foreign countries it travelled abroad. In France and England it was known as the *allemande*. By the same route, English and French dance travelled abroad, and the great cross-fertilization of dance throughout Europe had begun. And so, if we say that the dancing master has taught a 'German dance' rather than a dance from Germany, ethnicity is creeping in, and we are now embarking on the labelling of 'national dances'. The wheel has turned full circle and, travelling far from its basic roots when everyone followed the same pattern, national dance takes its place upon the world's stage, and is ready to make its own statement.

Boy circling the girl in a couple dance from Ibiza.

2 THE IMPORTANCE OF STYLE

What exactly do we mean by style, and why is it of prime importance in relation to folk dance? Style is, in fact, the most vital ingredient if we wish to reproduce dance that in any way bears a resemblance to how it appears in its country of origin. Style must surely be the most over-worked word in any examiner's or adjudicator's report vocabulary, which is as it should be, as style is the most essential ingredient in true folk dance. If we consult the *Oxford English Dictionary* to discover the exact meaning of the word style, we find several different definitions, ranging from manner, fashion, method of performing actions or customs, a mode of deportment or behaviour, to the manner of action of a particular performance. If we investigate further to establish the root of the word, we come to the old French *'manniére'* – the manner or way in which something is done and, most importantly, a person's characteristic bearing. This all points to the same thing, and we come back full circle to that most important word 'style'.

So – from where do people acquire their style, and why do styles differ? Most certainly when dance is performed by the indigenous people, it reflects the

Bulgaria, girls from Sofia.

Singers at a Czech folk festival.

character of those people. It might be interesting to comment at this point on a precept of which so many dance teachers are well aware, that when performing in many different dance disciplines, even the youngest children reveal much of their own character through their performance.

With reference to folk dance and its indigenous performance, it is now generally recognized that character is moulded by environment – initially affected by geography and climate. It would seem obvious that people living in a calm and temperate climate, and surrounded by a gentle and pleasant countryside, must surely develop a calm and temperate character and a friendly, outgoing nature. In contrast, extremes of climate coupled with harsh and unfriendly landscape must affect the nature of

those who have to live with them. Gentle landscapes and calm weather make life easier and more pleasant, while extremes of temperature and a hostile environment can turn life into a continual fight for survival. One example that comes readily to mind is Denmark, a country of gentle farmland and low softly rolling hills. Even the forests are light and airy, with no dark and threatening areas. The flower-filled meadows give way to grassy sand dunes and long, quiet beaches. It is a charming and relaxed country, and this is reflected in the nature of a friendly and out-going people. And so, Danish dance has a happy social quality, and to join in with a Danish folk dance group is to experience a great feeling of 'togetherness'. Similarly the landscape in the Netherlands is of wide horizons, with open skies reflected in endless waterways. There are no jagged peaks to disrupt the view, and everything looks calm and placid. Again, this is mirrored in the character of the people, and like their landscape, Dutch dancing knows no great 'heights and depths', rather it has a calm and amiable quality. It poses no particular technical challenge, but engenders a happy and satisfying experience.

If, however, we cross over the continent and travel eastwards to the Caucasian mountains, we arrive at the region that marks the edge of Europe. Here we are faced with a harsh and forbidding landscape. Sheer mountains raise their jagged peaks skywards, and valleys, even if offering a fertile oasis, are isolated from their neighbours by yet another range of precipitous slopes. This all contributes to forming a tough and self-reliant character, and helps to develop similar characteristics in the dance. The men's dances show the sharp and wary attitude of a warrior people, constantly on the lookout for danger. The macho quality of the male dance is clearly visible, even if one comes upon a lone dancer quietly improvising for himself. The movements throughout are a constant statement of strength and arrogance,

offering a challenging attitude to the beholder. In contrast, and in keeping with an eastern mentality, the women play a quiet and more supporting role. Their dance has a dignified and very feminine quality, showing off their beauty and grace. The contrast in style from east to west in Europe, could not be greater.

One final example is to look at our own environment. The English landscape is not given to high drama – even our most spectacular regions are admired for their beauty and not feared for their awe-inspiring presence. The English countryside for generations has supported us and, at its best, the English character is more inclined to a tolerant approach than to dramatic fireworks. Our indigenous dance has a pleasant social quality, and moves along in much the same way that we wish to live – a calm and controlled lifestyle. So perhaps in these things we can see that the foremost ingredient in style is our own selves, and what we bring to our own dances. And what other influences come to bear on the creation of a country's dance style? The very obvious and most important of all is of course the music.

Cypriot men's harvest dance, all carrying sickles.

3 THE LANGUAGE OF MUSIC

Evidence of early human discovery of music. An ancient bone flute found in the Dordogne region of France. In fact, a group of 20,000-year-old instruments was discovered in the Ukraine, which included a primitive xylophone made from mammoth bones.

The indigenous music of a country is strongly imprinted with the ethos of that country. There is no doubt that the language and folk music of a country are closely allied, and of the two, music has the benefit of international understanding. From the simplest and earliest folk music through to the classical works of their greatest composers, there can be no doubt about the country of origin when we listen to the music. Let us look for examples, and this time start at home.

English folk music has a calm and gentle sound, never dramatic rhythmically or discordant tonally. It is gentle, rhythmical and pleasantly lilting in quality, and the phrasing is basically very even. The tunes are melodic and, whether in major or minor keys, are easy to remember – not particularly exciting, but pleasant to listen to, and very easy to dance to. Because of the evenness of the phrasing, the dances also move in evenly balanced phrases, and the preponderance of 6/8 and 2/4 rhythms is reflected in the lilting quality of the steps – never too big or too small, but always evenly spaced. The frequent use of repeated 8-bar phrases produces a similar pattern in the dance – usually 8 steps to the left will be followed by 8 to the right. Forward and backward movements are always evenly balanced, and even changing arm movements carefully reflect the musical counts. Consequently the overall picture is of a calm, even quality – no sudden accents and no unnecessary elaboration. Music and dance literally go hand in hand. Even in the complexities and attack of the sword and morris dances, nothing untoward is likely to happen musically. Rather, they move along together, neither music nor dance claiming precedence. This same construction is evident in our classical music. To listen to Elgar is to be instantly aware that he is an English composer and, even in his heaviest music, it is a statement of quiet strength rather than aggression –

the calm even quality always shows through. Looking back in time, William Byrd, composer to the court of Elizabeth I, made a similar statement, writing in the language of his own period. Again, the music clearly announced its Englishness. Early instrumental accompaniment has supported this quality, with violins, lutes, viol da gamba, flute and shawm, all of which produce a gentle and mellow sound. Even the early drum, the tabor, was never used aggressively. Rather it provided a supportive rhythmical background, never unduly obtrusive. We have mentioned the alignment of language and music, and here again the language of Shakespeare, our greatest writer, is never discordant. It is always harmonious with a flow that swells and carries us forward. At its most demanding it inspires us with a desire to listen, and even when it carries a grandiose message, it falls kindly on the ear.

Scotland is so near geographically, and yet has developed her own very distinctive musical idiom. The use of the Scottish bagpipe produces a very specific sound, which is immediately identifiable with Scotland, and to which no other country – even those with bagpipes of their own – can lay claim. The development of the 'snap' – the use of a dotted quaver at the beginning of a phrase – is the exact opposite to the more usual folk rhythms. In these the opening accent usually has a downward emphasis on the first beat of the bar, whereas the use of the 'snap' gives lift to the movement, and the accent is immediately up rather than down. The building of many Scottish melodies on the pentatonic (5-note) scale also produces an easily identifiable sound. To experiment with this, most of the simple Scottish folk melodies can be played on the five black notes of the piano – try for example, *You Take the High Road*. A combination of these special effects make a very strong national statement, and all combine to affect the quality of the dance movement. The dance in both the Lowland social dance and Highland solo dancing has a strong and carefully prescribed technique, which produces a lightness and controlled upward movement and strongly propelled travelling steps, all supported by a firm non-varying rhythm. The country dance has an eminently social feeling with firm and responsive partnering, and the general attitude of the dancers throughout is to take a pride in their performance. Great attention is paid to

correct footwork, and a well-developed understanding of spatial awareness makes for clearly defined figures and patterns. Even on the most relaxed social occasion, one is conscious of the pride taken in a caring performance. The music never achieves a dramatic effect, rather it moves forward with strength, always leading the dancers on. The overall impression, both in music and dance, is of lightness, controlled strength and virility. The occasional tunes which in contrast to those accompanying Country and Highland dancing seem more suitable for step dancing, have been left behind by the waves of emigrants that left Scotland for North America in the nineteenth century. They took with them their dances and little trace of the old step dance was left in Scotland, but some of the old tunes lingered on in isolation. They can, however, still be found, alive and

Young musician from Finland.

Romanian folk musicians.

well, accompanying the step-dance competitions in Nova Scotia, where this style of dance, no longer popular in Scotland, has put down new roots.

Irish music has straightforward time-signatures, usually 6/8 and 4/4, but has an almost impelling rhythm. Each bar of music, within the confines of the time-signature, is 'full of notes', and the effect is of an incessant forward-thrusting rhythmic quality. This is reflected in the dance, which has a powerful, rhythmic quality – a feeling of non-stop movement, in which the strength of the rhythm supports the complexity of some of the steps. The music in fact supports two facets of Irish dance: the social country dance, which although energetic and lively has a casual approach; and the world of the competitive Irish step-dancing, which has grown up around what has become one the country's most popular activities. Here people dance to the same tunes, but any shadow of the casual approach is non-existent, and every note is made use of with military precision. Although the almost universal use of the violin as an accompaniment, and the many well-known Irish tunes, help to create an easily recognizable image, Ireland also has its own native instrument, the clairseach, the Irish harp, which brings its own especial flavour to the music. This, along with the bodran, the traditional Irish drum, which looks like a tambourine without jingles, combine to evoke a truly Irish sound. One other instrument that we should mention is the whistle. This humble instrument in skilled Irish hands brings a totally new dimension to whistle-playing, and is particularly suited to the light monosyllabic melodies.

Welsh music has a very strong melodic quality, and the whole country seems immersed in music. The Welsh language itself has a distinctive musical quality, and the people as a whole are natural singers with a history of superb choral music. The Welsh harp is almost universally played throughout the country – it is a well-loved and much-used instrument. It is certainly not a 'tinkling' instrument, rather it brings a vibrant quality to the folk music, and this quality is only too apparent in the quality of the dance, which is lively with a strength of definition and impelling rhythm. The whole impression created by music and dance is of joyful energy and a strong declaration of national pride.

For a comparatively small island, the United Kingdom has a great deal to say about folk music and dance, and is an excellent example of how firmly rooted indigenous qualities can give rise to a statement of proud individuality. One interesting point may be to look at the music of these neighbouring countries and to realize what can be done within one bar of 6/8 rhythm, and how its interpretation can affect the entire quality of the dance. We should bear this in mind when requesting our musicians to play a 6/8 rhythm, and be careful to specify from which folk-music vocabulary it should come. All this complexity from such a relatively small area, and we have not yet even considered what can happen to our 6/8 time further afield. Looking for more examples of the same hypothesis, we can travel north to Scandinavia and see how the music and dance theory applies to these countries.

Sweden and Denmark are close neighbours, and share a large pool of music and dance steps, and even dances. Here again, the differences shine through and each country speaks clearly in its own idiom. Danish music is simple and melodic, and along with the huge folk-dance revival, has been open to development. Today it is usually arranged for a basic quartet of violin, viola, clarinet and cello or bass. This combination brings an almost chamber-music quality to the sound, and the lack of percussive instruments allows both music and dance to flow gently. In Denmark, dancing is something to be enjoyed, and the dance throughout has an amiable, strongly social feeling. Dance and music move as one, and neither seeks to take precedence over the other. The Danish composer Lumbye brought this same gently flowing musicality to some of the most delightful ballet music ever written, in his compositions for the Royal Danish Ballet. In Sweden the musical accompaniment is usually the violin, and as the Swedes have a love of playing folk music, there are often a number of violins playing in unison. This produces a very distinctive sound, unmistakably Swedish, and gives to the dance a quality of attack and surging rhythmical phrases. This is particularly true in the case of the hambo, the national dance of Sweden, with its impelling, almost hypnotic rhythm and distinctive repetitious step.

In Norway the picture changes a little more, as the national instrument is the Hardanger fiddle – a violin with two sets of strings. The second set of strings, the 'sympathetic', are not played but vibrate 'in sympathy' when the first set are played. This produces an unusual and very specific sound, and when the Hardanger fiddle accompanies some of the older, traditional dances, the combination of ancient instrument and melodies paints a picture in sound of their native country. I will always remember walking through a forest late at night, the rain dripping off the trees in the half light, and the incredible sound of two Hardanger fiddles coming

from a log cabin where two ancient men were totally engrossed in making music. It is a music that lays bare the country's soul, and permeates that of the listener, and is evoked in the music of their great classical composer, Edvard Grieg. Earlier the same evening we had watched entranced as several couples danced untiringly with a quality of movement that exactly reflected the impelling sound of the music; the men giving a non-stop exhibition of their strength and virility in an improvised dance, while the women circled round the room with a calm dignity. Music and dance were as one, and could only be Norwegian.

The blue lakes and endless green forests of Finland are immediately conjured up in the sound of

Finland, musician playing the kantele, the national instrument of Finland (c.1900).

31

its quiet folk music – a quality perfectly captured by their greatest composer, Sibelius. His great work *Finlandia* expresses the entire ambience of his country in sound. The folk dance has the same quiet, one might say, peaceful quality, and interprets the music with a charming dignity and style. To watch a group of folk dancers beneath the trees, beside the lake, as they move quietly to the gentle musical accompaniment, is to feel the peace of this beautiful unspoilt country envelop one. Finland has, over the centuries, endured the hardships and frustration of foreign invasion and occupation, but it has survived, and the soul of the country shines through its music and dance. Before we leave this search for examples of folk music and dance affinity, there are several that beg for our attention, and so perhaps we must look at them.

France is a country of huge diversity. Originally an area populated by several different countries, it has variety but also a strong vein of similarity, so in some instances we can safely say 'French'. The music, for example, as a whole utilizes only a small range of notes, very often within a compass of six notes, and certainly within the octave. Apart from the special bagpipe of Brittany, (the binyou) and the hurdy-gurdy, so often used to accompany dancing, the accompaniment used throughout the country is often pipe and drum, played simultaneously by the same musician. The consequent limited range of sound has a strong effect on the dance steps, which in turn tend to stay within a small compass of movement, and never travel very far. So the overall effect is of small neat steps and carefully contained figures. The music does not affect wide-sweeping phrases, and the dance stays closely with it. Over this underlying general quality, the different regions, as if remembering their varied origins, superimpose their own special flavour. So, in the east in Alsace, on the frontier with Germany, we find a strong injection of German folk-sound. Here the popular instrument for accompaniment is the accordion, and the fuller sound and possibilities for harmony in music are reflected in some of the dances, which show a broader and more flowing quality of movement. The hearty German sense of humour has rubbed off on some of the dances, and we find more interplay and a strong tendency to be 'dancing for fun'. There is, however, still a definite feeling that, although Alsace has belonged at times to both countries, it has no inclination to lose sight of its French origins, and carefully preserved among its folk dances there are examples that show direct descent from the dances of medieval France.

To look at a completely contrasting region, we should travel to the opposite side of the country, to Rousillon in the south-west. Here, guitars and mandolins bring to the music a strong melodic content and freedom of movement, and the dance accordingly follows and moves with a more sweeping style. The strength of the sound produced by a combination of these instruments leads to more attack in the dance, and the whole picture is of a pulsating and lively partnership. As the people of Alsace speak their Germanic-based dialect, the people of Roussillon speak Catalan, a Romance language, and the music in each case speaks as strongly as the language.

Travel to Brittany in the north-west, and the sharp staccato movements of the Breton dancers, with their highly specialized arm movements, follow the music of their bagpipes in an exact rhythmic partnership. The music has a distinctive Breton 'flavour', unlike that of its neighbours or the rest of France. Indeed, this region in particular, with its ancient Breton language and Celtic heritage, makes a very clear statement regarding its position in the world. Language, music and dance are closely intertwined, and in spite of modern-day geography and political boundaries, we are never allowed to forget that this is Brittany, not France. In spite of its having to fight continuously to preserve its own distinctive identity, Brittany has survived, and the children are now allowed to speak their own language in school, and the growing number of folk festivals are proof of the strength of its folk music and dance. This is so very representative of much of France.

In the French regions of the Pyrenees, the Basque people still play their own folk music, and their distinctive dance (often almost balletic in the case of the men) closely follows the music, interpreting its special qualities – once again, a people with their own language, music and dance. In the far south, bordering the Mediterranean, we find yet another example. Here the dance can speak to us of ancient Greek colonization and, although the music is now

Folk musicians from France. Two ladies are carrying vielles (hurdy-gurdys).

generally of the pipe and drum typical French style, underlying rhythms and the dance quality that they influence tell us that ancient ties can survive over the centuries. So perhaps in referring to 'French' dancing, we should remember that, although we can find many dances that tell us that they are indeed French, we must also give to the contrasting regional styles the respect that they warrant, and they in turn can tell us so much of their origins.

Italy is a lovely, living example of how much music affects the dance and how language affects the music. Italy is possessed of a dramatic and intensely musical language. Its expressiveness is unbounded. I well remember asking for directions to Castelamare from an ancient man who was digging a hole in the road. He paused to lay down his spade, and then launched into a positively operatic description of *La Bella Castelamare* and how to get there. His performance could have done credit to

the stage of La Scala in Milan. This operatic quality comes over clearly in the folk music and the flirtatious and often dramatic style of the dance. Both have a lively, almost forceful down-to-earth style – always a performance, no quiet, introvert quality here. Usually, nowadays the dance is accompanied by the accordion, which can provide the harmonies to support the tuneful melodic line. In Sicily, however, the music is often played on the jaw's harp, which produces a twanging, almost nasal sound. The common use of the 6/8 time, usually played at speed, gives to both music and dance a strong, almost percussive 'two beats in a bar' rhythmic accent. The tendency of the Italian male (many of whom have fine tenor voices) to burst into song, adds to the excitement of the music and underlines the playful drama often interpolated into the dance.

In contrast, Switzerland is a country of gentle, quiet music, and the dances mirror this completely.

OPPOSITE PAGE:
Italy, folk musicians at a festival in Mallorca.

Reserved, dignified in style, quietly rhythmical, and on the whole unadventurous – these are all the hallmarks of the dance in the peaceful isolation of a small neutral country set in the midst of an often war-torn Europe. Protected by its mighty alpine ranges, the music of the quiet valleys of Switzerland reflects their peace and prosperity and does not aspire to any great dramatic heights and depths. Even dances that have been adopted from surrounding regions are quietly integrated, and follow the music in developing a gentle and unhurried dignity of style. The overall feeling seems to be that music and dance are harmonious and quietly pleasurable, but that there is no need to go to excess in either.

On the other hand, Switzerland's near neighbour, Austria, has a lively and rhythmic musical tradition and matching dance repertoire. Present-day Austria is all that remains of the once vast and powerful Austro-Hungarian Empire, where music and dance were vital ingredients at all social levels. The peasants danced their lively and often complex dances to the impelling rhythm of the ländler, the strongly accented 3/4 rhythm of which pervaded the ballrooms of upper-class Europe as the valse. At this time, Austria held within its political boundaries an incredible array of different ethnic peoples – Poles, Hungarians, Czechs, Slovaks, Italians, Serbs, Croats – all were linked together under the all-powerful Habsburg rulers, and all contributed to the powerful mix that was the Austrian Empire of the eighteenth and nineteenth centuries. When a country is rich and powerful, its strength is reflected in its music and dance, and this is true at all levels of society. Polkas and valses were the backbone of the dance, and when Austria produced the famous Strauss family, the development of folk tunes and rhythm into lively, tuneful orchestral music knew no bounds, and the entire country danced, from the peasants in their villages to the social élite in grand ballrooms and royal court. From the assimilated countries of the Empire there was always an input into the dance repertoire, and this was taken up by the two prolific composers of the Strauss family, and reflected in the flashes of mazur and czardas, which appear from time to time in their works. Now a modern country in line with its European neighbours, Austria has never lost its affinity to tuneful music and its accompanying dance, and in the folk dance today the gaiety lives on in lively ländlers, polkas, and the men's very special *Schüplattler* with its wealth of clapping, slapping and stamping. Once a part of this great Empire, Hungary has a strong tradition of both folk music and dance. The Hungarians are a Magyar people, who, centuries ago, came from the east and settled on the Puszta, the vast fertile plains of Hungary, where they became farmers and, in particular, horse breeders. Their music is very distinctive, owing nothing to Western Europe, and its especial added quality owes much to the fact that for centuries, the music of Hungary has been in the hands of the gypsies. In most Hungarian villages, the gypsies lead a settled life, living and working within their own communities. They inevitably have become the local musicians, and as such, are called upon to play for all the village's social occasions. The preponderance of violinists, and their distinctive 'glissando' style of playing, has had a strong effect upon the traditional Hungarian tunes. This in turn has influenced the folk dance, and the music and dance of Hungary today is distinctive in its impelling, percussive rhythms. The ornamentation of the basic tunes is mirrored exactly in the steps of the dance. There is certainly no way in which either could be mistakenly assigned to any other country. The classical composers of Hungary have taken their inspiration from their folk music, and the compositions of Kodaly and Bartok speak strongly in their native tongue. Even when adopted by others, for example, in Brahm's Hungarian dances, the sound rings through clear and immediately identifiable.

There are many examples of the effect of the quality of sound upon movement and how the tune played on different instruments can change the syle of the movement. For example, the popularity of brass instruments in Germany, and the use of the brass band as an accompaniment, brings an almost boisterous strength to the music, so that even some of the simplest dances are presented with virility and attack. This is a classic demonstration of the translation of sound into movement.

Musician from Finland.

Try, for example, playing Kreuz Koenig on the piano, and then listen to a recording of it by a German village brass band. The difference is quite amazing in roundness of tone, and this applies to the dance, where with a strong brass accompaniment the movements are rounded out and strengthened.

The breadth of movement in the Russian dance comes most surely from the melodic content and wide-sweeping phrases of the music. Tsar Peter the Great, in his efforts to westernize his country, forbade the use of the traditional musical instruments, the balalaika and the bandoura, which had always accompanied the dance. If the people wished to dance their traditional dances, they had to look elsewhere for their music, and so they sang. If different levels of voices come together, the development of harmony is not long delayed and Russia now has a vast store of choral music, with excellent choirs at every level of society, attached to different industries, occupations and social groups, and particularly to the army. And so, as the music resounds with the tonal quality of deep harmony, the dance follows with its own depth of movement. Strike a note on the piano with the sustaining pedal held firmly down, and listen to the ongoing waves of sound as they die away. The same quality is there in the Russian basic steps – an ongoing deep flow of movement. The examples are endless, but the proposition remains the same – soak yourself in a country's music, and the style of the dance will look after itself. This is the only safe way to go about this music and dance partnership – watching and trying to copy a style in any other way can only lead to a puppet-like and over-theatrical interpretation.

Before leaving the subject we should consider the overall picture in the Balkan countries. Here there are other aspects to consider. In Greece, for example, many of the ancient circle dances grew out of the rituals that in turn gave way to a more social development, with people moving rhythmically in a circle while they recited the tales of gods, warriors and the stories that were already laying the foundations of what today, we refer to as mythology. In these circumstances the movement reflected the rhythm of the spoken word, and through the centuries this rhythm has remained constant. When eventually the words faded and the movement became social dancing, music gradually became a required ingredient and was accordingly moulded to the existing rhythms. So here we have the opposite statement that music inspires the dance, as in this case we find music added to existing dances, often with complex rhythmic consequences. The popular use in Greece of the slow, quick, quick rhythm, translated very artificially into

Bulgaria, musicians accompanying the Kukeri mummers.

our Western 7/8 time, is a direct descendant of the ancient rhythm of the spoken word and it is Greece that gives us our vital word 'rhythm' derived from the ancient word '*rheo*', which means to flow, and surely the flow of the music is the most vital force in the affinity of music and dance. In the Balkans the musical instruments are in no way a quiet and gentle support to the dance, rather they are strong, almost aggressive and strident in tone – pipes, drums and basic stringed instruments, all very ancient in lineage, and strongly asserting their place in the music/dance partnership. In the case of most village musicians, they tend to lead the dance and set the pace. As they pick up a basic dance tune (often requested and paid for by one of the dancers), they take over the melody and, like the jazz musicians in America, they build on it with constant, ever more complex improvization. They play until they tire of that particular piece, and so the dancers follow. I have witnessed lengthy dances, where music and dance proceeded without pause for breath for long periods of time. I was once caught up in a chain dance that continued for a breathless twenty-five minutes. I did not dare to 'let the side down' by creeping out to early retirement, but hopped, jumped and ran as hard as I could to keep up with

the ancient village ladies who untiringly led the dance. By the time the musicians decided that drinks were overdue, I sank gratefully into the shadows, my research for the rest of the evening handed thankfully over to my husband and his video camera. So dance in these regions, although now a purely social event, has a very different aspect to that of Western Europe, where the accent nowadays is on securely choreographed and carefully rehearsed dances. In the villages it has an underlying, almost primitive, dimension, while even in the hands of the most professionally oriented folk groups, it makes us very aware of its ancient roots, at present unsullied by too much 'modern development'.

What of the indigenous musical instruments of Europe? We can safely offer the equation that:

traditional instrument = special tone

which creates a distinctive quality in the folk music of its country, and this, as we have seen, dictates the quality of movement in the dance, which brings us full circle to style. The list of instruments is enormous, but the following are the ones most universally known, and I would most heartily recommend any folk dance *aficionado*, whether teacher, student

Bulgarian folk musicians.

or amateur 'happy dancer', to take every opportunity to build up a collection of music played by a country's traditional instruments. In this way, the translation of sound into movement will never present any difficulties.

Accordion (International) In many shapes and sizes, and with or without piano keyboard. Easily portable and with a full sound, they are ideal for accompanying folk dance and have become widely popular. The accordion can trace its origins back to the bandaoline of 1822, and is now regarded as a traditional instrument. Unfortunately it is becoming so commonly used internationally, that it is replacing many older traditional instruments, and this in turn waters-down the true ethnic sound of a country.
Adufe (Portugal) A square hand-drum or tambourine held upright by one corner and drummed with the fingers of both hands. Sometimes pieces of tin are added to the rim to make a jingling sound.
Alboka (Basque country) A small horn, looking like a pair of cow's horns stuck into a hollow block of wood with finger holes. One horn is blown and the sound comes out of the other.
Bagpipe (International) There are several types with a variety of names. It can be either mouth-blown or played by the use of bellows. In various forms it has been in use for centuries, and there is even a reference to the fact that the Roman Emperor Nero could 'play the pipes'.

Balalaika (Russia) A triangular instrument with three strings.
Bandoubria (Spain) A type of guitar.
Bandoura (Ukraine) A type of zither. The strings are either strummed or plucked.
Biniou (Brittany) A small bagpipe.
Bodran (Ireland) A drum-like large tambourine without jingles. Played by being struck with a small stick held like a pencil.
Bombarde (Brittany) A reed instrument held like a recorder.
Bomdo (Spain) A large drum.
Bouzouki (Greece) An eight-stringed instrument.
Castanets (Spain) The most popular instrument in Spain. It takes its name from the chestnut wood from which it is traditionally made. Castanets are played in pairs: male, deep sound used to mark the beat, and female, lighter in sound and used to develop the rhythmic pattern. Usually they are tied over the middle finger, but when used for flamenco they are looped over the thumb.
Caval (Romania) A flute.
Chitara (Italy) A type of guitar.
Clairseach (Ireland) The Irish harp. The oldest example of this instrument known as the 'Brian Boru' harp dates back to the fourteenth century.
Cobza (Romania) A type of lute.
Concertina (International) Dating from 1844, the concertina has developed so that both hands pressing buttons can each play chromatically.

Cymbalon (Hungary) A stringed instrument hit by hammers. The cymbalon gives to Hungarian music a very distinctive sound, which in turn brings a percussive quality to the dance.

Defi (Greece) A tambourine.

Diabelskie Skrzypce (Poland) Translated means the devil's head. It is a type of violin decorated with a devil's head.

Doedelzak (Netherlands) A bagpipe.

Draailier (Netherlands) A hurdy-gurdy.

Duda (Hungary) A bagpipe.

Ferrana (Spain) A tambourine without a skin.

Fiddle (International) A violin, particularly popular in Scandinavia, also used extensively as a dance accompaniment in Ireland and England.

Flahutet (Provence) A flute. Held in the left hand. It has three holes.

Fluier (Romania) A primitive pipe.

Gaida (Greece) A bagpipe.

Gaita (Spain) A bagpipe.

Goc (Serbia) A bass drum.

Gousla (Bosnia) A one-stringed fiddle played with a bow.

Guitarra (Portugal) A lute-like instrument. The wire strings are plucked with a piece of tortoiseshell.

Hardingfele (Norway) The Hardanger fiddle

Hommel-Vlier (Netherlands) A type of dulcimer. Laid flat on a table or on the player's knees. The strings are plucked with a plectrum.

Kantele (Finland) A triangular-shaped dulcimer.

Rommelpot (Netherlands) A type of friction drum. Usually made out a pig's bladder stretched over a pot, with a central hole for the stick. It makes a distinctive 'grunt'.

Shawm (International) The forerunner of the oboe. Held like a recorder.

Stringa Di Pan (Italy) Panpipes.

Syrinx (Romania) A panpipe especially associated with Romania. It gives a special quality to the folk music, almost bird-like.

Tabalet (Spain) A drum.

Tambal (Romania) A cymbalon.

Egyptian musician.

Folk instruments.

Folk instruments.

Norwegian violinist with Hardanger fiddle.

Tambourin (Provence) A drum flung over the left arm and hit with the masseto (drumstick) held in the right hand.

Toumbeleki (Greece) A percussive instrument made of pottery or metal with a skin at one end.

Traskofiel (Sweden) A clog fiddle – a type of fiddle.

Txistus (Basque Country) A drum.

Uileann (Ireland) A bagpipe. Not blown but played with bellows strapped over the right arm.

Vedel (Netherlands) An old-fashioned fiddle.

Vielle à Roue (France) Literally means a 'wheel fiddle'. It is played by a wheel turned by the right hand.

Viola da Franca (Portugal) A Spanish guitar.

Whistle (Ireland) The humble whistle in skilled Irish hands gives a new dimension to whistle playing. It is said that Aileann, chief of the Tuatha De Danaan was able to lull the defenders of the royal residence at Tara to sleep by playing fairy music on the whistle.

Xirula (Basque Country) A flute.

Zarrabete (Basque Country) A hurdy-gurdy.

Ze Peteira (Portugal) A large drum.

Zoumas (Greece) A type of shawm now found mainly in the Peloponnese and Macedonia. Elsewhere it is being replaced by the clarinet.

Zourna (Bosnia) A shawm.

These are just a selection of the many ethnic instruments still to be found. They may give some idea of the diversity and yet overall similarity of musical instruments – their basic construction, materials used and method of playing. Even today, our modern instruments reflect humankind's first discovery of the principles of making musical sounds – blowing (pipes), beating (drums) and plucking or 'bowing' strings attached to an instrument (stringed instruments). Throughout history, the pattern has always been the same – from the moment that music entered the dance scene, it has taken the lead and dictated the quality of movement. Even with the advent of the professional dance, music has led the way. Composers have been commissioned to produce the musical scores for the great classical ballets, while dance has patiently waited its turn to speak and, coming closer to home, all dance teachers I am sure will agree that once they have located suitable music to illustrate their chosen theme, dance follows hard on its heels, and the next school performance is well on its way.

4 THE DEVELOPMENT OF COSTUME

We have already noted that the use of the description 'national' can have political connotations, but with the growing proliferation of international folk dance festivals introducing groups representative of their countries, there is a tendency amongst onlookers to refer to 'national groups' and 'national costume'. We have seen that political frontiers can cross over ethnic and tribal boundaries, and in no way give a true picture of whom they represent. So we can conclude that the title 'national costume' is too generalized a description. We may refer to a national flag but not fairly to a national costume, unless, in the case of some professional groups, a costume has been specifically designed to further some aspect of their performance. Where then can we start to look for our costume, the costume of the common folk? For it is amongst the peasants that we shall eventually find both the roots and true development of our present-day costumes.

We first begin to be aware of the existence of the ordinary people through the medium of Europe's great portrait painters. Originally portraits were always of the rich and famous portrayed in all their magnificence. The paintings show the high fashion of the period, with royalty and nobility posing in their finery. However, if we look closely we become aware that the noble Duke is not alone in the picture – the ordinary folk are also present as small figures going about their everyday tasks. In these early pictures, the fashion of the day was to depict a backdrop showing a highly stylized classical landscape and it is against this lavish setting, often complete with its Greco/Romano ruins, that we see the small figures of the peasants toiling in the fields.

Portugal. The couple are wearing probably the most representative of Portuguese dress.

Netherlands, couple from Middleburg. The girl is wearing the bonnet described as the angel's wings.

Easily recognizable in their roles of rural husbandry, they are otherwise faceless, almost formless, little people and whichever country we look to at this period, they share a common appearance. They are uniformly clad in shapeless tunics and leggings, not linked to any particular region and unmarked by religion or specific custom. They could belong to any place and yet these unknown peasants form

the basis upon which future fashion and regional costume will build its mighty edifice of expanding variety of form and design.

As we move on in time, the pictures start to tell another story, as artists, who are in tune with the common people, begin to give them a more prominent role in their paintings. The people themselves are also beginning to develop their own identity, and already the tunics and leggings are giving way to a more recognizable style of dress. Bruegel, in his sixteenth-century paintings of the Netherlands, shows us a very clear step forward in dress, while at the same period Theodore de Bry in France and Hans Sebald Beham in Germany have left us with many illustrations of peasants dancing at village weddings, fêtes and so on.

Although dress is certainly moving forward, there is as yet nothing sufficiently definite to point to any particular region or country, and the everyday garments of the common people still have an overall similarity, so that a medieval man or woman from England would not have looked out of place in France, Germany, Spain or any other European country of the period. Shapes especially were very similar – shapes evolved to give maximum ease of movement and comfort in a hardworking life. Simplicity in construction was also an essential factor when everything was home-made by people who already suffered an over-burdened lifestyle. People, everywhere, were dependent upon whatever materials were available to them locally, and in an era when their lives were governed by strict social strata, even choice of colour was carefully proscribed and rigidly enforced. Certain colours were reserved for royalty and nobility: purple, silver and gold for the former; reds, blues and all the rich colours for the latter; leaving very little choice for the peasants – greys, browns, greens and russet, all of which blended in with the landscape, a landscape that provided the dyes used to colour their homespun fabrics. Mosses, lichens and leaves all provided dyes and were cost-free to the hardworking non-salaried peasants. Fabrics also reflected local availability, and people wore their own homespun wool and linen. Warmth in winter and cool comfort in summer were the important criteria. So, for a long time all people in all countries looked very much alike, the only

Netherlands, ladies from Middelburg.

considerations regarding dress being weather and occupation, and even more important – availability.

With the release of the peasant from bondage, and the emergence of a middle class, things began to move more quickly. As wage-earners took their place in society, independence brought with it freedom of choice, and people could purchase the things that they desired, and which were in any case probably beyond their own capability of making. As always, reflecting their social development, people begin to be upwardly mobile and the newly emerged middle class promptly aspired to the dress of the upper class. They became very fashion-conscious, and the clothes of the nobility were readily copied by people who now had purchasing power. This adoption of fashion quickly became a landslide, so that as more people had better clothes,

there were more cast-offs to be handed down, and as garments began to circulate, even the poorest working-class people began to fit in with the appearance of developing society. Increased wealth also brought with it a new aspect of life – leisure time – and with time on their hands people discovered and developed other skills, and a whole range of handicrafts developed. Embroidery, lace-making, braiding, beading, knitting, all made their appearance, and it now became the norm to add decoration to costume. At this point each community could only look to its own environment for inspiration and therefore local, even regional, influences began to creep in. As all this was happening, the upper classes did not tamely give way to the rising tide of imitators copying their clothes; rather they too looked for every opportunity to

ABOVE: *Denmark, typical bonnet pattern. May be found in several different regions with variations in embroidery pattern and colour.*

RIGHT: *Portugal, boy wearing the* verde gaio, *the green cap named after the jay.*

state their position in society, and the pursuit of ever more fashionable clothes was unstoppable. The fact of their determination to be the leaders of fashion of course led them to look further afield for new ideas, and with increased trade and travel, more often than not they looked abroad, so that they, for the moment at least, do not feature in our search for regional costume.

With more freedom of choice in colour and materials, people began to look around for new inspiration. Regarding colour, they were initially influenced by their surroundings. This is well-illustrated by some of the Danish regional costumes, which clearly mirror the colours of a northern heathland, with pinks and purples reflecting the glow of a heather-covered landscape, and the soft grey-greens of lichen-clad stones. Again, in Denmark, in the exquisite embroidery on some of the bonnets, the flower motifs are indicative of a country full of wild flowers – scarlet and gold pimpernel, blue cornflowers, yellow and white daisies, poppies, wild lupins, lavender-coloured scabious and pink sea-thrift. In less than an hour in one small field I collected sixty different flowers. Many I remembered from an English childhood, but now sadly missing from our chemically treated countryside. The summer hedgerows of Denmark with their veil of sweet-scented wild roses in shades of pink and white, are a constant source of inspiration both for colour and lace patterns. Similarly the flower motifs of Swiss embroideries clearly show the flowers unique to Alpine meadows and mountain slopes – white eidelweiss, red alpine roses, brilliant blue gentians, golden and white alpine meadow flowers – all make a clear statement regarding their origins.

In Brittany, the swirling scrolls of embroidery are evidence of a Celtic inheritance, with the spirals so often seen in rock carvings appearing in wide bands of embroidery on skirts and bodices. Frothy white lace and blue ribbons, reminiscent of white waves and blue sea, are found in many coastal areas, and even folk memories come to bear on dress; for example, the elaborate white lace head-dresses of Normandy carry the memory of the medieval headgear of the Norman noble ladies. From early folklore, people also draw on colours for their embroideries – yellow for the sun, red for life's blood, green for nature annually reborn and blue for the summer skies. This is especially relevant in northern countries where the choice of bright primitive colours reflects the people's yearning for summer in a region where winter is a long period of darkness and the sun never rises above the horizon. The wildlife of a country can also supply ideas; for example, the green caps of the Portuguese cowboys from the Ribatego are modelled on the *verde gaio* – the green jay, a bird that inhabits the region, and whose head with its bright cockade has offered inspiration. Colours and patterns can travel – the brilliantly striped skirts of the Łowicz area of Poland were originally inspired by the striped uniforms of the guards who

Polish dancers. The girl wears the dress of Łowicz, with its brilliantly coloured stripes and floral embroidery.

accompanied the Italian Bona Sforza, daughter of the Duke of Milan and Isabella of Aragon, Princess of Naples and Duchess of Bari, who came as the bride of the Polish king, Sigismund I. (Incidentally, a similar uniform can still be seen today on the Vatican guard in Rome.)

Many things affect the development of costume. Wars and long periods of foreign occupation leave their mark at all levels of society. Even comparatively brief periods of exposure to another culture can influence the dress of the upper-class social level, regardless of origin, as people are only too ready to adopt the latest novelty and translate it into fashion, and an occupying army would most probably bring with it the officers' wives and all their foreign finery – creating a new look locally.

Two major influences have helped to shape the dress that we now recognize as folk costume. First, the constantly changing political boundaries in Europe eventually stirred up waves of patriotism, so that any facet of folk culture that furthered this cause was strongly promoted, and as the storm-clouds of revolution began to gather over much of Europe, people began to seek a political and cultural identity. Anything that could promote this desire for recognition was eagerly sought and determinedly fostered, so that costume was soon drawn into this statement of identity, and any individual development was encouraged and nurtured.

Having established a recognizable folk costume the next and even stronger, or at least longer-lasting influence was that of the Romantic Age. We must remember that the type of dress we are looking at was basically that of the peasant class, and it was with the dawn of the Romantic Age that poets, writers and artists began to look closely at the life of the common people. There was now a growing belief, particularly amongst artistic circles, that the life of the peasant could provide society with a valuable lesson in simplicity, honesty and true values. It even became the fashion in high society, court circles in particular, to dress up and, for want of a better description, 'to play at' being peasants. This trend had already started in pre-revolutionary France, when Marie Antoinette and her courtiers deserted the palace of Versailles for her country cottage, the Petit Tianon built in the palace

grounds, and there dressed up as shepherds and shepherdesses and lived what they considered to be the simple life. This, however, was more of a game rather than an altruistic attempt at embracing the simple life. A century later, with the advent of the Romantic Age and its attitude towards the peasantry, people were perhaps genuinely trying to learn from the simple life. Although the dress of the common people was most certainly not developed to please these observers and imitators, it thrived on their interest, and its development was guaranteed, as was its survival and continued progress in the years ahead. This outside interest from a higher level of society created a consciousness amongst the peasantry – a recognition that they had something that they could proudly display, and this certainly affected their approach to dress. Now, apart from the everyday clothes of their own lifestyle, people began to think in terms of special clothes for weddings, feast days and especially for church-going on Sundays. Eventually, of course, the appeal of the special costume spread and more people outside the peasant class began to affect their costume, usually of course adopting the more elaborate dress of the social occasion. So development speeded up and costume became more easily identifiable with region and country, and even with local custom – marital status, degrees of mourning and the requirements of religion and the church. Even royalty now adopted folk costume with some sincerity, and in Greece and Romania the reigning queens wore their costume on festive occasions. The dress adopted by the Greek Queen Amalia became identified with her goodness and popularity, so that it has ever since been a popular choice of costume nationwide. Its gold-embroidered velvet jacket, tasselled cap and long full silken skirt is now one of the most easily recognized of the Greek costumes. Queen Marie of Romania (grand daughter of our Queen Victoria) wore Romanian folk costume in her efforts to help promote a feeling of national pride and unity.

In Tsarist Russia, a heavily be-jewelled version of the peasant *sarafan* (smock) was affected by the royal family and their courtiers. Regional dress was now so firmly established that within the culture of the community it could make its own statement

Spanish costume, showing the elaborate jet bead embroidery.

ABOVE: **Netherlands. Family group from Hindeloopen. The two children, a girl and a boy, are dressed alike until the age of five.**

ABOVE RIGHT: **Netherlands. Costume from Hindeloopen. The woman's dress is made of batik print imported from the Dutch East Indies with which the sea-faring people traded. In her trousseau, the bride will have nine variations of colour, from the pinks and reds shown here through to purples and black. These dresses are to cover the different degrees of mourning, which are very strictly observed. The man is wearing the eighteenth-century sea captain's costume.**

regarding the wearer. It could show their occupation, rank, marital status and even religion. In France, for example, the skirts in Alsace – all of the same style decorated with black velvet bands – could be red for Catholics, green for Protestants, and mauve for Jewish women. Now it was even possible to identify from whence the wearer came. This brought with it a new outlook, as the costume of a community became so closely identified with that particular community that any innovation was regarded with suspicion, and not always approved and accepted. If someone went to live in another region (usually a bride from a neighbouring village),

they would be required to adopt the costume of their new home and discard their former dress. Incidentally, this custom has sometimes led researchers astray, as the beautifully preserved costume found in the attic of a remote farmhouse has sometimes been falsely claimed as local dress, whereas it was in fact, the discarded dress of a bride who had come from another region to marry the farmer and take her place wearing the costume of her new community, her former dress laid aside in the attic.

This development of dress could be carried to extremes in a prosperous community. One such example can be found in North Holland, where in the village of Hindeloopen a bride was expected to include nine different dresses in her trousseau. The pattern for all was the same, but the colours covered the lifestyle and various degrees of mourning observed in the community – light reds and pinks for young brides through deep purple to black for the mourning of a very close relative. In between these two extremes the colours ranged through shades of light purple, lavender, dark blue, light blue, until the original reds and pinks could re-emerge. An expensive investment when dresses were long and voluminous, and, in this case, made of imported damask, batik prints and Indian chintzes. Another point of interest in this example is the import and use of new materials. Hindeloopen until the Zuiderzee became the Ijsselmeer, lay on the coast, and before the network of roads, tunnels and bridges, which now make all parts of the Netherlands easily accessible, it was cut off from the mainland by long stretches of water that took a great deal of time to circumnavigate. Consequently the people were outward-looking, away from the mainland, and their sea-faring menfolk brought home with them materials from the Dutch East Indies, this giving rise to a unique dress unlike that found in any other part of the Netherlands. The growth of imports gave rise to many developments in costume; for example, the sturdy knee breeches worn by the Danish farmers are made from a fabric simply called 'Manchet'. On enquiry, I found that the fabric was

Danish group representing different regions. From left to right the ladies are from Vendsyssel (north), a Skovser fisherwoman, Høng and Romó, an island off the west coast. The colour and pattern of the men's waistcoat fabric indicates their region.

Queen's costume from the island of Laesø, north-east Denmark. When the islanders rescued the ship-wrecked Queen of Denmark, she gave them permission to copy her costume. To this day it is worn by the islander's folk dancers.

group with the men in their red knitted woollen caps is like seeing as many flames. With a devotion to preserving authenticity of costume, the Danish folk dancer usually insists on knitting his own cap. This zeal often applies also to his hand-knitted white socks and the white linen shirt that he carefully sews – even down to the linen-covered buttons; a shirt that has not changed in shape since the Middle Ages. It is very akin to our own English smock, which itself is an example of how a garment can identify its wearer. The old English smock took its colour from locality, and sometimes also from occupation. So, for example, the woodsmen usually wore green, while the butcher often wore black. Blood stains do not show on black fabric, so cannot cause offence. The embroidered yoke on the smock was very important, in fact the special embroidery across the tightly gathered yoke came to be known as smocking. On this foundation, motifs were added that usually alluded to the wearer's profession. So, for example, a shepherd's smock might be embroidered with a crook. For Sundays and feast days a smock was always white. In fact, sadly, the very best of the smocks are no longer there for us to see, as usually a countryman would be buried in his best smock. After his wedding, the beautifully embroidered garment would be safely put away and preserved for his funeral.

So many small things have affected costume as we see it today. For example, in the eighteenth century, a German ship carrying black felt top hats *en route* for fashion-conscious men in London, sank off the coast of Denmark and the hats floated ashore. An enterprising local trader collected them, added ribbons and sold them to local women. Since that time, the tall black hats have been a distinctive feature of the costume in Ringkobing. In another shipwreck off the north-east of Denmark, the Danish queen was rescued by the people of the island of Laesø, and in gratitude she gave the local women permission to copy her dress – hence the elegant long silk gowns and brocade aprons worn today by the folk dancers of Laesø. In order to 'keep up' with their beautifully gowned ladies, the men of Laesø have added a top hat to their otherwise simple costume. Yet another shipwreck – this time off the west coast of Portugal – gave the local people their

originally imported from Manchester, England. Paisley shawls from Scotland became an important fashion accessory for many women's costumes in Northern Europe – an interesting development as the pattern woven into the shawls was itself of eastern origin.

Historical events also propagated new ideas as news of them travelled abroad. The scarlet freedom cap worn by the French Revolutionaries found its way into Denmark, where it was adopted with enthusiasm by the men, and has now become an integral part of their costume. Watching a Danish folk dance first sight of Scottish tartans as the survivors were brought ashore wrapped in their plaids. The Portuguese adopted the tartans but brought their own love of bright colour to bear on the designs, so that today, in the fishing village of Nazaré, the shirts of the men and skirts of the women appear in bright checks and tartans, like so many liquorice allsorts.

Head-dresses have always been an important feature in a costume. They too can signal information regarding the wearer – most often regarding marital status or religion. They have changed a great deal over the years. Often starting life as a small neat cover for the head, in some cases they have grown out of all proportion, even to the extent of becoming so unwieldy that they eventually had to be abandoned. This exaggeration is particularly true in the Netherlands. At the beginning of the twentieth century, the neatly fitting bonnet worn in Volendam had small, hardly noticeable wings. Gradually the latter have grown until they have taken over and the huge winged bonnets now seen on Sunday mornings, as the people walk to church, look like ships in full sail and are just as unwieldy in a high wind. It is the Volendam costume, incidentally, which everyone identifies with Holland, and inevitably appears in children's dance competitions in England. Unfortunately, as regards authenticity, this is one of the two main non-dancing regions of the country. Volendam, known historically as the 'land beyond the dunes', has very little dance history apart from the basic chorale (sung circle), which disappeared over a century ago. Rather it is a region of song with some excellent choirs. It is on listening to these choirs that one is reminded of another piece of the region's history. When the Spaniards were forced to withdraw from the Netherlands in the sixteenth century, a number of them, having lived all their lives in the country, had no desire to go to Spain. Accordingly they 'disappeared' and in the wild untamed country behind the sand dunes, they settled and stayed. The sound of Iberia can plainly be heard in the singing today and one can still meet a rosy cheeked, blonde Dutch girl with the dark brown eyes of her Spanish forefathers. The other completely non-dancing region centres on the small town of Staphorst, where the people wear folk costume as their everyday dress. It is a very puritanical community and this is reflected in their costume, which is basically very simple: black and with a small amount of embroidery. They are very resentful of tourists who come to stare and treat the village as a theme park, and photographers are certainly not welcome. A very closed community, the people take great offence at their costume being regarded as 'fancy dress'. Over-persistent tourists have been known to suddenly see their cameras sinking gracefully beneath the waters of the canal. Perhaps this is a salutary reminder that we are talking about something that is a treasured part of a people's culture and not a musical comedy outfit. Interestingly, recently, the people of Staphorst gave permission for a well-known Dutch folk dance group from Alkmaar to wear their costume for some of their dances. The condition for granting this? – they must promise never to wear it for dancing on Sundays.

In the south of the Netherlands, in the region of Brabant, a classic example of a head-dress 'out of control' is the poffer. This is a large, nay huge, white hat, flat in shape and with generous folds of fabric hanging down the back. Originally this was a simple hat that signalled the girl's confirmation and as a plain white head-dress was usually paid for with the money raised by the girl cutting her hair for the first time. The hair was sold to the wig-makers of Paris, whose agents have always toured the rural areas of Europe seeking natural unspoilt hair. After the confirmation, the poffer would be carefully put aside until the next important occasion – the girl's wedding, but it was not forgotten meanwhile, as the back-packing peddlers who travelled on foot throughout Europe visited villages where the girls were only too happy to buy small quantities of whatever lace and ribbon they could afford. Small quantities initially, but over the years the investment grew, and as a continuous supply of decorations were added, the poffers also grew. The latest fashion in silk flowers from Paris, handmade lace from Brussels, embroidered ribbons, pearl beads, were all gradually added until the resultant headgear could put anything seen at Royal Ascot to shame, and a bride's poffer was a work of art. The rise in the popularity of riding bicycles saw the decline in the wearing of poffers – to attempt to do

RIGHT: Netherlands. Couple from Brabant. The lady is wearing a poffer.

BELOW: An example of a 'poffer' head-dress.

both on a windy day was a recipe for disaster. Too precious to discard completely, the poffers waited quietly in cupboards and drawers, until some years ago, a local clergyman visited a colleague in England and witnessed that very English institution – the church jumble sale. Remembering the precarious state of his own church roof, he returned home and promptly advertised locally for 'jumble'. Out came the poffers, and he was inundated with all the redundant finery. Realizing that this was a part of a priceless heritage, he commandeered the local almshouses, which for years had lain empty, and the bonnet museum was born.

One of the most distinctive head-dresses in Germany comes from the Black Forest. Here the women wear a large wide-brimmed straw bonnet decorated with eleven huge woollen pompoms – red for the unmarried girls and black for the married women. The marital status of their menfolk is also marked by a special hat and the colour of his waistcoat. The bridal head-dress from this area is a truly remarkable confection. It is a massive construction entirely covered with glass beads, and tiny glass witch balls in every conceivable colour. In Germany also, in the mountainous region near Tribourg, the women wear high top hats in brilliant shades of red, orange or yellow, each colour denoting a specific area of origin – yellow from Schönach, orange from Prechtal and red from Elztal. The fur hats worn in Bavaria are purely for decorative 'best dress' occasions and not for warmth, and so can be seen at any season. Throughout Germany, Austria and Switzerland, the distinctive 'sun wheel' appears. Usually mounted on a small cap it stands up like a large halo. It can be made of chenille trimmed with gold lace or covered entirely in gold thread.

In France the head-dress varies from the Bigoudon – the high white lace conical hat from Brittany in the north (incidentally comparatively small at the beginning of the 20th century, but still growing in height) to the flat straw hat of the south. This latter was designed to protect the wearer from the sun. It is embroidered with flowers, taking its motifs from the flower fields where the people work at picking flowers for the scent factories. Throughout France one finds an array of regional lace bonnets, and then in the east in Alsace on the German border, a very

Bridal crown, Germany, the Black Forest. The decorations are made of blown glass – like Christmas tree baubles.

different head-dress appears, in the shape of a gigantic bow of stiffened silk in either red or black.

Bonnets have always been a popular form of hat – easy to construct and comfortable to wear. In central Europe – Czech Republic, Slovakia, through to Hungary – they are lavishly embroidered, often trimmed with sequins, flowers and a profusion of ribbons, and in some parts of Hungary with a mass of brilliantly coloured pompoms. One remarkable example of laborious hand-work in Hungary is the bonnet worn by the women of Kalosca – completely covered with ruched ribbon and brilliantly coloured embroidered flowers. At this point we are reminded that the entire costume of Hungary is an acknowledgement of how much work someone is prepared to put into creating what must be one of the richest costumes world-wide. The wealth of

Hungary. Front and back views of a man's coat.

BELOW: Polish girls wearing the distinctive floral head-dress from the Kraków region (note all the coral beads).

colour and embroidery, beaded and sequin work is impossible to put into words. On enquiring from a lady wearing the costume of Kalosca how long it took to make it, she said simply that it was started when the baby girl was born and was the result of many years of work, first preparing the handwoven linen with drawn thread-work in various patterns before finally adding the elaborate flower embroidery. Both men's and women's costumes are equally decorative, and both wear high boots, which give a special quality to the dance steps. The men wear either tight-fitting trousers or white linen breeches cut like a culotte. The women's skirts are enormously full and supported by many petticoats. As a costume for dancing both bring tremendous colour and a special movement to the dance.

Peacock feathers are a favourite decoration for men's hats throughout the Czech Republic, Slovakia and Hungary, and appear again in Poland decorating the square white hats of the men of Kraków. Local lore tells us that peacocks were originally brought to the Polish Court from Italy – their cast off feathers were carefully collected and highly

prized by the peasants, who regarded them as lucky charms. The girls' head-dress in Kraków is a flower wreath with coloured ribbons cascading down from each side. This compliments her ribbon-trimmed flower-patterned skirt and the floral embroidery on her velvet bodice. Poland possesses a wide variety of costumes. Because of the long years of occupation by Russia, Prussia and Austria, the Poles have clung fiercely to anything that symbolized their own identity. So the regional costumes became their statement of that identity, and vary from the plain darker costumes of the north-west, to the brilliant stripes of the Łowicz area, with many permutations of ribbon decoration, lace overdresses and floral prints for the girls and the long-coated, booted costume of the boys. In the mountainous regions of the south-east we find in the Carpathian mountains the people known as the *górale*. Here the people wear the costume that has evolved in a comparatively isolated community. Hand-woven woollen fabric left in its original cream colour forms the basis of the men's jackets and straight trousers, and jackets for the girls. Fur-lined coats are worn in winter, as this is a region of heavy snowfalls. The men are usually employed as wood-cutters, and their long-handled axes feature in their dancing. Footwear is usually a soft laced-up leather moccasin. A similar costume and lifestyle can be found on the Slovak side of the mountain ranges, where the people also work as wood-cutters and shepherds.

People living in high alpine areas tend to evolve their own culture, as the mountains act as a protective barrier against too much outside influence. This applies to Switzerland, which, although a small country in the centre of Europe, with French, German and Italian speaking regions, as well as the ancient Romansch language spoken in the more remote areas, preserves a strong feeling of its own identity. It has even managed to retain neutrality throughout two world wars. Switzerland has an interesting variety of costumes. Here the dresses are very specifically regional, even varying from valley to valley, so that one can at once pinpoint the origin of the wearer. Although many Swiss costumes have been preserved over the years, there are also some revivals. One striking example is found in

Spain. Girls from Mallorca. The lace head-dress is native to the island.

the High Engadine, where the revived medieval dress is of bright scarlet with embroideries of Renaissance design. The most well-known man's costume is, of course, the *lederhosen* – leather shorts or breeches held up by braces with beautifully embroidered flower motifs. This costume is also found in Austria and southern Germany. There is a considerable variety of hats and shapes vary from small round pill boxes through to the large straw hats of the French-speaking areas. An especially attractive head-dress is that of Schwyz. This is made up of two upright lace frills mounted on a small cap and looking like two wings. Traditionally the lace is black for the girls and white for the married women, and the wealthier ladies add roses between

ABOVE LEFT: *Portugal. Bride from the Minho region wearing her dowry of gold jewellery. Her wedding dress is made of heavy black silk.*

ABOVE: *Portugal. Shepherd from the mountainous region of north-eastern Portugal. His dog is wearing the heavy spiked collar as a protection against wolves. The latter always attack the throat of their adversary.*

LEFT: *Portugal. Woman carrying the 'cargo' on her head.*

the two wings giving rise to its name – *Rosehube*. A particularly notable head-dress is the golden lace halo worn by the women of St Gall, another reminder of the sun-wheel of early European religion.

With the development of costume, the buying power of the wearer begins to show. In Portugal, where the peasants have been almost uniformly poor, the dress in many regions is still relatively simple, with little decoration and uniformity of definition, so that in some of the poorer villages it would be difficult to give a description of costume other than a general 'blouse, skirt, apron'. Colours and fabrics are very mixed. There are, however, notable exceptions, and in the wealthier regions, such as Minho in the more fertile north-west, the costumes are bright and in beautifully woven fabrics. Here the overall style is clearly stated and colours are bright – royal blue, red, emerald green and yellow – giving a richness to the costume. In these wealthier provinces, the value of a girl's dowry shows in the heavy golden chains and ornaments that adorn her long black silk wedding dress. The mountainous region of north-eastern Portugal is an inhospitable area offering only a meagre living for the people. Here the shepherds live with their flocks in order to guard them from the packs of wolves that roam the mountains. To protect themselves from the harsh climate, they wear a massive cloak made of straw. When the weather is particularly bad, the shepherd stands his cloak upright on the ground and uses it as a tent. The straw is so thickly woven that it is waterproof. An interesting legacy of the ancient Roman occupation of the country remains in the costume of the sea-weed gatherers – a short Roman-style tunic and a sou'wester-type hat reminiscent of a Roman helmet. Of the numerous Portuguese folk dance groups that we see at international festivals today, it is only very occasionally that we find one that makes any attempt at a theatrical spectacle. Rather they remain constant to their region of origin and, should it be a poorer area, the simplicity of their dress reflects this, with the girls' basic blouse/skirt/apron style appearing in a variety of colours and fabrics. The women wear a diversity of scarves and shawls for head-gear, often with a small padded ring that supports the heavy loads, the 'cargo', which they often carry on their heads. This small pad is often referred to as the 'mother-in-law', an allusion to the heavy hand on the young wife's head.

Bordering Portugal, Spain presents a very different picture. Here, if we are not very careful, we can easily be side-tracked from the genuine folk costumes by the proliferation of elegant dresses worn by Spanish classical dancers and the flamboyant array of the Flamenco dancers in the tourist areas. In such a large country the range of costume is immense, with each region offering its own specific variations. Generally the basic shape is of bodice, skirt, apron and shawl, but with many areas showing intricate detail in style and exquisite handwork. In Galicia (north-west), for example, the costume can only be described as elegant – smooth lines and massive use of black jet bead embroidery, while in the region of Zamora (north-central) the wealth of embroidery and sequins is breathtaking in its scintillating colour and glitter. The men's costume generally throughout Spain offers a sleekness and elegance of line coupled with a macho style of wearing it that is immediately identifiable with its country of origin. From the plain black trousers and jacket of the classical dancers, through the three-quarter length trousers, jacket and short cloak of many peasants, to the ultimate flamboyance of the bull fighters 'suit of lights', the Spanish men's costume cannot be mistaken.

Italy has its own legacy of a strange episode in its past. In the Middle Ages the country was divided up into many small city states, each with its own overlord. When riding around their estates these noblemen did not like to see poorly dressed peasants working on their land, so very often the workers were issued with special costumes or accessories. This was especially the case when visiting nobility were present. It is even said that Leonardo da Vinci was called upon to design some of these special outfits. Eventually, as time passed and circumstances altered, the peasants inherited these garments, and in an effort to preserve them added over-sleeves and aprons. A combination of these strange developments has left its mark on some costumes even today. The head-dress most readily associated with Italy is the *tovaglia*. Made of white linen, it is folded to make a flat shape on the head with folds of linen

Norwegian trio showing the contrasting style of the revived folk costume.

hanging down the back. This is the hat seen at every dance competition and is immediately identifiable with its country of origin. Originating in the province of Naples, it is always associated with the tarantella dance.

One country which makes a very positive statement in costume is Norway. Here the folk costume disappeared entirely as people adopted the uniform dress of everyday modern life. With the proliferation of folk-dance groups and a growing awareness of their native culture, however, costume has undergone a complete revival, and now each region sports its own fully-fledged costume, complete in every detail. Norway, for several centuries, was first part of Denmark's dominions and then

belonged to Sweden, and only in comparatively recent history has gained full independence. When occupied by foreign powers a country always looks to its language, folklore, music, folk-dance and any special feature of costume as a means of preserving its identity. In Norway today there is still a strong chauvinistic attitude to preserving all things Norwegian – in particular, the wealth of regional costume has been carefully re-created and is worn with immense national pride.

In Sweden costume is seldom seen today outside the folk-dance groups. Where they do still exist they are carefully preserved and no new fashions are allowed to creep in. As in other parts of Scandinavia, newcomers must adopt the local costume. Preserving old styles, a bride often borrowed her wedding dress from the local church. With this special dress she wore a high crown of flowers and beads. Beneath this bridal head-dress in some areas she wore the 'virgin's crown'. This small silver symbolic crown was completely hidden from view, but it is said that in a typical village community everyone would be aware of its presence – or whether it was missing! One popular costume that typifies the country is the blue costume of Halland – a blue skirt, jacket and shawl worn with a white blouse, brightly striped apron and small white cap. The man wears the same blue fabric in his jacket worn over patterned waistcoat, white knee breeches and blue stockings. The one costume that may still be found in Sweden today is from Dalecarlia. This is certainly the richest to be found in Scandinavia. It is of red fabric, almost completely covered with floral embroidery. The sleeveless jacket is of plain bright green, and the apron is also completely plain – often a dull gold colour. The bonnet matches the dress – red with bright floral embroidery – and is shaped very much like the old English sun bonnet. The man's long plain coat has bands of the same embroidery, and this also decorates the cuffs of his knee breeches.

The Baltic Countries are often regarded as one region both ethnically and linguistically, but they are in fact three countries – Estonia, Latvia and Lithuania – all of different origins and speaking different languages. Estonia, in particular, is of very different origin, the people being descended from

Lithuanian dancers.

Girl from Estonia wearing the distinctive embroidered head-dress.

Finno-Ugrian tribes who migrated to Europe from much further east. Their very distinctive language can also be found in Siberia, and its closest relatives in Europe are Finnish and Hungarian. The whole area has suffered for centuries from constant foreign occupation. Overall the three countries tend to offer a similar silhouette, with long-sleeved bodices, or sleeveless jackets over full-sleeved blouses, and long heavy skirts. A distinguishing feature of the Estonian women's costume is the very large exquisitely worked breast buckle, which seems to belong exclusively to Estonia. They also wear necklaces of coins. Full sleeves with embroidered bands at wrist and elbow are often a feature of the blouses, and aprons are generally either of striped or checked

fabric. If plain, they have decorated borders. A tight fitting cap is covered with a handkerchief tied under the chin. The bridal head-dress is a very distinctive high crown.

Probably due to foreign occupation (Lithuania has had Russian, Scandinavian and German occupiers amongst others), the ancient costume of the Lithuanian people has long since disappeared. However, they have evolved their own dress. In the north the people favoured brightly coloured imported fabrics brought in by travelling pedlars. These were made into bodices and skirts and latterly, aprons. Originally aprons did not feature in the Lithuanian costume but the fashion seem to have been brought into the country by immigrants. More recently also, the old-fashioned striped jackets showing Polish influence, have been replaced by checked or plain coats. A white linen head-dress has survived from earlier times, called the *namilka*, and is usually worn by the older women. It is believed that the *namilka* was originally worn by women who had been baptized as the country became Christianized and signified that they were no longer heathen. The men long ago adopted modern dress, but occasionally can still be seen wearing the fur hats and even wooden shoes of older times. A revival of the older costume is worn by men in

Latvian girls. The crown-like head-dress is a distinctive feature.

the folk dance groups, where knee breeches, waistcoat and shirt are usually worn under a long overcoat. Head-gear can vary from knitted woollen caps to a variety of felt hats.

The Latvian women's dress is notable for the richly embroidered border on the skirt. The bodice is unusual in shape, with a deep heart-shaped neckline, tight waist and flared basque, worn over a full-sleeved blouse. A large brooch is usually worn. A special feature is a high-crowned embroidered head-dress. On the feast of St John (midsummer's

eve) the people wear garlands of oak leaves, a relic of the ancient nature worship, which predated their conversion to Christianity. The costume of Finland appears in two distinct forms. The first shows the influence of the long Swedish occupation of western Finland, while the second is the true Finnish costume. The 'Swedish–Finnish' costume usually features the typical Swedish striped skirt with long-sleeved blouse, bodice and apron, while in the truly Finnish areas, the old-fashioned smock-like dress can still be found. The men's dress mirrors the general north-European pattern of knee breeches, waistcoat, shirt and long coat, although the more ancient men's costume in Finland also retained a connection with the older style, with a loose smock-like tunic worn over straight trousers. The footwear in Finland is often a sandal make of birch bark. The old saying was not, 'How many miles?' but rather, 'How many sandals?', as the traveller would stop *en route* when his sandals wore out and make another pair from the bark of one of the millions of birch trees that cover much of the country.

In Denmark, the emancipation of the peasants at the end of the eighteenth century brought great changes to their lifestyle and consequently their dress. Independent farming meant that now the women were working alongside their menfolk to establish their new farms, and had no time to spin and weave their own flax and wool. To compensate for this, the new farmers found themselves with surplus produce that could be sold to provide money with which to buy ready-made clothes. The local dress gradually faded out and the cash now available opened the floodgates to imported silks and cottons, never before available. Costume was once again on the brink of change. A gradual development in the pattern of women's dress had already taken place, with the division of the complete dress into a bodice and skirt; initially a fashion started by the wealthier classes, by the end of the seventeenth century it was common to all levels of society, and established the basic shape of today's folk costume. We should remember, when contemplating the blouse/skirt/apron approach to folk costume, all too often found in dancing-school performances, that the long-sleeved white blouse in

LEFT: *Denmark. Couple from Djursland. The man's silver buttons indicate the number of cows he possesses.*

BELOW LEFT: *Denmark. Girl from Amager. When attending a funeral the heavy gold clasps fastening the bodice are replaced by simple silver hooks and a black shawl is worn.*

BELOW: *Denmark. Bride from the island of Bornholm wearing her* nolle *(special bridal head-dress).*

Denmark is an undergarment, hidden safely beneath the long sleeved bodice. It would not be considered seemly to appear in public in one's underblouse, unless perhaps when working in the fields in the heat of harvesting. The one exception to this rule is the costume of Lyø. This is a dress used especially for dancing, with a long-sleeved white blouse over a blue woollen skirt and small white apron. The simple dark bodice fastens down the front and is worn with a red-patterned scarf. Broad white silk ribbons embroidered with pastel-coloured flowers hang down from the small bonnet; the married women tie their ribbons, the unmarried girls allow them to fall over the front of the bodice.

Regional variations are now clearly marked and, as in many countries, much more obviously in the women's costumes. The reason for this is the same in each case, in that from early times women have been home-based, while the men have often travelled both at home and abroad in their efforts to make a living; for example, as pedlars, drovers, soldiers and sailors. This has led to an early adoption of a basic dress that mirrors their work, and at home an overall similarity – in Denmark, as in Scandinavia generally, knee-breeches, shirt and waistcoat, with the colour (often stripes) of the latter indicating region.

One costume that can still be seen today is that of the women of Skov, a fishing village on the outskirts of Copenhagen. Working in the city's fish-market, they still wear their floor-length green woollen skirts, edged with red for unmarried girls and black for married women. The long-sleeved blouse is black patterned with white polka dots, and over this is worn a white shawl embroidered with red flowers and green leaves. The checked apron is voluminous enough to protect the skirt, and the white linen head-dress resembles a large poke-bonnet. Aprons are symbolic in Danish costume. The bride wears an embroidered white linen apron as a symbol of her purity, and the godmother at a christening often wore three aprons, symbolizing the Father, Son and Holy Ghost, in order to protect the child until it has been received safely into the Church. The apron is also believed to protect the unborn child from evil. Bonnets in Denmark, as with the French head-dresses, can identify the

exact origin of the wearer and for a comparatively small country the variety is immense, with hand-made white lace in various shapes, and a multitude of beautifully embroidered small bonnets of silk or velvet. The bonnet embroideries stem from an ancient superstition. Originally two eyes were embroidered on the back of the bonnet to scare away goblins and evil spirits. These creatures always creep up from behind but disappear instantly when you look at them. Small mirror-like decorations were also added to the back of the bonnet, so that if the devil crept up behind you, the sight of his own reflection would scare him away. A strange fashion appears on the island of Fanø, off the west coast of Denmark, where the women wear a black face mask to protect their faces from the stinging blast of the sand whipped up by the wind. Combined with their turban-like head-dress it can look quite sinister.

Gradually, as in many countries, things 'grow and grow' and the Danish bonnets developed into works of art covered in gold and silver embroideries. At the height of the 'bonnet mania' the very wealthy families would even dress their nursemaids in gold or silver bonnets as a status symbol – an early version of the Rolls Royce syndrome!

On the island of Bornholm in the Baltic Sea, the bride wears a special white lace bonnet wreathed in artificial flowers. This is called the *nolle*, and after her own wedding it is carefully preserved to wear at any weddings she may attend in the future, for without a *nolle*, she could not be counted amongst the guests present. If you do not possess your own, you must surely borrow one for the occasion, as when heads are counted, the number of *nolle* present signifies the social status of the wedding. In many countries cloaks are considered an essential item in the wardrobe. Often it is the bride's father's wedding present to his daughter. If he could not afford one he would buy her a long heavy skirt instead, and this could be turned up to cover the head.

In Ireland the cloak has always been important, with the heavy black hooded Munster cloak offering an all-engulfing 'cover up' and protection in a wet climate. Here also a skirt could be used as a cloak, and the crimson skirt of the ancient Irish costume would often be actually worn separately over the head. This crimson skirt, worn with a

Irish step-dance group.

black bodice and shawl, was very much part of the Irish tradition until it fell into disuse after the years of famine. It was indicative of the Irish love of bright colours. This love of colour has spilled over into life today with the revival and theatricalization of Irish dress. It is an accepted tradition that in ancient times the Irish had a beautiful dress that reflected their Celtic heritage – a simple tunic-like garment embroidered with Celtic symbols. This has today been translated into the short embroidered dress worn by Irish dancers in performance and competition. Now choice of colour is completely free, resulting in many startling colour schemes. The present-day dress is usually overloaded with embroideries, often trying to present genuine Celtic motifs, but sometimes in great danger of 'over-exaggeration'. The lovely line of the old Irish cloak has shrunk until it is merely a small highly deco-rated panel. The incredible variety and array of

these modern dance dresses, seen at Irish dance competitions, is quite remarkable, the intricacy of the embroideries in most cases matched by the technical virtuosity of some of the very young wear-ers. The proliferation of Irish-oriented shows, fol-lowing in the wake of *Riverdance*, has again taken the same style and developed it in an even more the-atrical manner – sadly moving even further away from their Celtic roots.

Wales clings firmly to its Celtic traditions. Always circumscribed by England, it has clung fiercely to its costumes and traditions. The most distinctive fea-ture of the women's costume is the high, black, beaver hat. This can vary according to the region; for example, the hat in Gwent has a wide brim, while in Cardigan the brim is narrower and the hat very tall. A white frilled cap is worn under the hat – the frills cover the ears but do not show at the front. The dress consists of a petticoat and gown, the latter

looped up and pinned at the back. A tight bodice with a basque may be worn, and there are always several petticoats, the top one usually striped. Aprons may be checked, striped or plain, and the shawl or large neck scarf is usually worn crossed over in front and tied behind. The men wear knee breeches, shirt and waistcoat and a long top coat, usually black. For special occasions a ribbon-decked straw hat may be added.

In England, dancing has been a social event for centuries, and people wore the prevailing fashion. Regional costume has never developed in England as it has in most European countries – possibly owing to the early urbanization and rapid industrialization, which took place at the time when other countries were developing their regional costumes. In England at this period people were leaving the rural areas to seek work in the fast-growing industrial towns, where they were left with very little time or energy to follow their old customs.

The exception has been the special costume worn by sword and morris dance teams. Every sword dance team has evolved its own costume, encompassing many variations in style and colour, and in many cases of comparatively recent invention. Morris dancers generally fall into two categories of dress: the Cotswold morris teams wear white trousers and shirts, coloured baldricks, ribbon rosettes and bands of bells round the calf; while the processional and border morris dancers wear dark knee breeches, white shirts and coloured waistcoats, often with bells attached to their shoes or clogs. In both cases the hats can vary from top hats to straw hats of various shapes. All are usually profusely decorated with

ABOVE LEFT: **Cotswold morris man.**

LEFT: **England. Abbots Bromley Horn Dancers in their longways set (2004).**

flowers, feathers and ribbons. Notable exceptions are the Bacup coconut dancers, who wear white kilts over black woollen jumpers and leggings and white turbans. They always appear with blackened faces and hands, and carry white handkerchiefs, or half hoops. They wear clogs, which adds to the repetitive rhythm of their dance. The other exception is the Abbots Bromley Horn Dance, where the men wear a revived medieval costume and carry enormous reindeer horns of ancient origin. In all these specialist dances there are a number of strange characters in attendance, each in a fantastic dress of their own invention. Apart from this, the sun-bonnets of the women and country smocks are the only indications of region or occupation and these certainly vary considerably from one district to another.

Scotland is synonymous with a large number of clan tartans in a wide variety of colours and checked patterns. Each clan has its own especial tartan and, in some cases, in addition to the designated clan tartan, they have a special tartan for hunting (usually in shades of green – useful camouflage in the countryside) and a dress tartan for festive occasions. An example of contrasting normal clan and dress tartan is especially marked in the Royal Stuart, with the bright scarlet for day-wear and the white for evening. Incidentally, this is the one tartan that may legitimately be worn by a non-clan member. In every other case only true members of the clan may wear its tartan, but in the case of the Royal Stuart, any subject of the reigning monarch may wear it. It was the voluminous plaid wraps worn by the Scottish immigrants that carried the seeds of heather to North America two centuries ago and spread the swathes of heather seen today in Nova Scotia.

As with folk dance, folk costume carries so many clues as to people's origins, and with the relaxation of the old rigid class system we have seen how people were free to make a statement regarding their status through the medium of their dress. Even small things, for example, the number of silver buttons on a Danish farmer's best coat indicating the number of cows that he possessed, while the number of large silver medallions on a Dutch man's belt were a proud announcement of the number of his sons. Again, large silver ornaments worn by the women in the fishing villages off the north coast of Europe advertised the fact that a sea-faring husband had brought back his earnings in a tangible shape.

So many small things, but all add up to progress – people moving forward and feeling free to claim their place in society and to dress accordingly. All this is relevant to Western Europe. In the east – the Balkans – the picture is a little different. Although the Balkans is a comparatively small area when compared to the rest of the European continent, it contains a remarkable number of countries. Starting with what might be called 'the rump' of the former country (which disintegrated in 1990) Yugoslavia, today comprises Serbia and Montenegro. Part of the old Yugoslavia, and now independent countries, are Slovenia, Bosnia, Herzegovina and Macedonia. (There are also regions of Macedonia in Greece and Bulgaria.) In addition the Balkan countries comprise Greece, Albania, Bulgaria and Romania. This entire area has had a completely different social development from the rest of Europe. One might even say, that until the end of the nineteenth century, when they freed themselves from Turkish control, that life under foreign occupation had left no space for very much social development of any kind. Consequently, without outside influences and the emergence of different class strata, people remained very much within centuries-old village community life. This of course precluded the development of fashion, and people tended to be self-sufficient, following familiar established life patterns. This latter in particular, was their chief support in view of their lack of freedom and centuries of foreign occupation.

So costume remained the same, and in fact until freedom brought with it a tendency to adopt modern everyday costume, no deliberate attempt was made to build on their original style of dress. This is particularly true of the men, as they would be the first to leave their villages to look for work in the towns, and in doing so begin to adopt modern dress. Sadly, with freedom from the overall control of Turkey, the newly freed countries of the Balkans embarked on continual wars amongst themselves, until they were finally drawn into two World Wars.

So, in the villages people still followed their old ways and wore their traditional costume, and whereas in the West the overall shape of costume was generally that of blouse and skirt, plus regional accessories

Typical Balkan men's costumes at a Bulgarian folk festival.

such as jackets, bodices, scarves, shawls and a variety of aprons, the main style in the East remained basically a long dress or shift. Again, this reflects the early smocks of people who have never been in a position to use clothing to make a statement regarding their status, or even more importantly their ethnicity.

What did emerge with freedom from Turkish occupation, however, was the rise of a long-suppressed ethnic consciousness. Now for purely chauvinistic reasons, writers, poets and musicians all had something to say regarding their own emerging countries, and this gradually filtered through to dress, so that for the first time diversity was consciously sought and fostered. Greece was the first country to regain her freedom, and is the one that has retained her identity ever since. This could be a pointer towards explaining the diversity and richness of Greek costume today,

with its contrasting and in some cases exotic range of regional dress.

In the poorer Balkan countries, which are only just emerging from centuries of the inhibitions of occupation and continual warfare, the tendency has been to follow the old styles, reflecting local influences in fabrics and colours. The exception here has been with the rapid development of the many folk dance groups encouraged and often funded by the Communist Governments which emerged in eastern Europe following World War Two. These groups were quickly recognized as a viable export to the West, both as a financial asset in bringing home much needed hard currency, and particularly as political propaganda presenting an exciting and colourful picture of the people happy under Communist rule. To further this cause, costume development received a massive injection of both conscious theatrical presentation and financial investment. So, for example, a festival-winning Bulgarian group dressed in their scarlet, black and gold costumes bear little genuine relation to the simplicity found in the villages – villages now so poor that they often remain only as the houses of an older generation, as the younger people leave their rural lives to seek whatever security they can find in the towns. As tourism gains recognition as a useful means of making a living, local people in the tourist-favoured areas are beginning to look for ways of enticing and entertaining these paying guests, and revivals of ancient customs and folk dance occasions are beginning to proliferate. This is a two-edged development, as dance as a commercial enterprise divorces it completely form its ancient traditions and in doing so is just one more step towards the tragic loss of the people's inheritance, while from the altruistic point of view it makes some, however diluted, acknowledgement of the true culture of an ancient people, while helping to provide a living for their descendants.

To attempt a detailed written description of any one particular costume could run into several pages and still not necessarily paint a satisfactory picture.

Couple from Slovenia.

Bulgaria. Village costume.

In the case of a country it would be of encyclopaedic proportions, as we have now reached a high peak of detailed regional development, and in many countries the diversity is enormous. Sufficient to say, in fact vital to acknowledge at this point, is that before us we have a vastly complex picture, and we must realize that describing a 'French' or 'German' costume is of little use unless the description is allied to a specific dance or region. Rather, if we wish to dress a dance we must start at the beginning and ask from which region of the particular country does the music and dance originate, and then look for the correct regional costume. So often at dance competitions one sees, for example, 'A Polish Dance' and the child performs a very creditable dance based on the mazur. Unfortunately she is wearing the costume of Kraków, a region with its own very special costume, music and dance. France is another country that suffers greatly in the dance competitions. Rarely is the diversity of her many regional costumes acknowledged, and all too often an easily recognizable Breton costume is used for a 'French Dance' – an added insult to Brittany, a region that has its own ancient and closely guarded dance heritage, which owes nothing to the rest of France.

So please remember, a winged cap and clogs do not make a Dutch dance (the Dutch do not use their clogs for dancing) any more than a '*stein*' (beer mug) or a string of sausages are the required properties for a German solo. So – in order to further this study with any degree of integrity, let us all become 'collectors'. In every holiday place, postcards of regional dress can be found amongst the recipes and views, and from museums and from visiting folk dance groups costume pictures are to be had. (The former can also usually offer pictures of the historical antecedents of today's costumes and the cultural attachés of many embassies will readily supply information.) Taking your camera to an international folk festival can provide a wealth of material. We have never yet found anyone unwilling to pose for us, and even to offer detailed explanations relating to their dress. By these means, hopefully, we can begin to build up a more truthful picture of costume, and in doing so open the door to a most exciting and rewarding subject for research.

Polish dancers in the costume from Kraków.

5 WHAT BECAME OF THE ANIMALS?

At the beginning of our discussion we travelled back in time to observe the early cave paintings in which our prehistoric ancestors depicted themselves wearing animal guise, and in some cases most certainly appearing to dance. Since then we have journeyed a long way along the road of dance development and have continually been absorbed in discovering what humans did next. Perhaps, however, we should not leave our friends in the caves without pausing to look and see what they did and what happened to the animals. Are the creatures merely a shadowy memory of long-forgotten ritual, or have they travelled silently alongside us and are even with us today? The answer is a very definite 'yes' – the animals are alive and well and throughout Europe, in fact world-wide, make their presence felt on many occasions.

Of all the facets presented by dance throughout the ages, the animal dance is one aspect that has fired human imagination to the extent that, over a time-span of several thousand years, it is still with us – ancient ritualistic elements now forgotten but nevertheless clearly delineated and, judging by the reception it receives from today's onlookers, it still possesses the power to involve and excite. If we take just a brief look at some of these animals in their present-day guise, it will surely point to the fact that those early paintings were laying the foundation for an extraordinarily long-lived cult. Chief among the survivors are the stag, the horse, the bear and the goat, and today they all have their own especial 'stamping grounds', where they appear in lively and virile guise. To pursue their appearances and antics in detail would be to leave the confines of our present study, but for those with a desire to

Prehistoric cave painting from Les Trois Fréres Arriége, France. It depicts the masked dancer named the sorcerer.

71

follow the trail further they should seek out Violet Alford's book *The Hobby Horse and Other Animal Masks*, which contains a wealth of detail based on securely researched information. Sufficient to say that the animal cult has proliferated and that throughout Europe, whichever way you turn, there will be in all probability a fearsome creature looking over your shoulder. I do not use the term 'fearsome' lightly, as over the centuries these creatures have grown in strength with a determination to survive, so that although our modern-day sense of reason reminds us that beneath the masks and costumes there is an ordinary human being, no more supernatural than ourselves, the combination of an inborn folk-memory, and the aura of strength that emanates from the creature, puts us firmly in our place and back alongside our less-knowledgeable and more superstitious ancestors.

So perhaps we should take a brief look at some of our own 'home-grown' beasts, then at best we do not run the risk of arousing their ire at being left out of the story. The animal that has travelled through the centuries in step with our English dance history is the horse and, as the hobby horse, still demands our attention on its special days. The *New English Dictionary* quotes, 'Hobby, Hobyn, Robin, Robbie – a small or middle-sized horse'. Of the many hobby horses, which annually make their appearance throughout the country, the two most widely known are the Old Hoss of Padstow and the Minehead Horse, both from the West Country, a region which has a long and complex history of horses and the part they have played in local ritual. In Padstow there are now two horses. The original 'Old Hoss' lives in his stable behind the Golden Lion Inn, and it is said that at end of the Great War, the local women carried him out, as there were no men left to carry him and a break with tradition was unthinkable. This Old Hoss is made up of a large wooden hoop covered with a black tarpaulin, which falls to the ground like a curtain. The hoop is about 4½ft (1.4m) in diameter and is carried on the shoulders of the man beneath. The man wears a tall pointed cap and a strange face mask with grey whiskers and a long red tongue hanging out of its mouth. He is accompanied by a group of strangely named attendants, an accordionist, and a character named

'Lively Mac' known as the 'Teaser'. Lively Mac carries a club marked with the sign of the Hoss and facing the creature, dances a mysterious, almost hypnotic dance. Periodically the Hoss sinks to the ground, to be revived again by the white-clad singing girls who follow him. According to custom, the Hoss pursues the local girls who run away shrieking. To be caught and dragged under the tarpaulin cloak was considered lucky – a relic of ancient fertility magic, when the 'luck' signified a new baby. Traditionally, the Hoss appeared at midnight on 30 April, and with its entourage of men and boys serenaded important townsfolk and special visitors with their 'night song'. The recipient of this honour must let the singers know that he or she is awake and hearing them. This continues throughout the night, until the dawn of May Day, when the little

England. Abbotts Bromley Horn Dance. The hobby-horse.

72

horse, now known as the Blue Ribbon Horse, joins in the fun, but always keeping a watchful lookout that it does not encroach on the Old Hoss's activities. The new horse was created by a group of temperance-oriented young men (hence its name) as an antidote to the somewhat wild drinking habits of the Old Hoss's retinue. On the afternoon of May Day following a substantial feast at the Golden Lion, both groups converge on the town square where the maypole stands, decorated with greenery and flower wreaths. Here both horses and their attendants dance, the Teaser allowing specially selected onlookers to hold his club and dance with Old Hoss. This is taken very seriously and all those selected for the honour appear fully versed in the intricate steps of the dance. And so the festivities continue through the streets, with Old Hoss repeatedly dying and reviving. Death and resurrection – a plain message carried to us over the centuries by an extraordinary long-lived animal ritual. At last the Hoss returns to its stable at the Golden Lion and the whole amazing ceremony is over for another year.

The Minehead Horse is the sailor's horse. He is about 7 feet (2m) long and originally had a head covered by the skin of a hare and snapping jaws, now sadly lost, but he still sports a long tail made of rope. Originally this was a cow's tail. His cover is made of canvas covered with a variety of coloured strips of cloth, and his carrier wears a tall conical head-dress, which covers his face. His retinue is made up of a group of sailors and an accordionist. The Minehead Horse is regarded as the true bringer of spring and there are records dating back over a century describing how on the night of 30 April he would go out to a nearby crossroad, where to the beat of a drum his attendants would dance round him. On the morning of 1 May, the horse would dance and the prettiest girl in the accompanying crowd would become the May Queen. Originally there was also a May King, thus symbolizing the sacred marriage of ancient spring ritual and the May Queen would be carried around on the horse's back.

During the course of May Day morning, the horse and its retinue descend on the streets of the town and again we have shrieking girls supposedly fleeing in terror. Traditionally the procession visits

Bulgaria. 'Kuker' character who appears during Lent.

Dunster Castle where they are received with honour and so the festivities continue, another living relic of our ancient past. These are just two of the innumerable examples of how the animals have kept pace with us, but they serve as a reminder that no aspect of dance ritual is ever lost, rather it accompanies us along the way, biding its time until

at a propitious moment it can claim our attention, with its strange and often bizarre behaviour and whatever the context, reminds us quite forcibly of 'where we came in'.

TOP: *Bulgaria.* **Kukeri** *animal characters in procession during Lenten ritual.*

ABOVE: *Bulgaria.* **Kukeri** *animal characters.*

6   FOLK DANCE IN EDUCATION AND ITS TEACHING

This title in actual fact immediately poses two questions: What exactly do we mean by 'education' and what by 'folk dance'? And how do the two parts complement each other? The meaning of education for us today is a fairly straightforward proposition. It is basically the tool that we use to launch our next generation into the world, furnishing them with the basic skills needed to make their way in life. In our present day and age, this usually constitutes a knowledge of reading, writing, mathematics and then all the extras – history, geography, the sciences, languages, art, music and so on. Gone from the Western world are the survival skills taught by our ancestors, although in some parts of the world such knowledge is vital to survival and lessons learnt from Nature and the importance of being in harmony with Mother Earth are still the cardinal values of primitive

education. Each itinerary is relevant to the community that it serves. Higher mathematics would be of little use to the children of hunter-gatherers and subsistence farmers, while today's children would have little or no access to the materials required for survival in a primitive society. In that primitive society, however, dance has already raised its head and will walk alongside humans mirroring their every development, until in the fullness of time, it becomes the mainstream of dance as we recognize it today. And the meaning of folk dancing? We shall come to this very soon.

So, looking at our own vision of education and folk dance, how are they compatible in furthering the education of our young people today? The question takes me back over forty years to when I was a director of a combined theatre, arts and educational school. I well remember one of the regular

Lithuanian children in a mushroom-picking dance at the Llangollen International Eisteddfod.

75

England. Young morris dancers, dancing a hey.

inspections carried out by the ministry of education. For two weeks, a team of high-powered educationalists watched over our every move, attending lessons, examining text books and scrutinizing the children's work. One thing began to worry me. The last period of each day was given over to my folk-dance class and starting from day 1, my audience grew until by the end of the second week, I had a complete row of observers, intent on all our work, from our dancing in circles, chains and couples, to the children sitting on the floor discussing the origins of folk culture, costumes, music – the 'whys' and 'wherefores' of the dances. Eventually even our 'audience' began to join in with a few tentative questions, usually reflecting their own academic field and paying grave attention to the children's comments. When they finally departed, I summoned enough courage to enquire of these die-hard educationalists what had brought them into our little world of folk dance. 'Little', the chief inspector replied, 'was a total misnomer'.

What they had seen was one of the greatest forces in education that they had ever witnessed. Each member of the team had seen us learning about their special subject – history, geography, religion, economics, art, music and languages, and all through a simple medium with which the children easily identified and clearly loved. They could not wait to discuss the possibilities afforded by this fascinating subject – folk dance in education.

Over the intervening years, I have never forgotten that comment and throughout a lifetime of learning, have never ceased to value the doors that have opened to me through folk dance. What I had previously done intuitively, became an integral part of my teaching and of those who have joined me over the years. Now a dance is not just an enjoyable physical experience, but rather another book of knowledge waiting to be opened. So – let us start to bring the two parts together and consider how they can bring a richness to a child's education.

One of the questions posed by those visitors of long ago came from the historian of the group. It arose when we moved from our local English dances to a Balkan Circle. The question was, 'Is this one a traditional dance?'. This gave rise to considerable thought and discussion amongst the children and the answer given, in basically childish form, proved to me yet again that children, at any stage of their development, have a native wisdom and an in-built concept of the many facets of dance. The carefully thought out answer was, 'No'. 'This is a folk dance because we are learning it in a folk-dance class at school. If, however, we lived in the village from which the dance originally came and learned it from our parents and grandparents, you could call it traditional, as it was taught to us without any thought of technique and performance.' Someone else volunteered the information that it might even be the only dance that they knew, as they had never been to a dancing class. A third voice interpolated that it might not even have a name in the village, just something that they danced to a particular song or tune. This surely gives us the answer to our question as to what is the meaning of folk dance.

So, lesson no.1 had been assimilated and these twelve-year-olds were already aware that people dance for different reasons, and that behind the folk dance of today lies a vast reservoir of traditional dance, a form of dance that springs from the very roots of the people, as natural to them as living and breathing and as old as the moment when human beings first stood up on two legs. This first lesson opens the door to an educated look at the dance. Even as folk dancers, if the dance has to have any meaning other than the physical satisfaction of the movement, we must surely know something of the culture from which it comes, the 'raison d'être' for any particular dance. The immediate question is that of why people, unhampered by the decrees of a dancing master, move in a certain way. In fact, what shapes people into a particular mould.

Popular opinion today would place most of the emphasis on environment. So, let us take out our maps, open our geography books and the education has already begun. Children are always interested in how their contemporaries in other countries live and find no problem in the concept, for example, that living in a flat, lush green country

English clog dance team performing at the International Folk Festival in Mallorca.

Portuguese dancers in action.

can be very different from being in a rocky, mountainous region, or a hot and dusty area where farming is hard and unrewarding. Now the exciting part begins: the search for and discovery of examples and through individual research, the development of these examples into project work and its many ramifications. Humankind has certainly not lost its hunting instincts and children are natural hunter-gatherers. Snippets of information, the discovery of a picture, a story, a map, a piece of fabric, scrap of lace, even a recipe for a local speciality, all are grist for their mill and each one opens up yet another avenue for their enquiry, another trail to follow. And follow it they will. One fourteen-year-old sleuth, on hearing that the pretty evening bag, bought by her mother from an antique shop in Copenhagen, was in fact made from a nineteenth-century Danish bonnet, spent many happy hours looking for bonnets in books, museums and among folk dancers, until she had compiled a dossier on Danish bonnets, which was outstanding in both its conception and detail. She was adamant that her best source of information came from a folk-dance group, the members of which were cognisant with every detail of their costume, from whence it had originated, to how to reproduce it today. During her research she had also managed to learn several Danish dances, a folk song in the language and acquire a Danish pen-friend. All in all, one might say, a useful contribution to her education.

An example that always appeals to English children is the tuneful music and easy-going dances of the Netherlands. They find no difficulty in relating these to the character of the people and the geography of the country. Given art-materials and a large table, I have seen a veritable map of the Netherlands appear before me, as the children created winding canals carrying fleets of miniature barges, cardboard windmills, rows of multi-coloured bulb-fields, farmhouses surrounded by plasticine models of sturdy black and white cows and delightful cardboard houses reflecting the wide variety of Dutch architecture. All these things, so much fun for the children to create, initiate thought processes, which in turn give rise to considered opinions in even the youngest children. For example, the varied silhouettes of the older houses brought a comment from a ten-year-old that, as the Dutch did not have any hills or mountains, they 'landscaped' their houses to make the scenery more interesting. Could this observation give rise to a future interest in architecture? So, from the pleasure of learning some simple Dutch dances, children who have not yet ventured abroad, can visualize and appreciate the lives of the people who created the dances. Geography has never seemed more pleasurable.

History came upon the scene when, teaching dances from our own region, I threw the ball once more into the children's court. What could they find out about when and where we used to dance.

Suddenly the children became aware of the fact that their grandparents could prove to be a mine of information. Rummaging amongst old photographs, newspaper cuttings and tattered copies of sheet music, the grandparents were able to furnish the required information. Of course it did not stop there. Great-grandfather did not have a car (a thought-provoking point – nobody at that time had a car), so how did he take great-grandma to the dance in the next village? So, horses and traps now appeared on the scene and country road conditions discussed. Did they have refreshments at the dance and if so what? Ancient family recipe books came under scrutiny for information regarding long-forgotten cakes and even more exciting, the brewing of nettle beer. Another point of interest arose when the fact that most of the dancers had to be home in time for the morning's

milking pointed to a situation when cows were milked by hand, deliveries made by horse-power and farms operated efficiently without electricity. Enquiring minds considered how cattle and sheep were transported before the days of our grim cattle wagons and here I was able to help, as my father when a child, often accompanied his father to isolated farms and the great northern cattle markets to buy sheep. The answer to the transport question was simple – they walked the animals home. And, I was always told, the animals set the pace. There was no point in arriving home with an exhausted beast. As these walks could take several days, the all-important question with the children of food and rest *en route* quickly raised its head, and now the strange names attached to various local farms began to take on a new meaning. Names like 'Catch all', 'None go by' and 'Drovers Rest' began

Children's group from the Czech Republic (photographed at a folk festival in Mallorca).

to make sense, indicating that originally they were Drovers' Inns, where animals could be safely pastured overnight, while tired men could rest and eat. The drovers' dogs also knew their way around the inns. In the days when a man might drive his herd from Scotland to London, he would often have business to transact in the city and would send his dog home. And home it went on foot, seeking shelter at those same inns, where it was recognized and made welcome, his master paying for its food on his own return journey.

From the simple pleasure of dancing the old Dales dances, we find ourselves immersed in our own history. Music is a most obvious sphere of learning and 'sound equals style' is well understood. The quality of sound and rhythm are easily recognized by children as giving each ethnic dance its own particular flavour. Young musicians are always eager to perform and it becomes obvious that as much pleasure may be had from accompanying the dance as in actually performing it. The question of who the musicians are in the traditional situation and the continued use of the old folk instruments in many countries is always of absorbing interest. Access to native instruments is usually impossible, but a desire to 'try out' the tunes on something more easily available – recorders, violin, piano, can often spark off a real interest in folk music and even in home-made instruments, as children are remarkably inventive on this score.

Throughout Europe the remnants of many ancient work-dances speak to us of past lives and conditions, and children relate to these very easily and with an understanding of what people used to do. I have been intrigued by a group of youngsters who decided to invent their own work-dances, reflecting today's occupations – a thought that pointed to the fact that centuries ago someone had come up with the same idea.

And so it continues, this fascinating study of the world through dance, each individual dance supplying yet another snippet of information, so that like a gigantic jigsaw puzzle in 3D, we begin to build the picture of a people's history, music, art and religion, and the geography, climate and economics of their country. Surely with this evidence before us, we can believe that there is no surer way of creeping up on our pupils and administering a good dose of education, happily accepted in the form of folk dance.

One question only now remains to be asked, how to teach folk dance successfully. Perhaps the answer lies in our remembering that it is unlike many other dance forms, where a technique must be established almost before one can move. Rather it is a language – a language to which we all instinctively have access and, as in studying any language, we must start from the beginning, building up a basic vocabulary. The steps are the words, the figures and patterns the sentences and paragraphs, and the reward for fluency is to be able to join comfortably in the dance. From the huge reservoir of information available, always set the picture into its true frame – children love a story and in their innate wisdom they know that there is much more fun to be had in joining in a dance when we know what it is all about. The whole of childhood is spent in learning by seeing and hearing, but if we can stimulate their natural curiosity, the learning process is soon accelerated. Listening to music, looking at maps, pictures and a great favourite, costume dolls, all bring the subject sharply into focus and if you can take your courage into both hands and suggest that they could bring any memorabilia to class, which they might have from the holidays of family and friends, the response can be enormous. The French dance that they are learning suddenly comes to life and becomes French children 'planting the oats' and not merely English children performing a pale copy of a living dance. Be careful in your planning, as this can be a 'snowball situation'. I was once taken by surprise when the class had decided amongst themselves that our coffee break should be relevant to the subject in hand and the end of term class was inundated with cakes and cookies from the countries that we had been looking at.

This subject is so vast that all we have discussed so far is merely a skeleton of the whole. Without our skeleton of course none of us would stand up, so as teachers it is up to us to flesh out that frame and breathe life into it. Surely then we will be able to tap into an endless supply of teaching material and inspiration and find ourselves with a class full of happy achievers. And the greatest reward of all – if we handle this wonderful opportunity with the infinite care that it deserves, we may find that we have launched another generation of folk dance *aficionados* and that we can leave the future in safe hands.

PART TWO

COUNTRY BY COUNTRY

7 AUSTRIA

From early times, interplay between boys and girls has been a significant factor in Austrian dance. This has carried through to the present day, when the basic motif of many dances is that of the boys wooing, and the girls affecting a shy rebuttal. This is demonstrated very clearly in the *ländler*, the popular waltz dance with its many turning steps. The *ländler* originally came from the province of Land, in the heartlands of Austria, and was in the first instance an improvised dance with no set format. The couple danced individually, the girl quietly turning with modest demeanour, while the boy showed off his strength and virility in a series of athletic steps circling his lady and crowing loudly. At the end of the dance they came together with a waltz hold and turned together in a real waltz. There are various descriptions and illustrations of these old dances; one dated 1900 describes a wedding dance from Syria in which the bride dances backwards alone, while the bridegroom follows her with a great display of athletic prowess, slapping of thighs and feet, and even turning cartwheels. From this original simple courting dance, three variations in style developed: the turning *ländler* couple dance, which we see today, and in which the accompanying song originally played an important role; second, the *steirer*, in which the courtship motif is pre-eminent; and last but certainly not least, the *schühplattler*, probably the most easily recognized Austrian dance, in which the boys give free play to a great deal of clapping and mock fighting. The *schühplattler* is always associated with a special boys' costume, the lederhosen,

leather shorts or breeches. Nowadays there is a tendency to generalize and to refer to all these dances as waltzes, and the old accompanying songs have long disappeared. But apart from the mass of dances based on the waltz rhythm, there are, in Austria, many other popular dances – polkas, polka-mazurkas, galops and *schottische*, are all well represented and in constant use.

The wheel figure, symbol of the sun, is a popular theme common to many Austrian men's dances. It is usually danced by eight men, four of whom support the four making the wheel. A good example is found in the Appenzell region, where the herdsmen perform their mill-wheel dance in this way. In other regions the wheel is shown by four couples joined by interlocking hands.

There is certainly, in Austria, an accent on men's dances, and of men taking the lead when the women are included. A popular dance is that of the lumberjacks, which shows off work actions such as chopping and sawing, and often develops into a trial of strength between two boys trying to pull each other over. Austria also has a maypole tradition, again with a male accent, as originally it was danced by men only. Not confined to May, the dance can be seen both in summer and winter. In the early part of the year the maypole is a fir tree that has been stripped of all its lower branches. The remaining top branches are then decorated with coloured tinsel and candles. Long coloured ribbons are attached and the dancers weave these into patterns as they circle round. Interestingly, a dance for men only, up to the Second World War, the dancers usually wore masks, and the dance was made up of weaving, snake-like spirals, and the inevitable ancient sun-wheel.

Another example of the dance scene dominated by men was the *maschkerertanz* from Salzburg. This was, as the name indicates, a dance in which the performers wore masks. In this the dancers were coupled together representing compatible male and female characters; for example, dairy man and maid, gypsies, moors, farmer and wife, butcher and cook, and so on. Originally for men only, the dance is now performed by both men and women.

In the Inn valley, the egg dance used to be popular. Using complicated footwork, the dancers were required to manoeuvre several eggs into a basket. Originally attached to particular Easter celebrations, in which the egg has always been an important symbol, it was also sometimes taken out of context and presented as an entertainment. There is a record of one occasion when it was performed in 1498 by two couples at the wedding of Margaret of Austria to Philip, Duke of Savoy. For this performance, over one hundred eggs were laid out on the ground, and the couples were required to dance round and over them without breaking any. The reward for a successful performance was permission to marry, surely a most public and daunting way of declaring one's devotion. It is recorded that on this occasion it took three attempts to achieve success.

There are many references to sword dances in Austria. These are especially related to the mining regions, where the danger involved in their work ensured that the miners were superstitious to the point of creating special rituals designed to protect themselves. One of the most important of these was the sword dance in which they carried metal swords, and consequently even today in the Salzkammergut, these dances are still preserved in the villages. The Salzkammergut has always been a very important mining region, with mines producing gold, silver, tin, coal, lead and particularly the salt from which it derives its name. Here the mining tradition dates back to prehistoric times, so that in the surviving sword dances we can still today see the remnants of work actions and ancient rituals reflecting the deep reverence of the miners for Mother Earth, to whom they owed their livelihoods and even their lives.

Hoop and garland dances are found throughout Austria today, and these are a reminder of yet another ancient ritual. Early humans saw the sky as a vast arch – the source of wind, rain, thunder and lightning. In their early dances this arch was represented by the half-hoop. This hoop could also represent the rainbow and, accordingly, was often decorated with multi-coloured ribbons. Flowers and fruits were also added to the hoop in the hope that this would stimulate Nature to be bountiful. The hoop and garland

Girls from Innsbruck, Austria, wearing their distinctive black felt boaters rimmed with gold cord.

dances seen today are usually attended by strange characters who often describe themselves in verse – perhaps a hunter or a witch, or even one who steals wood to sell in the market to raise money to spend on getting drunk. Originally there was always a man–woman figure, this latter reflecting the ancient belief in the conjunction of both sexes as a vital requirement for human survival.

There are also dances with fools who are believed to bring luck to farms and fields. Their costumes are covered by little tabs of various coloured cloth, and it is regarded as lucky if one can pull off a tab from their clothing. If this is placed under a hen it ensures a good supply of eggs.

Animal dances are also a part of the ancient tradition. Performed by men only, they imitated a variety of animals, birds and even frogs. This motif is still seen today in the *schühplattler*, where the men crow and flap their arms imitating the mating dance of the black cock as they circle their partners.

Morris dances, very similar to English morris dances, can be found in some of the more remote mountain regions. The steps and figures are very like those of the English morris, with the dancers using handkerchiefs and sticks, and even similarly dressed in white clothing, ribbons, bells and flower-decked hats. Most of these ancient dances were eventually absorbed by the guilds and became a part of the grand processions and spectacular performances at public festivals. Although they lost many of their more ancient ritualistic aspects, at least their adoption and promotion by these powerful societies ensured their basic preservation. Today a great deal of the Austrian dance heritage has been absorbed into the 'Tyrolean dance evenings', so popular with the tourists. Although nowadays it appears as an entertaining spectacle, we should remember the depth and wealth of the dance history from which it has grown, and which offer limitless inspiration to any serious choreographer.

8 THE BALKANS

In the region of Eastern Europe known as the Balkans, there has been little or even no change in the style and form of the dances over the centuries. The basic dance form throughout the region is the circle and chain of antiquity, and at any point in history these would have looked much the same as they do now. The people here have their own approach to everyday life, and the segregation of the sexes has a great influence on the pattern of life. This is underlined especially in those regions that have had a strong Moslem influence. Men and women have their own individual place in the life of the community and only mix freely within the innermost family circle. This fact especially influences the dance, where the social and particularly the couple dances have not developed as in Western Europe. This segregation in the dance is only too evident in the villages far from the tourist influence. Here the pattern is always the same. When the musicians start to play, the men, led by the eldest, form their own circles and chains and begin the dance. This pattern is then followed by the women. Small boys join the men's dance, and their little sisters follow on the end of the women's dance.

The very fact that the dances follow the circle and chain patterns serves to limit dance development, as the act of moving forwards, sideways or backwards on the same line, usually with hands joined, has inhibited the development of steps, so that complexity has come from rhythmic development – the creation of elaborate rhythm patterns – rather than steps. Complex time signatures are the norm, 5/4, 7/8 and 11/8 are commonly used, and phrasing is seldom even, as in Western music. These compelling rhythms suggest an early origin and the possibility of a rhythmic accompaniment other than the tunes now played. For example, in Greece in ancient times the stories of history and mythology were recited. In an era when people were illiterate it was essential that these stories should be passed on to the next generation and story-telling became an initial factor in ensuring this, taking the place of formal education and preserving their history. As usually happens when the same tale is often repeated, the recital develops its own rhythm, which would eventually be reflected in music. So in Greece the rhythmic count of 7, to which many of the ancient stories were recited, is reflected now in the 7/8 time of the *kalamatianos*. As people began to read and write, the necessity for story-telling gradually disappeared, but habit dies hard, and the custom of story-telling is still a part of Greek village life today. I have often witnessed such a gathering when after the days' work was finished, the people would come together in the cool of the evening and listen avidly to tales told by the village story-teller. We have ourselves sometimes become a part of the 'tale' as the natural curiosity of the peasants led to endless questions regarding our lives and families. All of which was translated and passed on to the audience with a suitable dramatic presentation. So, as the circles and chains, which accompanied the original recitative, fell out of use in their old form, they gradually, with the ancient rhythms intact, became dances, and so passed into the social life of the people.

In Greece the dance is rooted far beyond the confines of history and it is in the realms of mythology that we find endless references to dance. Dancing was an important feature in religious ceremonies, and it is recorded that at the ancient feasts of the gods, maidens in long robes would dance. Even with the advent of Christianity, dancing held on to its place, and in the Greek Orthodox Church today the priests circle the altar during the marriage ceremony. Since the age of Classical Greece, dances of many

*ABOVE: **Bulgaria. Various regional costumes.***

*RIGHT: **Typical Greek peasant work dress, Ionian islands.***

different types have been performed – religious, martial, athletic and with a dramatic tale to tell. Greece was well supplied with suitable venues for the performance of their dances, as there were temples, huge sport stadiums and of course theatres readily available. Terpsichore, muse of dance was greatly honoured, and all forms of dance were highly esteemed.

The continuity of tradition in Greek dance spans many centuries, and if we look at paintings on Greek vases today, and the remains of bas reliefs in the ruins of temples, we immediately recognize poses that can be seen in Greek dance today. The suggestion of steps in the ancient illustrations are highly reminiscent of those still danced in Greece, and it would seem that songs and dances are even now alive in much the same form as they appeared throughout Greece and her colonies over 2,000 years ago. The music still follows the 5/4 and 7/8 rhythms, which, as we have seen, in all probability retain the rhythm of the spoken word. Today, as in ancient times, every celebration has its own accompaniment of song and dance, and every village has its own dancing space – the *chorostan*. This is quite often the village threshing floor, with its level, well-beaten floor. Even the monasteries, of which there are many today in Greece, have their own special dancing space, an acknowledgement of the fact that song and dance have always been an accepted part of religious ceremonies historically and in modern times. It is interesting to note that, whereas in Western Europe the Church has tried constantly to ban the dance, the Greek Church has inherited and preserved a rich tradition of dance. In the works of Homer, the Greek poet (eighth century BC), there are frequent references to dance. In the *Iliad* there is a description of a circular

85

dance in which only men took part. They danced in a circle round the musicians who were standing in the centre, while the women watched from the windows of their houses. This description closely follows the *sirtaki* danced today. Although nowadays the women, particularly the younger generation, make some attempt to join in the dancing, in the rural communities this is still very much frowned upon, as the men regard it as their especial prerogative, and prefer the women to keep to their role of a respectful audience, keeping their distance. The women do in fact have their own special dances in which the men would not dream of joining in. Even the smallest boys would not presume to join the women's circles, although on some occasions, the chain may be led by a man.

The fact that the majority of the dances in Greece, even today, are still circles and chains, underlines the difference in the social development in Eastern and Western Europe. The segregation of the sexes in the east has precluded the development of the couple dance to the extent that they are very rare indeed and, probably in every case, an import. One of these rarities is the *ballos*, probably introduced by the Venetians over 800 years ago. It is found mostly in the Ionian islands, and is usually danced by one couple. With its interplay between boy and girl there has been some speculation that it might stem from the harem dances of the Moslem invaders in past times. Certainly it does not fit in with the more usual segregation of the sexes found in the Balkans.

ABOVE: **Greece, bridal costume.**

RIGHT: **Greece, Ionian islands, bride from Corfu.**

Typical Balkan costumes. Left to right, from the regions of Kustendil, Karnobut and Dimitrova.

There are several examples of circle dances that belong to specific groups of people; for example, *hassapikos* (dance of the guild of butchers), *klephtikos* (dance of the *klephts*, mountain warriors) and *tsamikos* (dance of the guerrillas on their way to battle). The popular dance of the islands today is the *sirtos*. Every village taverna has its own version of the *sirtos*. It is essentially a men's dance but, in recent years, a girls' variation has been arranged and this is permitted providing that the ladies are wearing trousers.

The most famous Greek dance is, of course, the *kalamatianos*. The leader, carrying a handkerchief, improvises and, when exhausted, passes the handkerchief to another, who then becomes the leader. The basic step and 7/8 rhythm remain the same, but variations are introduced for different occasions, such as weddings and patronal festivals. An interesting version is seen at weddings, where members and friends of the two families alternate in a chain, which then winds up into a tight coil. When they can move no further, the priest blesses the union of the two families and sprinkles holy water over the linked dancers. The chain may be linked in three different ways: hands joined in the 'W' formation, usually this is in a large circle; holding shoulders with dancers in a straight line; and

the basket hold, usually when dancers are following a curved line.

It is important to note the part that dance plays in the life of Greek men. Through the dance he expresses his own personal feelings – happiness or sorrow – and this is a very inward-looking, private emotional experience. Zorba the Greek introduced the phenomenon of a lone male dancer to the western world, but we must remember that in real life there are deep underlying emotions at play, and we should 'keep a respectful distance'. We shall never forget the time when, returning to a village after a long absence, the old peasant man who had been my husband's special friend, literally 'danced for joy', expressing his happiness at the reunion. It was a deeply emotional experience.

The region which for many years was collectively named Yugoslavia, has now reverted into its individual ethnic groups. In all these groups we can recognize subtlety of movement and contrasting rhythms, which give individual style to the dances. Circles and chains predominate throughout, and in these regions the circle is the *kolo*. Serbia is the predominating country, freeing herself from Turkish rule at the beginning of the nineteenth century and establishing herself as a fiercely proud and independent country. This strength of purpose and national pride shows in the dance, which varies from light to vigorous, but is always full of vitality. The dancers move with dignity and pride, always high-spirited, sometimes to the extent of appearing aggressive. Most certainly they make a statement regarding who they are. Unlike the rest of the Balkan countries, in Serbia there is a tendency to dance on the ball of the foot, which produces a swiftness of footwork. It also helps to make possible the many variations on basic steps and the ability to cope with the many intricate rhythmic patterns. In Serbia the chain dance and straight-line dance predominate. The dancers very often grasp their neighbours' belts on either side with their arms crossed. Every region has its own dances and style, which can vary from easy and light to soft and subtle, and to strong and vigorous. In every case the overall impression is of gaiety and light-heartedness. The northern region of Serbia, Vojvudina was under Austro-Hungarian rule until 1918 and here one can still find couple dances and even dances for three – a boy and two girls. The province of Croatia was under the rule of the Austro-Hungarian Empire until 1918. Again the dances are basically chains and circles, some rooted in very ancient rituals. On the coast and Adriatic islands, ancient ceremonial dances have been preserved, and here we can find sword dance and the *morisca*, the dance-drama depicting a struggle between the Moors and Turks over a Moslem girl. In the area around Zagreb there is a strange 'shivering dance', in which the whole body of the dancer vibrates as though they are being shaken. The style generally in Croatia seems to reflect the easy-going temperament of the people.

MACEDONIA

Situated in a region of continual warfare, Macedonia was not released from Turkish rule until the Balkan War of 1912. The dance here shows evidence of this long occupation and many elements of Turkish dance have been assimilated. A general oriental influence can be recognized and parts of some Turkish dances have been absorbed into the native dances. One of the main characteristics of Macedonian dance is the complexity of the rhythms, which in turn leads to syncopation in the steps.

The most commonly used form of dance is the open *kolo*, and it will be noted that the leader keeps his free hand behind his back with fist tightly clenched. This is symbolic of the ever-present resistance to the Turkish occupiers. Many of these dance leaders are highly skilled dancers, and often improvise with solo, very complex steps, as they lead the chain. The style can vary from region to region and generally reflects the life and background of the people under foreign occupation; it can vary from heaviness and sadness through to a high-spirited, almost flighty manner. In the regions of the old Turkish feudal estates, the style recalls obligatory subservience of the workers, while in other regions the peasant farmers dance with a more natural gaiety. There is considerable difference in the style of dance of men and women, the latter dancing with much more restraint.

Greek Macedonian costume.

MONTENEGRO

In a region encircled by high mountains, Montenegro was best able to preserve itself from foreign occupation. This preservation of their native culture and freedom of spirit shows in the free style of the dance, with its high leaps. Singing is an important part of the dance scene, as otherwise the beating of the feet is the only accompaniment. There is no instrumental music in Montenegrin dancing. In the *kolos* the sexes are divided, the women following the men's lead, here dancing with much more restraint, but there are couple dances, the most lively one being called '*to crnogorski*'. The style throughout is always lively, energetic and with an almost joyful freedom of movement.

BOSNIA AND HERZEGOVINA

The people of Bosnia and Herzegovina have suffered a long history of occupation by foreign powers. First under Turkish rule, and then under Austrian rule, they have had every possibility of losing their own folk traditions and identity. This may have contributed to the fact that folk music plays little part in the dance scene. For the most part the dances are silent, without musical accompaniment and depending on rhythm alone. This does not inhibit the dance in any way, rather it produces its own excitement, as often after a quiet beginning, the dance grows in speed and exhilaration. The beat of many pairs of feet working in precision, however complex the rhythm, can have an hypnotic effect on the listener and can produce more exhilaration than the folk music would. There are in fact many *kolos* that can be performed with or without music, and there are some lively and expressive couple dances that are possibly a legacy of the Austrian occupation. The style is always lively and full of vitality and usually follows the pattern of a calm and quiet opening, which eventually explodes into an almost ecstatic performance.

BULGARIA

The wide repertoire of steps and rhythms found in Bulgarian folk dance suggests the influence of a long and involved historical background. Geographically, Bulgaria most certainly lies in an area of complex history – both ancient and modern cultures and ethnic interchange meet and overlap in this region. The majority of the dances are social dances belonging to the whole community, the most important being the *horo*, either in circular or chain formation. It forms the basis of village social life and is danced on Sundays and Feast Days, and it is an important part of the wedding ceremonial. It is danced on every possible occasion, even in the fields at harvest time. At village fairs the *horo* circles non-stop throughout the day, dancers and musicians being replaced when necessary. Groups of people try to out-dance each other, and vie with each other to pay the musicians and 'call the tune'. The chain is a living symbol of democracy – everyone, rich or poor, can take their place therein.

Every region has its own *horo*. In the western regions the dances are lively and the steps very small. In the north, the dance is much wilder; while in the south-east it is much slower and solemn in performance, with considerable difference between the style of men and women. The chain dance is called the '*vodemo horo*', the 'led dance', as the chain requires a leader. The most exciting led *horo* is the 'crooked' *horo*. This chain has a leader at each end, the first and last dancers, and they wind the chain into a spiral and unwind it at an astounding speed. Both leaders frequently carry a handkerchief as insignia of office. The innumerable names given to *horos* can, in some cases, indicate their place of origin. For example, some *horos* have migrated from the mountain regions to the plains brought by shepherds, soldiers, harvesters and gypsy musicians. Other names would suggest a more distant place of origin, when we find names such as the Serbian, the Greek, the Wallachian, all of which propose another country of origin. There are endless local names, which might indicate connection with work; for example, sheep, hare, goose, all suggest aspects of rural life. Other *horos* are named after local heroes, and there is a very quick *horo* named 'lentils', and a slow *horo* with a limping step called 'the cripple'. There are several of these 'limping' dances throughout the Balkans, and they have connections with very ancient rituals concerning the limping God. The limping God appears

ABOVE: Bulgaian costumes. A special feature is the embroidery on the stockings.

RIGHT: Bulgarian man's costume.

in many guises – the Greek God Dionysus is the classic example (Robert Graves' *Greek Mythology* gives a full account of this phenomenon). The dance link with the limping God is the limping step that appears in many old dances – particularly in Eastern Europe and very often in funeral dances.

One of the most important dances is the *rachenitsa*, a dance of improvisation and endurance. It can begin as a couple dance, and end up as a group, as more and more of the onlookers are drawn in.

It is done at weddings by grooms and bridesmaids leading the bridal procession, and is included in several parts of the ceremony, which is spread over a number of days. There is even a special *rachenitsa* danced at weddings by two puppets.

The special *horos* for men have small steps and are very agile and lively in performance. They have names that suggest that originally they were associated with certain trades; for example, the butchers', the shepherds', the masons' and the potters'.

ABOVE: Bulgaria. 'Camel' seen in the background.

RIGHT: Bulgaria. 'Kuker', a Lenten character.

In these *horos*, the movements very often reflect the movements used in certain work. There is a hare dance in which two men mime the chasing and leaping of two hares, and they flap their hands to represent the hare's ears, sometimes real ears are fixed to sticks. This dance sometimes includes a comic mime with a huntsman. The dance 'how black pepper is sown' is a dance for ten men who mime all the actions of sowing, harvesting, pounding and threading on strings to dry. It is performed at weddings and belongs to the category of agricultural, sympathetic magic dance-games.

There are dances with masks that appear at carnival time, and the week preceding Lent brings out the *kukere* with their fantastically dressed dance-drama. At certain times an immense hobby-horse creature – a 'camel' – dances during the night, the camel's leader blessing the houses and ensuring fertility; the farmers pay him with wheat. During Whitsuntide, the *rusali* appear in many villages along the Danube. They dance to cure the sick and to bring general fertility. The name *rusali* comes from the

Bulgarian girl. The colours red and black with a white blouse are very typical.

Latin *rosalia*, which was connected with the custom of hanging up garlands at the festival of *rosales escae*. These dances are made up of small, very rapid stamping steps and the dancers carry small staves.

The ancient custom of fire-dancing is still alive. This takes place on 3 June. The dancers step with bare feet on live coals to the music of bagpipe and drum. The drum is preceded by processions carrying icons, and *horos* in many separate chains are danced. The women's *horos* are often accompanied by singing and are quiet and often slow. The Saturday before Palm Sunday is an important festival for the girls, when, forming themselves into companies, they go from house to house singing and dancing to 'bring the spring'. They have special costumes for this important occasion, often wearing richly decorated head-dresses. They are led by an older girl – the *kumitsa*, and their songs have suitable words for each household approached. For example, a newly married couple will be serenaded with:

> For the good health of this house,
> For its health and abundance,
> Dance for this young bride,
> And for next years' cradle.

The girls are made welcome everywhere and are rewarded with gifts of money, bread and eggs, feasting on the latter in the evening when they allow the boys to join them in the *horo*. These dances are the remnants of ancient pre-Christian spring, fertility rites.

Singing was always a feature of Bulgarian dancing, often with a peculiar style in which one person will sing the melody, while two others will keep up a strange droning accompaniment. Today, however, instruments are replacing the singing and the musicians are frequently gypsies. Young men returning home from service with the army are gradually introducing wind and brass instruments, so that many villages now have their own small brass band. The violin, introduced by gypsies during the Turkish occupation, has now become a popular instrument for folk music. In spite of five centuries of Turkish rule, Bulgaria has preserved the purity of its dance and there is no sign of the eroticism that one identifies with Turkish dancing. However lively the dance becomes, it always retains a dignified quality.

ROMANIA

The two most characteristic dances of Romania are the *hora* and the *calus*. The *hora* is a simple chain or circle dance and is the chief dance of the people. Although there are few specific dances, in fact no more than nine or ten in living practice, there are innumerable variations and each village has its own *hora*. According to research, there are over 2,500 different variants. It has always been the custom in the rural communities for the peasants to meet together on Sunday afternoons to dance the *hora*. It is a dance in which everyone could take part, joining and leaving the dance as they felt inclined. It has always been such an important part of the people's lives that 'to enter the hora' meant that boys were approaching manhood and girls were of marriageable age. The villagers used the *hora* as a standard of morality and if anyone of dubious morals attempted to join in the circle, everyone would cease dancing, thus making a public condemnation of the guilty person. If people were in mourning, the period of mourning was officially ended when they once more joined in the *hora*.

There are two forms of the *hora*: the *hora mare*, the big *hora*, for as many people as wished to join in, and with everyone facing the centre of the circle; and the *hora tarameasca*, a dance for two couples in a circle. In this the two men take turns in directing the circle to the left or to the right. There are *horas* for every possible occasion – for weddings, births and every possible feast day and social occasion, and the dance is known by many different names, usually descriptive of who dances that particular variation. There are the gypsies' *hora*, the girls' *hora*, the fairies' *hora* and very many others. The bride's *hora*, which is danced to open the wedding celebrations, is very important. It is danced outside the bride's house, with all the guests dancing in a huge circle. The *hora* is also a part of the church ceremony, as following the crowning with marriage wreaths, of the bride and groom, they join hands with the priest and with their parents and dance round the altar.

The word *hora* in Romanian means a circle, but the word is of Greek origin and comes from the Greek word *chorus*, to dance. The other important dance in Romania is the *calus*. This is a men's ritual dance and

Young boy from Romania.

its origins are lost in pre-history. The men who dance it are called *calusari*, and they are medicine men who dance to cure the sick. The *calus* is danced at Whitsuntide, a period called *rosali*, the festival of roses, which pre-dates Christianity. The dance must be performed by an odd number of dancers. Originally the group comprised nine men from nine different villages. They meet on Whit-Sunday, when they take a solemn oath to their leader and raise their flag. This is garlanded with garlic to ward of evil spirits.

Romanian boy. The red and black embroidery is very typical in pattern and colour.

They tour the village dancing in the yards of the houses to expel evil and to ensure good fortune for the householders. The *calusari* are able to exorcize evil spirits and if a person is cured, they pay for their treatment by feeding the dancers during *rosali* for the following three years. The name 'calusari' means little horses. In some regions the men do not speak during the week while the dancing lasts. As in all the countries of Europe, the position of leader of the chain is immensely important, and is always given to the best dancer in the village, regardless of his social status or whether he is a poor man or a rich man. When leading the chain he becomes the most important person present and is respected by everyone. There are many other ritual, fertility, work and healing dances, but none is as important as the *calusari*.

One dance with very ancient ritual connections is the *capra*, the goat. This belongs to New Year's Eve with its hopes and promise for the coming year. On this occasion men dressed as animals sing and dance at the villagers' houses led by one dressed as a goat. The goat man represents the devil and therefore cannot enter any church. The man dressed as a mare carries the bag for presents and the dancers receive gifts from the villagers, a different wish being made in exchange for each gift. Often the group of dancers will stop passers-by and start a *hora* around them. If the passers-by are not sufficiently generous in handing over money or presents, the goat howls loudly and the *hora* continues around the mean people until they remedy the situation.

There are so many ritual connections to be found in the dances and owing to the traditionally patriarchal life of the Romanian peasant, much has been preserved, and has a great deal to offer to the researcher. Over the centuries the peasant dancers have continually added to the vocabulary of the dance, and the fact that so many variations on skips, hops and stamps have survived until today is indicative of their importance in the eyes of the dancers. From ancient ritual to more recently developed social dances built on the old patterns, dance is preserved and treated with respect. With its gay character, ease of movement and all-embracing welcome, the dance in Romania has created and maintained its own dignity and rhythmic approach, and has certainly become the favourite pastime of the people.

9   THE BALTIC COUNTRIES

S ituated in the north of Europe and bounded by cold northerly seas, the countries of Lithuania, Latvia and Estonia have had a long and often turbulent history, frequently suffering at the hands of powerful neighbours. Nowadays when watching Lithuanian groups at folk festivals, the programme is largely made up of couple dances, quadrilles, figure dances and polkas, often with mime introduced, reminiscent of a children's game, and the whole impression is of a lively social dance scene with everyone enjoying the dance.

Lithuania, however, has a wealth of dance that reflects the working life of a rural community. Under work dances we can list: *malūnas* (the mill), a dance with rhythmical movements imitating the working of the mill; *rugeliai* (rye); *piovéjai* (mowers); *gyuataras* (hedgerows); *audéja* (weavers); and *kubiuas* (wash tubs); all are made up of actions expressive of the work they illustrate. There is also *jungas* (jokes), a special men's dance in which the men illustrate ploughing with oxen. Animal dances include cocks, racehorses and kids.

Dancers from Lithuania.

Girl from Lithuania.

In the spring, the prettiest girl in the village is crowned as May Queen, and swathed in birch branches. She sits beside the May Tree, while everyone dances round her. On St John's Day and at Whitsuntide the growing seed is ritually inspected. Families walk through the rye fields and there is feasting outside. The young people make flower wreaths and dance in the fields. There are also dances imitating growing plants – plants that are important and must be encouraged. Amongst these are *dobilélis* (clover) and *aguonéle* (poppies). With the coming of harvest the last sheaf of corn is named *boba* (grandmother) and this is drenched with water before being danced round by everyone. There is an axe dance,

the *kirvio šoks*, but on this occasion it is the girl who carries the axe. She stands in the middle of the circle of dancing men and when she throws the axe up into the air, the man who catches it is entitled to claim a kiss.

There are records of two hat dances, *skrybéliv sokis* and *kepurline*, in which the men dance in a squatting position around hats placed on the floor. Dances associated with important occasions in the people's lives include *nuotakos šokis*, which was a Lithuanian bride's dance. The dancers, carrying lighted torches, form a circle round the bride and perform little jumps, while the bride dances with each member of the groom's family and finally with the groom himself. Another important wedding dance was the *saduté*, a dance that expressed the sadness of the bride's family and friends at losing her. On the eve of the wedding they come carrying flowers to bid farewell to her. They bring a wreath of flowers, which was placed on her head to symbolize her leaving the status of maidenhood for that of a married woman. Another dance associated with weddings was the *piršlio šokis*, the matchmaker's dance, which was humorous.

Also closely connected with the lives of the people were the dances performed as part of the ceremonial rites at wakes. A charming description of a Lithuanian dance comes to us from a nineteenth-century Danish author. Referring to the *blezdingéle*, the swallows, he wrote:

> I saw this dance one Summer evening in a little birch grove. Couple behind couple take up positions in two sets facing each other. They swing around, head down and pass through quick as a flash, so that really in a way it reminds one of the swallows' twisting and rapid flight.

The dance is the girls' farewell to the swallows as they fly off to warmer lands. The boys have their own ceremonial dance, the bear dance, which is performed at carnival time.

In Latvia there are early references to dance. According to Latvian mythology the sun danced:

> The little sun danced on the silver hill, gold shoes on her tiny feet.

Latvian girl's costume.

The legend continues:

> A bush with white blossoms grows on a rock in the middle of the sea, and thence every evening the sun goes to dance.

An interesting point here is the fact that the Latvians refer to the sun as female, whereas in the majority of cultures the sun is the male god, while the moon is the female deity. Certainly there is evidence of the ancient roots of dance in Latvia, and its constant presence through the centuries. The Latvians combined dancing round their trees with the midsummer bonfires. On St John's Eve a wooden barrel filled with burning pitch would be set upon a pole and left to burn throughout the night. On this special night, the countryside was alight with these burning beacons and with fires alight on every high vantage point. People went from village to village singing and dancing and then going in search of fern blossom.

Throughout history in the mountainous regions, early people would come together at holy places to carry out their religious rituals and make sacrifices to their gods. These rites were also carried out in woodland groves, which offered them suitable sanctuaries in which to make offerings to the gods. These ceremonies took place under specially chosen trees, which were considered to be holy – in particular the oak and the lime – and offerings were hung on the tree branches. A description of these ancient rituals comes to us from 1606, written by a Jesuit priest, who had observed them:

> In diverse places they set light to pyres, and threw into the flames offerings and then began to dance round the trees.

In times of drought they prayed to their thunder god, Pērkons, making offerings of a black goat, a black calf and a black cockerel. They danced three times round the pyre, drinking beer from a goblet and sprinkling the rest on the flames. Animal dances in which the dancers actually impersonate the animals are found in Latvia, and also dances connected with animals exist. In the latter for example, there might be one step or movement reminiscent of a specific animal, perhaps the pawing step or galloping of a horse. Pigs, for example, have their own patron saint, and it was believed that St Tenis would dance at the back of the pig sty and the number of footprints left behind by the saint indicated the number of piglets that would be born there. On 17 January, Saint Tenis' Saints' day, it was the custom to let the sow and piglets dance to make them strong and healthy. In the evening everyone went to the inn, where they danced with the swineherd to ensure the growth and health of the pigs. On 4 December, St Barbara's Day, Latvian shepherds danced through the rooms of the farms. They hopped in a crouching position copying the movements of their animals. On Märtin's Day, children put on masks and dress up to perform the märtin's dance in which they imitated birds.

Sea-borne commerce has carried English country dances to every part of Europe, and Latvia has also been a recipient. Country dance figures are found in several of the indigenous dances; for example, in *alkops*, *sudmalinas* and *jandalins*. Latvian dance can certainly prove and demonstrate its ancient lineage, and many remnants are to be seen in children's and adults' dance games today. The overall picture of dance nowadays, when seen at folk festivals, is very much that of a happy social occasion. There are many couple dances and couples in figure dances to draw on, and often folklore is woven into the scene choreographically, so that the dances are fun to watch. The style is always of ease, genuine enthusiasm, and with a lively flow of movement and supportive partnering.

In this trio of Northern countries, Estonia is ethnically the odd-man out. When the Finno-Ugrian tribes from the east came in search of new homelands in Europe, they divided up, so that one group turned south and settled on the vast Hungarian plains, while the others travelled onwards, and turning north settled on the Baltic coast in what is now known as Estonia. Ethnically they differ from the other Baltic people, and have always retained their own very unique language, totally unrelated to any other European language with the exception of Hungarian. As one would expect in a country with such a complex history, Estonia has many ancient customs and dances. The oldest circle dances are those seen at weddings. At weddings also, the chain dance appears, either with dancers holding hands or in a column formation with hands on the shoulders of the person in front. Either in chain or column, it wends its way round the farm led by a fiddle player. The dance is called the

Estonian girl wearing her special crown-like head-dress.

98

pulmarong, and can be performed with either a walking step, a polka or a step in triple time. On the way to the church and back the bride must have a supply of small gifts to present to relations. These are usually socks, mittens or belts, all of which must be beautifully handmade. To provide such an amount of presents, the bride needed help with her preparations, and friends and relatives would join her at 'sewing parties' before the wedding. On these occasions the groom would invite his friends along and then all would join in and dance. Often the route to or from the church would be barred to force her to pay forfeit in order to continue on her way. At the wedding reception they would have to wait until the pastor had left before the dancing could commence, as the Lutheran Church regarded dancing as sinful. Even today the thought of dancing, on what should be a solemn occasion, would shock the older people.

There are plenty of work dances to give evidence of the peoples' occupations over the centuries and one of the most popular still in existence is the *kingsepapolka*, the men's shoemaker's dance. In this the men dance eight bars of polka steps, and then mime hammering, pulling the thread and licking their fingers to make the thread pointed. Couples dance the *voor-saukadi*, a wood-cutting dance. The name of the dance indicated the noise of the sawing. In the *kalames* the fishermen show an 'after work' dance, as they dance stiffly and with difficulty after rowing their boats. Gradually, however, they loosen up as the dance progresses. In *kivikasukas*, which means beaten by a stick, the dancers represent the workers limping home, but as the music speeds up the dancing becomes livelier. There were also occasions for dance rather than work dances, as, for example, when help was needed with the spinning of the flax, girls from neighbouring farms would come together to help out with the work, often bringing along their own spinning wheels. Another occasion for communal work was the preparation of feathers for stuffing eiderdowns. Often at these communal work parties, the boys would join the girls later for dancing.

Animal dances are numerous and varied with dances in which the men imitate the movements of bears, frogs and birds. There is a magpie dance, the *kittsakatants* in which two men dance a polka and then jump clapping their hands in front and behind. There are many stick dances, which have arisen out of the practice of men carrying sticks to ward off the wolves which were very prevalent and dangerous. In the *konnatants* the men imitated the actions of frogs, and the dance was made up of squatting and leaping movements, or bouncing around in a 'press-up' position – a dance that required energy and determination. There is a women's harvest dance, the *targa rehealune*, which suggests the threshing of the corn. *Rehealune* means threshing floor, and the dancers move forwards bending and stamping their whole foot on the floor, flexing their knees and keeping their heels down. They sing as they dance. The *kaarasiim* is a stick dance for four girls each carrying two sticks. This comes from Setu, a region in which the women dance alone. There is also a 'limping' dance from the same region, which indicates the age of these dances. It is a dance, *setu kargus*, performed only by women. The 'limping' step is the equivalent of the Russian pivot step. From the island of Saatemaa, off the Estonian coast, comes a crossed-stick dance, the *riskulkade tants*, again performed only by women. In Estonia the women very frequently danced as men because the men were often absent for long periods, either working as fishermen or in military service. On the island of Saaremaa there is a dance for two girls and one boy. It is called the *raksi-jaak* and has the usual motifs of flirting and rivalry. Again, this threesome could indicate a shortage of male partners.

Christmas brings the usual customs and dancing occasions common to these northern countries. In Estonia a special cake, the Christmas Boar, is baked on Christmas Eve, and this is left on the table until New Year's Day, when it is fed to the animals. So it can be seen that there is a great involvement in dance in the Baltic countries, and where nowadays ritual has given way to pure social dance, it is always performed in an easy manner, and with a great sense of enjoyment.

The Baltic countries are well represented on the international folk-dance scene, and with their obvious pleasure in recreating their folklore are always well received. They all produce a wealth of children's groups, which augers well for the future.

10 BELGIUM

Belgium, in its geographical position, has much the same pattern of dance today as its neighbours, containing elements common to both French and Dutch dance, but if we look beyond the confines of contemporary folk dance in its social context and at festivals, there are some interesting developments that are uniquely Belgian. Chief among these are the sword dances. We have seen how the sword dance holds on to its place in the folk culture of many different countries, and in Belgium in particular there have been constant references over the centuries. There are descriptions of dances performed by the guilds, which were paid by many town councils to provide dancers at carnival time. In Liège the sword dancers appear with a hobby-horse, and records of their performance date back to the sixteenth century. In the seventeenth century there are descriptions of the sword dancers in procession on the occasion of the entry into the city of the Prince – Bishop of Liège. These are a brief acknowledgement of the many that have existed, but one that we must include is the *trawanteldans* of Westerlo. It is firstly famous for the complications that have been added to the original hilt and point sword dance and which have resulted in a dramatic and complex performance. To the intricacies of the sword dance, complicated manoeuvrings with a hoop have been added. The dancers carry sticks and must negotiate their bodies through the hoop without letting go of their sticks, and while passing the hoop to each other. Originally the dance was performed by various guilds but today is only danced by the Guild of Marksmen of Kempen. Presumably the dance was performed with swords, but at some time these were replaced by sticks. In the Flemish archives there are many prohibitions on the use of swords and in 1548 there is a reference to the sword dancers carrying

sticks. The *trawanteldans* is long and complex and contains many interesting and unusual elements; for example, the formation of a star in which the sticks crossed like a star are beaten in time one against the other. There is a dramatic pause in the drumming that accompanies the dance, almost as if the moment of execution has arrived, the drum beat stops for a moment and then the drummer gives one loud bang, followed by five beats made by the sticks. The dancers finally ride away using their sticks as hobby-horses. There exists a lengthy and very detailed record of the dance by Edgard Wanters, who describes the dance as performed by the Guild of St Sebastian Westerlo.

One other special feature of Belgian folk culture is the involvement with giants. In a country where the hobby-horse tradition is strong, *Le Cheval Bayard* is a veritable giant amongst his kind. He is first recorded in Ath, the name of the place where the hobby-horse was first recorded as having appeared, in 1461 and there is a description of him paraded through Brussels in 1571, carried by six porters and accompanied by a normal-sized hobby. He measures about 20ft (6m) from head to hooves, is beautifully painted, caparisoned with black velvet or felt, and decorated with small coats of arms. A hollowed-out portion of his back holds four little benches, which accommodate the four children representing the sons of Aymon safely tucked inside, but with false legs dangling outside. In fact the legend is that far from being an ordinary hobby, this gigantic animal is descended from the magical steed that carried the four sons of Aymon to safety from the wrath of Charlemagne. In 1850, he is described as wearing a high ostrich feather headdress and many tassels, and being pushed along on his wheels by squads of men. In recent years it has been necessary to use long poles to raise the electric

The Goliath D'Ath.

wires so that *Bayard* may pass underneath. The taste for giantism in Belgium is well established and many cities own their own particular civic giant, which lays claim on the citizens' loyalty. One of the first things to spring to life at the end of the war was the Belgian giant – the government immediately made money available to renovate the giants, which had been safely hidden, and to replace those that the occupation forces had wantonly burned, so that in a very short time historical colossi like the *Goliath*

d'Ath were on parade as an expression of patriotism, which no invader could ever have understood. So, returning to our giant horse, we find that he has left his hoof marks here and there, and his incredible leap to safety with the four children saw him safely on the far shore of the river Meuse. According to legend it is here in the Forest of Ardennes that he can be heard neighing on the Eve of St John (Midsummer's Eve). And here we will take leave of the Belgians and their giants, and move on in our journey.

11 THE CELTIC INFLUENCE

The Celts were a group of tribes who had more influence on Northern Europe than any other people. Related by language, culture and religion, they began to emerge as a distinct people in the eight century BC and became the creators of the first civilization north of the Alps. They were the first people to use iron and were the first people to develop tools and weapons superior to those of their bronze-age contemporaries. This, combined with their superiority as warriors and horsemen, made them invincible, so that they were well able to subject the tribes with whom they came into contact, and impose upon them their own language and culture. These then were the people who colonized Scotland, Ireland and Wales. Although they never founded their own Celtic Empire, they succeeded in laying down the foundations of North European civilization wherever they settled, and in social, economic and artistic activities, their artefacts and jewellery can be easily identified in the grave goods of Europe's prehistoric cemeteries. Their most well-known design is the spiral motif, and this appears in many different forms, from rock carvings in Ireland, to the spiral embroidery patterns commonly found in Brittany, where they are used to decorate some of the women's costumes. Throughout the fringe of Celtic countries we are constantly reminded of their unbroken connections with their original Celtic roots.

SCOTLAND

The second wave of colonists who invaded Scotland were the Gaels, a Celtic tribe culturally and linguistically sufficiently strong to impose their language wherever they settled. So, the Gaels gave their name to the ancient language of Scotland – Gaelic, which is still very much alive today. Incidentally, they also settled in north-west Spain, where they similarly gave their name to the province of Galicia. The people of Galicia have certainly inherited much of their Celtic ancestry, and still today claim their ancient Celtic heritage in preference to being regarded as Spanish.

An observer writing in the nineteenth century commented at length on the Scottish love of music and dance, which 'amounts almost to a passion'. The writer notes how the young men and women, after a long day's work, would walk a considerable distance to take part in a dance, returning home with renewed energy for the next day's work. Their enthusiasm for dancing has helped to negate the efforts of the Church to eradicate what it referred to as promiscuous dancing. A very strong feature of the Gaelic culture was the practice of poetry and music, and this has become an important aspect of the Scottish heritage of which dance has become an integral part. Although little had been written down about the early dance, there exists a ballad, the *Colkelbye*. written in the early fifteenth century and in which about twenty of these early dances are named. The ballad gives detailed descriptions of the music and the musical instruments in use at that period in Scotland, information which would otherwise now be forgotten.

Dancing was always an important part of the celebrations at Royal marriages, and there are descriptions of the festivities on several of these occasions. With the return of Mary, Queen of Scots, the introduction of fashionable French dances at the court undermined the native love of dance, as the patriotic Scots did not welcome these foreign imports. This served to strengthen the arm of the Scottish Reformers who condemned promiscuous dancing as a violation of moral and spiritual laws, so that Mary's lavish round of non-stop dancing eventually goaded John Knox into preaching in denunciation of the sumptuous balls and foreign dances.

Scottish dancers wearing the 'Flora MacDonald' dress.

Despite the temporary gloom cast over the dance scene by the Reformed Church, the Scottish love of dancing survived and quickly began to re-establish itself as an acceptable and important part of social life. It raised its head in triumph once again with the introduction of the immensely popular Highland Games and the world-wide recognition of highland dance. Although a comparatively small country, Scotland has a considerable diversity of dance, which has been of prime importance at all social levels. Today the greatest contrast is between the highland and lowland dancing, the highland being the highly competitive professional level of dance, while the lowland encompasses all the social dances. Originally the highland dance offered a wide repertoire of solo dances but, in promoting the competitive element, many dances have been discarded and lost, as in order to simplify things for the adjudicators, only a limited number of dances have been retained and polished to a high degree of performance. The standard is now so high that in some instances only a series of highly perfected steps are shown, which sadly means that even now more and more complete dances are being lost for posterity.

Regarding the lowland dances, these are social country dances of which the Royal Scottish Dance Society have a vast store. They are based on an easily recognizable vocabulary of steps and figures and even on the most casual of occasions, Scottish country dance is never undertaken lightly. Steps are rehearsed to as high a level of perfection as possible, and the calm social aspect is always to the fore, with the dancers fully aware of their place in the figures and progressions, so that the patterning is always pleasing to the eye, steps correctly performed and partnering gracefully undertaken. Neatness and elegance are the norm throughout. Highland dancing on the other hand is a demonstration of the performer's dance ability and athleticism, and demands the highest possible technical dexterity. Also we have the demands of the solo performance in contrast to the group activity of the social scene and this requires a completely different approach, both mentally and physically, from the dancers.

Originally in the hands of the dancing masters, highland dancing was taught in private classes and performed in public at the Dancing Masters' Balls, which were the social culmination of each term's classes. For these occasions, special solo dances were arranged by the dancing master for his pupils, and these appeared on the programmes printed especially for the ball. For example, Miss Fraser's Hornpipe or Miss Murray's Jig would identify the solo dancer's *pas seul* on these important social occasions.

The history of the dancing master in Scotland parallels that of northern England. While in the towns there would, in all probability, be a resident teacher to whom people would go for tuition (in fact, in 1698 Aberdeen has its own official public dancing master), in the rural areas, the dancing master would arrive in his chosen territory and take up residence locally for a few weeks, often with a local farmer or similar homestead. For several weeks he would teach locally, classes or private lessons, arranging special dances for pupils booking private lessons and choreographing groups for some of the classes. The dancing was all based on the old step dancing and was often given a special theme with a costume designed and often made by the dancing master himself. So we have records of step dancers dressed as clowns, jockeys and even with blackened faces, all of which would be presented at the Dancing Master's Ball, which would be the culmination of his local dance course. The indigenous country dances would of course be on the programme.

Always preserved in Scotland has been the sword dance in its various forms. Descriptions of sword dances danced on various special occasions have been well-notated. As in every culture, sword dancing with metal swords originated with the mining communities, but as they were taken up by other workers, the workers' own tools were substituted for the swords of the original dances. This ancient heritage of sword dancing, common throughout Europe (as opposed to the 'over the swords' of today's repertoire) has survived in Scotland, though in many cases the swords have been discarded and more easily available work implements substituted. So, for example, from 1633 we find a description of the Perth Glovers' Company carrying work tools instead of swords in their dances. In this case the tools were the scraping implements used in their trade. There is an account of one of their performances given for King Charles I, describing the performance by thirteen members of the guild wearing green caps with red ribbons and bells about their legs. They were carrying scrapers in their hands, and danced their sword dance with 'many difficult knots'. In the same account there is a reference to the mounting of one ring of dancers upon the shoulders of another ring, a figure still seen today in widely scattered areas, from Greece to north-eastern Spain. There are in fact many clear references that bear witness to the strength of the sword dance through the centuries. From 1590 we hear of a sword dance and a 'hieland' dance being performed for Anne of Denmark, wife of James VI of Scotland. The performance

took place in Edinburgh and was presented by twelve men whose hats were decked with flowers.

When Sir Walter Scott visited the islands in 1814, he noted down an early Shetland dance, and from these notes the islanders of Papa Stour have been able to re-create their ancient sword dance now named *The Seven Champions of Christendom*. The dancers carry swords made of strip steel, which have replaced the straightened-out herring barrel hoops originally used.

A description of a dance notated in 1924 referred to an eight-man sword dance performed fifty years previously. It describes two men with swords crossed on the ground while six men danced round them. The centre two must avoid both the swords on the ground and those of the other dancers who point in toward them. The dancers change places until all have been in the centre. This description would seem to link the highland sword dance with hilt and point, but the highland sword dance of today, *ghillie callum*, is really in a very different category and there are many different stories regarding its possible origins. Little is genuinely known about its origin, but stories vary from it being a dance performed before a battle in dedication to some ancient god of war, to a dance of victory in which the victor danced over the crossed swords of victor and vanquished. The dance was brought to the lowlands by the highland cattle drovers who, when trekking had been completed, relaxed by competing amongst themselves in dancing, playing the pipes and in feats of strength. It is from these local 'games' that the highland games of today came into being.

Another very complex and elegant highland dance is the *seann triubhas* (grey trousers). One popular story about this dance is that it was created for the highlanders, who, forbidden to wear their kilts and tartans following the 1745 rebellion, refused to dance their ancient highland dances while wearing trousers. However, this theory can be discarded, as the trews were commonly worn in the highlands long before the Jacobite rebellion with its subsequent ban on highland dress. *Seann triubhas* is much more likely to have stemmed from an already ancient dance, which in the hands of the dancing master was transformed into the elegant dance that we know today. It was even adapted into a feminine and very graceful dance for girls to perform in the ballrooms of the period.

Towards the end of the eighteenth century, the newly conscripted Scottish regiments did much to promote Scottish dancing, inter-regimental highland games were regularly held at which *ghillie callum*, *seann triubhas*, and the foursome reel were the principal dances performed. In fact, dance became a method of recruiting young boys into the new regiments, as the splendidly attired Scottish recruiting sergeants attended country fairs and markets, where they rapidly attracted an admiring crowd. This inspired the local girls in particular and the boys, anxious to impress, were soon persuaded to 'join the army'. We shall see a similar pattern of events in Hungary, where special boys' dances, *verbunkos*, illustrate the story.

Ghillie callum is, of course, only danced as a solo, but Lochaber and Argyll broadsword dances are for four people dancing round four swords placed tip to tip in the shape of a cross. Eventually, even the sword dances were taken up by the dancing masters and some of the steps were adapted and introduced, quite out of context, into the popular ballroom dances of the day.

As is common everywhere, weddings in Scotland were an occasion for dancing and certain dances had a special part to play in the proceedings. The first dance after the bridal supper was the bonny briest knot, led by the bride and groom followed by the best man and chief bridesmaid. In the Western Isles, however, the first dance was the wedding reel, danced by bride, groom, best man and chief bridesmaid, and watched by the rest of the company. This dance is still performed in the Outer Hebrides. The bride would then dance with other men in the company, and it was believed that her first partner would be the next man to marry. The Scottish have always been very superstitious regarding fairies, and elaborate lengths were gone to at weddings to confuse the fairies who might be waiting for an opportunity to steal the bride. Two girls would steal away the bride while another took her place in the dance. The same thing would happen to the bridegroom, so the couple could be led to safety while the fairies thought that they were still dancing. The kissing dance was always chosen to close the wedding celebrations.

The most important of the great fire festivals of the Celts was in Scotland – the Beltane fire, which was kindled on 1 May. This was without doubt, originally an occasion for human sacrifice, and the ceremonial attached to it remained for centuries in the living folk customs of Scotland; fortunately it lost its sacrificial aspect long ago. The most recent detailed description dates from the eighteenth century. Written by the parish priest of Callandar, it describes the customs followed, which ended with the baking of an oatmeal cake, which was divided amongst the company. The cake was broken into small pieces and one piece was blackened with charcoal. All were put into a bonnet and everyone drew their own piece. Whoever drew the black piece was declared the 'elected' one, who would be sacrificed to the gods, to ensure a productive year. There is no doubt that in primitive times this would have led to human sacrifice. Fortunately in later years, without the need to placate the gods, the chosen one merely had to leap through the flames of the fire three times. In the north-east the fires were lit on 2 May and the herdsmen would drive their cattle round the fire to protect them from sickness. This was the night when witches were particularly active, and people would place rowan and woodbane over the doors of the cowsheds to keep out the witches.

Dance has been a part of every aspect of Scottish life – dances associated with the various harvest rituals, and even with the seaweed harvest, the latter being highly prized and used to enrich the soil for agriculture. A special dance followed the ceremony of wading into the sea to collect the weed. In 1548 the lowland shepherds danced in a circle, each one leading his wife by the hand, while the younger unmarried shepherds brought 'her whom he loved best'. From this round dance the square for three or four couples developed. The dance repertoire included reels, country dances, squares and circles, each originally having its own characteristics. The reel consisted of setting steps danced on the spot and alternating with travelling steps. The country dances generally followed a longways pattern with each couple progressing in turn. The square dance was a type of quadrille with four couples in a square – the lancers is a typical example of this formation. The circle dance was not a round dance but any dance in which the couple progressed round the dance floor. Of these four categories, the reel was the truly indigenous dance, belonging to all regions and all levels of society. Its style and formation made it very suitable for any space available. The country, square and circles started to arrive in Scotland from about 1700 and were rapidly assimilated and given a new dimension by the addition of native steps and figures. These new dances were originally imported for the entertainment of the upper classes, but in a country where everyone dances, they were assimilated into the general repertoire. The country dance came from England, the square dance from Paris, introduced by soldiers returning from the Napoleonic Wars, and the circle dance was also a continental import. In the early nineteenth century, the valse arrived, followed by the mazurka and the polka, so that Scotland had a wide repertoire of dances ranging from the oldest native dance through a complete range of social dancing. This has continued to grow through the efforts of the Royal Scottish Dance Society, which has continually collected and published Scottish dances and added new dances as they began to appear.

Another popular occasion for dancing were the hiring fairs, where both men and women came to offer their services for hire on the farm. As on every rural social occasion, an opportunity to dance could not be missed, and before departing to take up their new positions, a dance would be held. Custom demanded that should a man have several dances with the same girl, he must present her with a small gift – usually a box of sweets. This was called a 'fairin', and usually bought from one of the stalls that were erected for the occasion of the fair. A feature of the dancing on these occasions was the 'penny reel', when the fiddler would charge a penny for each dance played. Ceilidhs were a popular family entertainment in the croft houses, and on moonlight nights friends and neighbours would dance outside. The local laird gave annual balls for his tenants and neighbours, and everywhere the sound of fiddle and pipe could be heard accompanying the dancing. By the end of the nineteenth century, the majority of children took dancing lessons, and dance had become an important feature in the

rapidly growing highland games. Dance was held in equal esteem to sports and other arts.

One last aspect of Scottish dance is the step dance. This has now been lost in Scotland but is alive and thriving in Nova Scotia, where it was taken by the immigrants. The annual step-dance festivals are now a firm feature in the social calendar of 'Canadian Scotland', and as the competitive element has moved in, the dances not only survive, but are beginning once again to move forward as each generation of dancers develop new skills. So – what does this tell us about the overall picture of Scottish dancing? This style is clearly defined. A proud erect carriage, quality ranging from restrained elegance to a show of athletic strength, and always impeccable footwork, considerate partnering and a keen sense of spatial awareness in the social dances. I well remember attending classes with an elderly, testy, ex-army instructor who had divided the class into two sets to give us time to breathe, as we thought; he dismissed one half with 'Now, ye go and rest and while ye are resting, *practise*!'.

IRELAND

The Gaels, the second wave of Celtic invaders who invaded Scotland, also colonized Ireland, and again imposed their language and culture on the people. The Gaelic language still survives after 2,500 years. Ireland had an early history of music and dance, in fact it was recognized for its excellence and much admired in England before the wars of the Tudor times engulfed the country and brought about a decline in the more peaceful arts. Following the wars, the edicts outlawing everything Irish, including the language, served further to inhibit the actual use and development of the dance. In spite of this we can still find references to the quality of the native dance, for example, in a letter dated 1569, written by Sir Henry Sidney to Queen Elizabeth I of England, he enthusiastically describes the Irish jigs danced by the ladies of Galway, who he says 'are very beautiful, magnificently dressed and first class dancers'. Certainly, Irish music and dancing were very much in fashion in England during the latter part of Elizabeth's reign, and a chronicle of the period states:

The Irish delight much in dancing, using no arts of slow measures or lofty Galliards, but only country dances of which they have some pleasant to behold, such as Bulrudeny and The Whip of Dunbyne, and they dance commonly about a fire in the midst of a room holding withies in their hands and by certain strains drawing one another in to the fire.

Later we hear that in the time of Charles II, 'Graceful gentlemen were wont to dance with the fair ladies of the Court in the fashion of the Hey and the Fada'. This refers to the *hey*, which was, and is today in fact, a figure, while the *fada* means the *rinnce fada* or fading, a very important and ancient dance. A further reference to performing the *rinnce fada* before royalty comes from the reign of James II, when as the king landed at Kinsale, he 'beheld with delight the dancing of the Fading'.

It is possible that there is a link between the dancing of the *rinnce fada* and the fire festivals of the Celts. Fires have always been an important factor in Celtic folklore, and in the Celtic calendar there were eight occasions marked with the lighting of bonfires. Four were related to the movement of the sun and four to the moon. The sun's festivals were the winter solstice (21 December), the spring equinox (21 March), the summer solstice (21 June) and the autumn equinox (21 September). The moon festivals were samhain (1 November), imbale (1 February), beltane (1 May) and lughnasadh (1 August). On these occasions human beings were originally sacrificed. (The word bonfire is derived from the ancient word 'bone-fire'.) With the lessening of the demands for sacrifice by the old religion, effigies gradually replaced the human victims, and much of the ancient ceremonial attached to the occasion became a folk memory and purely dancing. The fires, however, have always had a deep significance for those who danced round them, leapt over the flames and drove animals through the magical smoke. Various characters are part of Celtic folklore, often appearing under different names according to the country. They are often associated with the fire festivals and there is an interesting description of one of these characters appearing at a St John's Eve festival (the summer solstice):

When the fire had burned for some hours and got low, an indispensable part of the ceremony

Young Irish dancers. Step dance group wearing hard shoes.

commenced. Everyone present passed through it and several children were thrown across the sparking embers, while a wooden frame with a horse's head fixed to one end and large white sheet thrown over it made its appearance. This was greeted by loud shouts of 'the white horse' and, having been carried by the skill of its bearer several times through the flames with a bold leap, it pursued the people who ran screaming and laughing in every direction.

This character is the 'white mare', which also appears in Wales as the *Mari Lwyd*. It would seem that many of today's social dances are firmly rooted in these early customs.

Another very important character connected with the spring fertility rites is the May Queen. In Ireland, the chosen queen retains her title for twelve months during which she presides over all dancing and festivities. There have always been dances connected with the maypole – the pagan symbol so severely condemned by the Puritans. Throughout northern Europe it makes its appearance at various times, from May to Midsummer, always with its own special singing and dancing. In Ireland, hoops covered with rowan and marsh marigolds are carried round the villages, and often gold or silver balls are hung within the hoops to represent the sun and moon, surely a reminder of the ancient Celtic festivals honouring these heavenly bodies.

The circle has always been a magical symbol, protecting whatever it encloses from evil. Sick people and animals placed within the circle can be cured when suitable charms are recited over them, and the bridal pair are ensured of fertility as the wedding guests circle round them. A remnant of the magic circle can be found in Ireland today, when on 11 August several places still celebrate their 'Puck' fairs. A decorated goat (the Puck) is placed on a platform round which the people keep a three-day vigil of dancing. Nowadays the celebration ends with the goat safely returning home, but undoubtedly this originally ended in a sacrifice. Again, the dancing was an essential part of the magic, and the dancing remains long after the original ritual is forgotten.

Seven has always been regarded as a magic number and it appears in the 'seven', the step common to so many Irish dances. The 'seven and two threes' (the side step) is the main step upon which many dances are built, and the same pattern of numbers can often be traced in other contexts; for example, in the knitted sweaters of the fishermen. The motif of 'seven' would be a chain to keep them safe, and the use of seven and three in the chain pattern is often used.

Dances with pantomimic actions also feature in folk repertoire, and often have links to ancient sympathetic magic. One example is a solo dance from Connaught in which the dancer mimes the growing of potatoes – an essential crop in Ireland. The dancer mimes the tilling of the soil, planting and the digging of the potatoes.

Another very important occasion in Ireland is the funeral wake, and on this occasion dancing was of very real importance. An English traveller described an Irish wake as follows:

> Sometimes they follow one another in a ring as they say fairies do, in a rude [basic] dance to the music of a bagpipe. At these meetings the young freye appear as gay as maybe with their holy apparel, and with pipers, harper or fiddler revel and dance the night throughout, make love and matches.

We are reminded that dancing was an important feature of Irish life by so many references to dance, often by travellers. For example, the fact that English country dancing had spread to Ireland was noted by an English traveller, Thomas Dinley, who in 1681 wrote that the people were much addicted to dancing the long dance in their country fashion. Country dances and figure dances based on the native jig and reel were popular in the early nineteenth century, when they began to replace the older, simple, country dances. Reels of three or four were followed by reels for eight or even sixteen (for example, Humours of Brandon) and dances developed from the quadrille, which was a popular dance in Napoleonic France, were introduced into the country by Wellington's returning soldiers. These imports were taken up by the dancing masters who replaced ballroom steps with native Irish steps and matched the tempo to the jig and reel rhythm. These quadrilles became popular throughout the country, particularly when they were adapted to Irish traditional tunes, and they remained in popular usage for over a century. Eventually they gave way to the demands of the revivalists who declared that only dances of the ceilidh were truly Irish and acceptable. The ceilidh started life as a social get-together for talk and gossip amongst neighbours, but rapidly developed into a social dance occasion in which form it remains unchanged today.

All we have looked at so far lies in the category of the social dance of the people, but the other very important factor in Irish dance (particularly in the wake of all the 'Riverdance' shows) is the Irish solo or step dance. This is now such a highly developed and integral part of Irish dance that we should perhaps look first at its simple origins in the life of the country folk. In early times a weekly custom in the villages was the 'cake'. In a village at a time when cake was an unaffordable luxury, every family contributed a tiny amount of either fat, flour or sugar, which would then be baked into a cake. The cake would be impaled on a pole erected outside the church on Sunday morning and following mass the village boys would compete in an improvised dance competition in an effort to win the cake for their family.

The earliest references to Irish step or solo dancing date from the late eighteenth century, and since that time they have been constantly polished by the dancing masters, until they are now honed to perfection. The hornpipe, reel and jig are the main dances in the category of solo and step dances. The steps have become ever more elaborate as the dances have progressed, and the men's steps include grinding, battering and drumming steps, always seeking more complex combinations. Formerly the pride of a relatively small group of people, the solo or step dance has now passed into the country-wide repertoire, and with the proliferation of competitions, it has claimed a huge place in the Irish dance scene. Today hundreds of schools have been established and literally thousands of people, adults and children, are studying step dancing with their specialist teachers. The perfection of technique amongst even the youngest children is quite incredible, and the flowering of talent seen in the competitions is quite breathtaking.

So in Ireland today there is a complete division between the two distinct forms of dance – the social dance of the ceilidh, where basic reels and jigs take pride of place and all can join in, and the highly polished competitive step dance, in which perfection is only achieved by tremendously hard work and commitment. We must, however, point out that although the gulf seems incredibly wide, the Irish love to dance and innate pride shines through, and at the simplest village ceilidh everyone is putting their heart and soul into their dance – there is no place for the uncaring. So the overall style lays claim to being Irish – erect carriage, an inborn sense of rhythm and all the energy put into the footwork. In the ceilidh, the arms are used for partnering, no other movements, while in the step dance they are held rigidly still.

WALES

As in the other Celtic countries, dance has always been a vital element in Welsh culture. There are many similarities, as one would expect, within the Celtic group; for example, the maypole dances of Northern Europe are common to Wales, where they are danced round the *fednen haf*, a flower-decorated birch tree, starting on Midsummer's Day and continuing for several days. The tree plays an important part in Welsh culture – couples were often married under a sacred 'marriage oak' and even after the arrival of Christianity, newly married couples would dance round the sacred oak and cut into it the Christian symbol of the cross. There is a dance called the *dawns blodau nantgarw*, in which the women carry long strings of wildflowers in each hand, which they alternately twirl overhead or throw them to the men they meet in the dance. This seems to have formerly been part of the maypole dancing.

As in all Celtic countries, the fire festivals were of vital importance, and in Wales the Festival of Lammas (originally Lughnasadh) on 1 August is still preserved as a fair in many parts of Wales. The lighting of the Beltane fires in Wales varied from 1 to 3 May, and required a special ritual. Here men would go into the wood to collect fuel and the sticks had to be from nine different trees. They also had to ensure that they were not carrying any metal of any kind. To ignite the fire one man rubbed together two sticks of oak until a fire was kindled. Round loaves of either oatmeal or brown meal were broken into pieces and placed in a bag, and the onlookers then each had to pick out a piece. Those who picked out a brown portion had to jump three times over the fire to ensure a good harvest, while those who had picked out the oatmeal sang and danced round the fire. One wonders if this had originally had some sacrificial connection, as the theme is common to the Celtic countries. *Dawns gwyl ifan*, the dance of St John's Eve, was danced round the midsummer bonfires and marked the end of the summer dancing.

At midsummer, cartwheels bound with straw and pitch were ignited and rolled down the hillsides. It was believed that this would strengthen the power of the dying sun, and if the flames burned until the wheels arrived at the foot of the hill, a bountiful harvest was ensured. Should the flames not survive, the harvest would be poor. There were special harvest dances and ceremonies, and, as was commonly believed in many countries, the last sheaf of corn left standing in the field was believed to shelter the corn spirit. There are many records of the different ways this spirit was released, but in Wales the men would throw their sickles at it until the sheaf was cut down, and the successful reaper was rewarded with a jug of ale. There are many references to the variety of dancing, latterly social, but in most cases with origins rooted in ancient ritual. Up to 1830, in the village of Bonnington on the Welsh border, folk would gather together on Ascension Day and decorate the holy well with flowers, greenery and rushes. They would then dance round it accompanied by the music of fife and drum. Another Well Dance comes from Glamorgan, where at Gellionen well, the people would perform a rain charm. They danced, scattering each other with flowers and herbs, singing and playing 'kiss in the ring'. The leader would then call out 'Bring in rain' three times and everyone then filled bowls from the well and splashed water over each other. Some water was carefully preserved and carried home to sprinkle on the garden. This would seem to be the remnant of an old fertility rite.

There were so many ancient rituals related to different aspects of work, but those showing sowing and harvesting were of paramount importance, as in primitive times they were an insurance to protect the essential supplies. There is an interesting reference left by a twelfth-century traveller in Wales, in which he described how both men and women danced as they sang – first in church, then in the churchyard, miming work that was not allowed on the Sabbath. He mentions ploughing, goading the oxen, preparing leather for shoe-making, weaving, spinning wool and so on. Again, dance was an integral part of the ritual.

There is of course also morris dancing, which has always been a part of the Welsh tradition. *Cadi ha* is a morris dance that moves from one place to another, with the dancers performing at their chosen venues. It is danced by eight men dressed in white with blackened faces. The dancers wear knots of coloured ribbon – pink if they are dancing on the womens' side, blue if on the men's side. They are attended by a boy carrying a birch branch decorated with flowers, a concertina player, a fool and a man–woman figure called the Megan.

An important custom still carefully preserved today is that of *Mari Lwyd* in which a horse's skull is carried round on a long pole, the carrier covered by a white sheet. The *Mari Lwyd* was a midwinter figure bringing good luck to the households. Nowadays, a singing, and sometimes poetry reciting, contest takes place between the householder and the *Mari Lwyd* and its supporters before they are finally allowed to enter. This is because, as the original ritual lost some of its meaning and became just a 'fun' occasion, the followers of the horse often degenerated into a noisy, drunken crowd, and the householders were not particularly anxious to let them in.

There are several descriptions of 'merry dances' in Wales. These were danced by sets of three people wearing hats and jackets decorated with paper ornaments. They would move from house to house and at each place performed a special reel only found in Wales; it finished with couples turning until they could turn no more. A description dated 1819 notes that 'the Welsh are very good dancers and are very fond of it'. It refers to their natural sense of rhythm and comments that the music was usually played on the Welsh harp, although 'the detestable fiddle' was beginning to supersede the native instrument.

There is an immense variety of dance in Wales, and the reputation of Welsh dance being boisterous and energetic was already recorded in 1138, when the people were one minute dancing on the

RIGHT: Welsh broom dancers. Boys dancing over the brooms.

BELOW: Wales. The boys are dancing over the brooms, with the Mari Lwyd in the centre.

green round the church and the next the 'wounded and unfortunates' circled the church seeking cures for their injuries. There is an article by the Reverend Richard Warner from 1798 (*Folk Dance of Europe* – Nigel Allenby-Jaffé, p.294 where the artcle is quoted in full) who described a ball that he attended while on a journey through Wales:

> Tis true there is no great variety in the figures of them but the few they perform are so complicated and long that they would render an apprenticeship to them necessary in an Englishman.

He comments on the agility and skill of the dancers, and was surprised to note that when the dance suddenly ceased and the harpist gave a signal, every gentleman saluted his partner three or four times 'with considerable ardour', after which the dance recommenced with renewed energy. He describes the test of agility between two brothers who danced two hornpipes with 'so much power, muscle, variety of step and inflexible perseverance as exceeded everything of the kind he had every seen'.

During the latter part of the nineteenth century, Wales suffered from the fanaticism of the religious

RIGHT: Dancers from the Isle of Man. Dance on the island shows both Celtic and Scandinavian influences.

BELOW: Couple from the Isle of Man showing the lively style of the local dance.

revival. The old traditional dances were persecuted almost out of existence. One of the reasons for the excessive zeal with which the Revivalists attacked the dance were the 'merry nights', which had long been a feature of the social life of the young people. On Saturday evenings the young people met together and whiled away the night with singing and dancing to the music of a harp until the Sabbath dawned. Before the Revivalists took over there had already been some murmurings from the pulpit regarding immoral customs gradually taking over. Dancing, as usual, was blamed for what was seen as corrupt behaviour, and such was the strength of the anti-dance movement, that Wales very nearly lost its complete heritage. Fortunately two collections of dances, the *Llangadgan*

and the *Nantgarn* were written down in an effort to preserve them and every opportunity was taken to preserve old customs in spite of the stern puritanism that had taken over the life of the people.

There has been an unbroken tradition with regard to clog dancing and Welsh clogging has developed its own very distinctive style. A mid-nineteenth century writer described Welsh clog as being 'exceedingly energetic and boisterous with its toe and heel clicking in perfect time with the music'. Certainly clogging is studied and performed with keen interest today and the standard in the clog dance competitions is remarkably high. The rapport between the solo dancer and his or her musician is most interesting to see – the dance is almost a challenge, a question and answer between musician and dancer.

Today the dance revivals have relaid the foundations of a great heritage, and there is a tremendous interest in the native dance in all its many facets. The numerous dance groups that have grown up, go to great lengths to 'get it right', preserving every possible detail. It is now possible to see authentic dances accompanied by traditional musical instruments, with the dancer wearing carefully created traditional dress. Once again everyone seems to be dancing in Wales, and the strong, rhythmic, lively style of the dance easily proclaims its Welsh origins.

Bulgaria. 'Kuker' character who appears during Lent.

horse, now known as the Blue Ribbon Horse, joins in the fun, but always keeping a watchful lookout that it does not encroach on the Old Hoss's activities. The new horse was created by a group of temperance-oriented young men (hence its name) as an antidote to the somewhat wild drinking habits of the Old Hoss's retinue. On the afternoon of May Day following a substantial feast at the Golden Lion, both groups converge on the town square where the maypole stands, decorated with greenery and flower wreaths. Here both horses and their attendants dance, the Teaser allowing specially selected onlookers to hold his club and dance with Old Hoss. This is taken very seriously and all those selected for the honour appear fully versed in the intricate steps of the dance. And so the festivities continue through the streets, with Old Hoss repeatedly dying and reviving. Death and resurrection – a plain message carried to us over the centuries by an extraordinary long-lived animal ritual. At last the Hoss returns to its stable at the Golden Lion and the whole amazing ceremony is over for another year.

The Minehead Horse is the sailor's horse. He is about 7 feet (2m) long and originally had a head covered by the skin of a hare and snapping jaws, now sadly lost, but he still sports a long tail made of rope. Originally this was a cow's tail. His cover is made of canvas covered with a variety of coloured strips of cloth, and his carrier wears a tall conical head-dress, which covers his face. His retinue is made up of a group of sailors and an accordionist. The Minehead Horse is regarded as the true bringer of spring and there are records dating back over a century describing how on the night of 30 April he would go out to a nearby crossroad, where to the beat of a drum his attendants would dance round him. On the morning of 1 May, the horse would dance and the prettiest girl in the accompanying crowd would become the May Queen. Originally there was also a May King, thus symbolizing the sacred marriage of ancient spring ritual and the May Queen would be carried around on the horse's back.

During the course of May morning, the horse and its retinue descend on the streets of the town and again we have shrieking girls supposedly fleeing in terror. Traditionally the procession visits Dunster Castle where they are received with honour and so the festivities continue, another living our and so the festivities continue, another living relic of our ancient past. These are just two of the innumerable examples of how the animals have kept pace with us, but they serve as a reminder that no aspect of dance ritual is ever lost, rather it accompanies us along the way, biding its time until

at a propitious moment it can claim our attention, with its strange and often bizarre behaviour and whatever the context, reminds us quite forcibly of 'where we came in'.

*TOP: **Bulgaria. Kukeri animal characters in procession during Lenten ritual.***

*ABOVE: **Bulgaria. Kukeri animal characters.***

12 CZECH REPUBLIC/SLOVAKIA

Situated in the centre of Europe these two countries were for almost a century linked together under the name of Czechoslovakia. In 1918, following the First World War, Bohemia, Moravia and Slovakia were united to form the new state of Czechoslovakia. They co-existed peacefully until, in 1990, with the collapse of Communism in Europe, Slovakia declared its independence. Fortunately, unlike many other countries that were now splitting up into their original components, the division was made peacefully, and the original state of Czechoslovakia now emerged as two independent countries: the western half as the Czech Republic, and the eastern half retaining its ethnic name of Slovakia. For the purpose of comparing dance from these two regions, the river Morava flowing through the central province of Moravia makes a useful dividing line. East and west of this line the two countries have very different lifestyles and cultural backgrounds.

The Czech Republic is a highly developed industrialized country looking westwards for its culture. Here folk culture is preserved through an acknowledgement of keeping up the old traditions, rather than the 'hands on' tradition of an agrarian community. Slovakia in the east, however, is a purely rural society with agriculture in the south and a pastoral tradition in the north. Here ancient traditions are still a way of life and folk customs are alive and meaningful. Even folk costumes are still worn in many areas. Slovakia looks eastwards to its roots and culture. This division is reflected in the dance of the two countries, with both similarities and contrasts quite clearly laying claim to both eastern and western origins. This is underlined when we look at examples of dances that share the same name and very similar melodies, but show a marked difference in style. A good example may be seen in *kalamajka*. Both eastern and western versions show elements of the same accompanying music, but the dances are completely different in style, with the western version showing a strong Germanic influence, both in quality of movement and musical interpretation, while the eastern version demonstrates a strong affinity with the dance style of its eastern neighbours, particularly Hungary, with more percussive footwork and a preponderance of beaten steps.

Another important contrast shows in the musical accompaniment. Although at times melodies can overlap, the general rule is that in the west the music is in the major key, in the east the minor key predominates. This reflects the general folk-music style of east and west, with a Slavonic quality in the east and a Germanic sound in the west. The various components of the village bands helped to underline this contrast. In southern Bohemia bands were chiefly made up of bagpipes, while in the north they could include a variety of instruments, violins, double bass, clarinets and even horns and trumpets. These instruments greatly influenced the sound of the folk-dance tunes; in particular, the bagpipe of this region was restricted to major keys. In Slovakia, however, the dulcimer took pride of place. This instrument is able to produce every tone and semitone within the scale (it has a separate string for each note) and the possibilities that this offers for melody, harmony and modulation have given complete freedom of range to the folk music. The usual accompaniment in Slovakia of dulcimer and violins has had a very definite influence on the quality of movement and consequently the style of the folk dances. Another significant input into the eastern music is the style of the gypsy musicians, who by the bravura of their interpretation of the indigenous folk tunes have brought a flexibility to the Slavonic dance in the same way in which they have influenced the dance of Hungary.

Looking back to the earliest dance form in this central European region, the most ancient step was the basic side and close – step right foot to right side, and close left foot to right foot, repeating to the left; this simple step, starting life in the old closed circle dance, has survived the centuries and forms the basis of many of today's dances. Again it looks both east and west. In the west it has a relaxed quality and easy musicality, while the eastern version mirrors the Hungarian czardas step with its distinctive 'double bounce' percussive quality. This simple step is preserved in its basic form in some of the old wedding dances of the women, in which, linked together in a chain, they dance in and out of the bridal house – out through the door and in through the windows. Early evidence of this ancient dance exists in a sixteenth-century chronicle.

In many children's games today we can find remnants of long-forgotten rituals, and these central European states are particularly rich in games that show traces of old Slavonic dances. Preserved in the girls' dance-games of today is the ancient Slav ritual of the 'little queens' – the *kracovnicky*. This is still performed at Easter and Whitsuntide; a group of nine girls dance in a 'V' formation, led by one girl dressed as a queen (nine is the magic number for women, as seven is for men). The dancers move in formation, casting off and making chains as they travel from house to house, singing and dancing to bring in the spring.

Another dance especially for women is the *vynaseni morany*, in which the girls carry with them a straw puppet. This is ceremoniously cast into the river at the end of the dance. The girls then dress another puppet in white and this is tied to a young sapling that has been newly felled and is now carried to each house in turn while the girls sing 'we carry death out of the village and bring the summer in'. Again we can recognize the theme of death and resurrection. There are special dances connected with Easter and harvest, which are the prerogative of women, as they are associated with rebirth and fruition. All these older dances have their roots in ancient Slav culture, and descriptions of folk dances dating back to the thirteenth century can still be seen today. Apart from the old circle dances, which provide a common root throughout

Europe, there are references to other dance forms; for example, chasing dances done by young men and girls, again showing the motif of courtship – the boy pursuing, and the girl pretending to spurn his advances – also very common in nearby Austria.

The geographical situation of this region in the centre of Europe, has ensured a steady input from its surrounding neighbours. In the sixteenth century there was an influx of Italian culture, when many

Children from the Czech Republic.

Italians were invited to the royal court. Their influence still survives in art, song and dance. In the eighteenth century the region was drawn into the vast Austro-Hungarian Empire, and here the influence was of a two-way nature, as Austrian music absorbed the native Slav form and rhythms, which were to surface again in the nineteenth-century music of Austrian composers such as Strauss. Strauss in particular incorporated many Slavonic themes into the popular repertoire of the day. He made great use of the polka, which one could certainly call the national dance of Bohemia. Popular belief is that it originated when 3/4 valse melodies introduced into the country were compressed into 2/4 time to accompany the indigenous dance steps. In his *World History of the Dance*, Curt Sachs refers to a Bohemian peasant girl who was the first to dance the polka at the beginning of the 1830s. Be that as it may, the polka grew and developed, so that now we can see polka steps flat, stamped, springing, forwards, backwards, sideways and turning. All of which contribute to the foundation on which much of today's folk dance is built.

Apart from the early circles and popular couple dances of the social scene, this central European region has a wealth of ritual dance, chief of which is the sword dance. Several of these are still currently performed and admit to very little change over the centuries. For example, in the village of Odamok, an ancient dance for six men may still be seen. They carry pliable metal rods and wear distinctive, highly decorated head-gear. Unlike Germany and Austria, where the sword dances have often been adopted by different guilds thus becoming very stylized, in the Czech Republic and Slovakia they have retained their original character, as done by the country people. In these regions it has kept its rustic quality and attendant folk characters and animal maskers. In Skani (Moravia) the swords are flat and broad, and are strung with small brass rings that jingle like bells. Here the dance is called *fasancare* (carnival) and the dancers visit the houses bringing good luck. At each house they perform their dance, often accompanied by a short sketch or part of a now long-forgotten ritual play. There is also a stick dance in which the dancers dance around sticks embedded in the ground and, similarly, there are dances in which axes are used in the same way. In the men's dance, *haydock*, the men carry axes and it is believed that this dance was originally performed by the seventeenth-century folk hero, the outlaw Janaosmou, who like our own Robin Hood, lived in the forest with his band of followers, robbing the rich and protecting the poor.

Interestingly, there are dance groups that dress in almost identical costume to the Cotswold morris men and perform very similar figures, waving handkerchiefs and clashing sticks. The bear and the ram are popular characters attendant on many ritual dance occasions. They also often appear at weddings, where they walk in front of the bridal pair, and also in the celebrations at carnival time.

The dance *pod sable* (under the swords) is found in its purest form in the Carpathian foothills, and although performed elsewhere, in this region it belongs particularly to the woodcutters, who have retained its original form. It is danced at the end of carnival by five boys carrying wooden sticks, which are painted red and inlaid with the brass rings used to decorate a horse's harness. Their leader carries a real metal sword but does not join in the dances. The dance commences with a promenade accompanied by singing and circles counter-clockwise, with one step to each beat of the music. During this the dancers use their swords like walking sticks. This is followed by different figures, stepping over, turning and forming a knot, in all of which the same jumping step is used throughout, and the swords are carried hilt and point fashion over their right shoulders. The boys are rewarded for their efforts by the housewives, who spear a joint of bacon on the point of the leader's sword. The dance was originally accompanied by a bagpipe, violin, cymbalon and clarinet.

A few original tunes for sword dancing may still be found in ancient manuscripts in the archives of the monastery of St Coruna, which is situated in southern Bavaria. These musical relics indicate that the dances in almost unchanged form were performed in medieval times. Dating back to the eleventh century, there are murals depicting musicians and dancers from the region that eventually became Czechoslovakia.

In Moravia there is a mining region that has a strong tradition of sword dancing, and more are to be found in the Carpathian and Tatra mountains,

Czech Republic. Boys carrying the axes that often feature in their dances.

near to Hungary. In Moravia, four men form a lock with the swords, while a fifth man carries a basket of small gifts that are given out to the householders to whom their visit is bringing good luck. This dance is accompanied by a mysterious song, the meaning of which is long-forgotten but seems to carry a vague suggestion that originally the dance enacted a ritual killing. Bohemia has various carnival sword dances. In Kaplitz the dancers form a special figure entitled 'the gate' through which all must pass. There is also

a dance with a straw man who jumps over the swords, the height of his jumps indicating the height to which the hemp will grow. In this dance, the mistress of each house visited must dance with the straw man to bring good fortune to the household.

Ponad flasku is performed by dancers carrying sabres. It appears at weddings and is danced round the bride as part of the ceremony. The dancers eventually lift her veil on the points of their sabres. In every country weddings have traditionally been the occasion for the enactment of ancient customs, dances and songs. There are several competitive dances for boys. Usually these are danced in a circle with ever more difficult steps and gradually increasing tempo. The dancers, when inspired, will run into the centre and take their turn at improvising more complicated steps. The *odsemek* is a competitive dance originally danced by shepherds around their flock.

The maypole tradition makes its appearance with the girls carrying a pole decorated in white, while the boys carry a 'guy' figure representing the tree spirit. In Bohemia the maypole appears on midsummer's eve along with the midsummer bonfire, on which it is ceremoniously burnt at the end of the celebrations. In Moravia the maypole is set up in the autumn and the men dance round it with high leaps. Again the height of the leaps would encourage the next year's crops to grow. There is a poppy seed dance in which the dancers mime the planting, watering, growing and harvesting of the seeds – even finally eating them. The step throughout is a high leaping step. This is a remnant of an old fertility dance that has now become a children's game. It can be related to similar dances found throughout Europe; for example, in England the 'oats and beans and barley grow', while in France there is 'how we plant the oats'. In both cases the mime of planting through to harvesting is indicative of the old belief in acting out the desired scenario in the hope that this would ensure its happening in real life.

In this same category there are other examples of sympathetic magic; for example, a dance for girls carrying flails, which are used to mime threshing. There is also a dance for washerwomen carrying the wooden bats that were used for beating the washing. There is a bear dance, *medvedka*, in which the dancers emulate the actions of the animal, with jumping and squatting movements. An almost identical dance can be seen in the film archives of the folk collection in Sweden. Another animal dance is the cock dance, *ko-tovy tanec*. This is found in Slovakia, where the dancers imitate the strutting of a cock, while the music reflects its crowing. This is danced on the night of the summer solstice and reflects the hope for the season's regeneration. The cockerel motif is found in many countries. It is particularly popular in France, where a wooden bird is placed on the midsummer bonfire. Its brief is to fly away in the smoke and bring back the sun the following year. This links up with an even older belief – that the bird was in fact the phoenix, the mythical bird that never died, but always rose from the ashes to live again – the eternal theme of death and resurrection illustrated in one of its most magical forms.

There are several fighting dances using the *valaska*, a long-handled axe, as a weapon. These axes have a metal head and wooden handle, and are decorated in traditional style with hammered patterns on the metal and painted designs on the wood. These dances are usually in the form of a mimed fight for two men. There are also solo dances in which the dancer shows off his dexterity in jumping over his axe and twirling it, both with a great deal of personal improvisation. The axe is also used in a country dance from the eastern regions. In this the man shows off his virility in the dance and his dexterity in handling the axe, while the girl performs her own jumping and heel-beat steps. This lively and strenuous dance is accompanied by a love song, which reflects its courtship origins.

The ancient rituals of good versus evil, fertility versus infertility, youth versus age, prosperity versus hardship, are all reflected in the tug-of-war dance game still performed by the girls of the Slovakian highlands. In all these tug-of-wars, the 'good' side must be allowed to win; for example, the young must beat the old, in order to ensure the re-birth of life in each generation.

An occasion on which one can be sure to witness unspoilt dance traditions is, of course, at weddings. On these occasions the whole cycle of traditional song and dance is recalled – not always in its entirety, but usually preserving some part of the original. This is true throughout Europe, with the central and eastern countries following the entire format the most closely. Slovakia, in particular, adheres closely to the original ceremonial. Here a master and mistress of ceremonies are appointed and under their leadership the seven-day cycle of ceremonies begins. The celebration follows a strict format from which no divergence is allowed, for to knowingly break with tradition would most certainly ruin any chance of a happy marriage. On the evening before the wedding, the unmarried boys and girls make crowns for the girls and buttonholes for the boys, of rosemary tied with white ribbons. The invitations are handed out prior to the wedding by the best man and chief bridesmaid, and on the morning of the ceremony the best man's first task is to go round the village accompanied by the musicians to summon the guests. He then collects the bridegroom, and on horse-back they go to fetch the bride. For this they are accompanied by the rest of the married men on horseback, the whole group singing and firing pistols. The church ceremony is followed by dancing at the village inn, until all are summoned to the wedding feast in the bride's house. Special songs and dances are performed to a carefully laid out format, the dancers all being of the old circle style. In one dance the chief bridesmaid stands in the centre of the circle cradling a large plate, as she would a baby, and collecting money from the guests for the hoped-for children. The dance is named *coubka*, the cradle. This is followed by *cedini*, a ring dance round the bride, and the *placek*, in which the bride's mother brings in a large wreath of plaited pastry. This is taken by the mistress of ceremonies who, after dancing with it three times round the circle, hands a piece to each guest. The guests then return to the inn and the dancing continues. The bridal couple in the centre of the circle drink from a jug of beer and then dance the polka together, followed by each couple in turn. This is the only time the dancers leave their circle formation. The following day, with a procession of horses and carts carrying all her new possessions, the bride travels to her new home. The procession is led by the musicians playing violins, clarinets and pipes, travelling in the leading carriage. More customs are carried out on arrival at the new home. The bride must be paid for with coins built into a bridge across the table. The chief bridesmaid then dances on the table and traditional songs are sung. All these special songs and dances are kept strictly for the occasion of the wedding and are never used otherwise. The final tradition is the exchanging of the bride's wreath for the head-scarf worn by married women. The bride must show her unwillingness by rejecting the scarf three times, but finally she accepts it and has now joined the ranks of married women. Another instance of special dances being used only on a specific occasion is the dancing seen at funerals. Again they are all ancient

circle dances, and are never used outside the funeral or funeral wake.

So in the western and eastern halves of this central European region, are two contrasting styles of dance and folk music, which yet retain some unifying elements. We can say that, apart from the older ritual dances we have been looking at (the sword dance figures, the ancient circles still used at weddings and funerals), then overall, dance today has left the group formation and the majority are couple dances. This is in line with the development of the dance scene today, which is part of the social scene and no longer tied to prescribed rituals and basic circles. The dances have a lively, social quality, and in both regions are performed with attack but, although we can hear similarities in melodic line and can recognize a common root in some steps, it is in the rhythm and tempo that we find contrast. In Slovakia, the ethnic dance can show constant change of tempo and can reflect the improvisation of the musicians, while in the west there are dances in which the measure changes but the tempo remains constant. This produces a very specific effect; for example, a phrase of three bars of 2/4 time followed by a single bar of 3/4 time produces in all a phrase of nine equal beats, and the dance steps follow this. So, although the music shows an interesting rhythmic accompaniment, the dance never falters – the impetus remains constant. An example of this 'mixed time signature' may be seen in *latovak* from western Moravia, in which the music follows a pattern of: A one bar of 3/4 and two bars of 2/4; B three bars of 2/4 and two bars of 3/4. These are alternated in a pattern of AAB AAB B B AAB, all of which is followed by the dance steps, while retaining a smooth even tempo. Apart from these musical clues, we can safely surmise that the western style shows a 'roundness' and constant flow, while the east has a sharper and more 'clipped' quality. This latter quality may perhaps also be indicative of a strong masculine input, which in turn reflects the male, militaristic style of Slovakia's nearest eastern neighbours. As ever, the musicians eventually 'call the tune'. The village bands of the west are already constant in their performance, so the dancers perform within a recognized framework, while in the east, the 'go as you please' gypsy musicians leave the door open for freedom of movement and constant change in interpretation.

13 ENGLAND

With an easy, even lilting style that exactly interprets the music of the social dance scene, along with the lively and more boisterous quality of the morris dancing and specialist clog styles, England has an immensely rich folk-dance heritage, encompassing a wide variety of dances related to many different occasions. We can list country dance, morris, clog dancing, sword dance (both long swords and rappers), garland dances and even broom and egg dances.

Country dances are social, danced for recreation by people of both sexes and any age. They have always belonged to all levels of society, and consequently have passed from village green to ballroom and back again as dictated by the prevailing fashion. Many of the dances are traditional and have evolved through countrywide usage, but just as many, if not more, have been choreographed over the years to suit the current popular demand. A perfect example of this 'supply and demand' is the emergence, in the seventeenth century, of John Playford, a London music publisher, who edited a series of dance collections, designed to meet the needs of the day. The first book containing 105 dances and tunes, was published in 1651, and most of these were, in all probability, already over a hundred years old. At a period when dancing was immensely popular, this first edition of *The English Dancing Master* was eagerly received and made an immediate profit, so that Playford continued his publications, presenting seven more editions, each larger that the preceding one. His son Henry continued the work, bringing out a further five books, while their successor, John Young, produced six more, bringing the total to

English folk dancers in a Playford dance and costume.

English 'country' dancers at a festival in Spain.

eighteen editions over a period from 1651 to 1728. The music for the early dances was generally made up of popular folk songs and ballades of the day, or even from an earlier period, but by 1690 music composed especially for dancing was becoming increasingly the vogue. The dances of the early editions were dances that were already well-known, many dating back to the reign of Elizabeth I or even earlier, but as these were gradually used up, choreography stepped in, and the dances of the later editions were composed especially for the books. This is reflected in the gradual change of style, from the informal 'fun dancing' of the earlier period, early folk dances often deteriorated into romps, through to the more formal and mannered dances of the later period. Here the influence of the dancing master begins to show, with the accent on deportment and good manners given equal importance to the dance steps.

We have seen how the simple melodic lines and even phrasing of English music combined to influence the dance, producing an easy, even, quality of movement with simple lilting steps with which everyone could feel comfortable. Following the Restoration of the Monarchy in 1660, social life once again changed its pattern and country dancing spread from court, stately home and gentleman's residences to balls given in public assembly rooms, when the newly emerging middle classes enthusiastically took up the fashion. The eighteenth century saw the heyday of the country dance, carried on a wave of public enthusiasm at all levels of society, and aided by the proliferation of dance publications in the wake of *The English Dancing Master*. (Many in fact blatantly copied from the Playford books.) The general enthusiasm for dancing knew no bounds, and the dancing schools, already established since the sixteenth century, did a roaring trade. A grand ball would commence with a minuet, followed by country dances, a pattern still repeated a century later, when it would start with a valse, again followed by country dances.

In 1706 Raoul Auger Ferrilest introduced English dance to the court of Louis XIV and English country dance became the height of fashion at the French court, from which it spread throughout the fashionable ballrooms of Europe. As environment influences development, so the country dances felt the wind of change in their new surroundings, and new dances, such as waltzes and quadrilles, began to make their presence felt. By the early years of the nineteenth century, the most popular of all the country dances, the longways set, was giving way to the new fashions. The reverse flow started, and new ideas from the continent began to appear in the repertoires of the English dancing masters and on the programmes of balls, so that by 1840 English country dance had almost disappeared from the fashionable ballrooms, giving way to waltzes, quadrilles, cotillions and even the polka and mazurka. By the end of the nineteenth century, the emphasis everywhere was on the couple dance, and the social scene was once again changing. In spite of this however, the country dance refused to accept obliteration and chose to bide its time in quieter corners, so that even today, in the villages of Northumbria, Cumbria and the Yorkshire Dales, one can still, at a local dance, suddenly find the floor cleared of quicksteps and valses, while the country dance takes over, and one and all, old and young, make up sets for 'Meeting Six', Cumberland square eight, la russe and even the occasional rant. As late as 1929, a programme of dances described by a Mrs Hall of Newcastle, listed Circassian circle, Morpeth rant, corn rigs and drops of brandy, along with the new veleta, St Bernard's valse and, of course, the lancers. The latter, popular both in village hall and ballroom between the two World Wars, is an example of a much travelled dance. Originally an English square set, it travelled to France, where after some elaborate additions, it made its way back home as a most popular ballroom quadrille.

There have been several instances of dances returning to their native shores. Since the Second World War, the American square dance, brought over by the American GIs, became very popular in England, and when we take a long look at some of them, we can recognize several of our early country dances, which travelled abroad with the emigrants and have now found their way back home, albeit in modified form. Fortunately, England has a

wealth of dance outside the collections, and the suppression of dancing by the Puritans has been greatly exaggerated. (There are references to dancing at the wedding of Cromwell's daughter.) In fact, even the Puritans realized the value of dance in teaching deportment and good manners.

Now the wheel has come full circle, and with the growth in popularity of the barn dance, the country dance again raises its head, often thanks to the enthusiasm of the revivalists, but also in many cases just quietly continuing in unbroken tradition, in a form of dance beloved by all who like to 'join in the dance'. Morris dance is a completely different form of dance. Originally a man's dance emanating from prehistoric spring rituals, it is a dance of strength and energy. In its high leaping steps, the men give out energy to strengthen the new season's growth, a reminder of the primitive times when people were totally dependent on Nature. In the morris dance we have a living relic of the rituals that these early dancers believed would ensure their future food supplies.

There are several distinct forms of morris dancing. The form most readily recognized by everyone must be the Cotswold morris. This is performed by teams of six men, half of which are referred to as the 'ladies' side', although of course they are all men. They are all dressed in white trousers and shirts decorated with coloured ribbons and rosettes, and usually with a baldrick – a wide ribbon or braid crossed front and back at chest level. Bells are attached to leggings worn round the calf. Hats vary considerably and may be of any style from straw trilby to top hat – the latter seems to be gaining in popularity nowadays. They are decorated with flowers, feathers, ribbons and so on, with a preponderance of flowers on the 'ladies' side'. The dancers carry either white handkerchiefs or sticks. The group is usually accompanied by any of a strange variety of characters; for example, a man–woman carrying a pig's bladder on a stick, a country bumpkin, usually attired in a smock, and particularly a fool, often dressed as a clown. The fool is usually given the job of carrying round the collecting box. There may even be a cake-bearer, who carries a special cake impaled on the end of his sword. Some groups have a hobby-horse in attendance, and one of the London groups even has a unicorn.

The dances are lively and energetic with a great deal of stamping and leaping, and great play is made of waving handkerchiefs or the clashing of sticks.

Owing to the decimation of the rural male population in the great war 1914–18, traditional morris had nearly died out by the early twentieth century. By the time Cecil Sharp commenced his research and collections at the beginning of the twentieth century, only 14 of the 250 sides known to be dancing in about 1800 had survived, and today there are very few teams that can claim an unbroken tradition. Of those that can legitimately make this claim, Bampton, Headington and Abingdon in Oxfordshire, and Chipping Camden in Gloucestershire are all Cotswold sides. (The latter are one of the few teams that dance hatless.)

Another important form of morris is the processional morris, found mostly in north-western England. They may usually be seen escorting one of the rush carts that appear at the end of the summer. Traditionally the rush carts carried freshly cut rushes, which were laid on the floor of the church in the days before there was any form of heating. The highly decorated carts travel in procession accompanied by the processional morris men, marching in twos and twirling sticks decorated with ribbons and bells. There is usually a large number of morris men, some leading and some following the cart. They wear dark knee breeches, white shirts trimmed with coloured ribbons, stockings and iron-soled clogs, often decorated with bells. Hats are elaborately flower-trimmed, usually with fresh flowers, and sometimes a patterned waistcoat is worn. The three most famous traditional processional morris dances are the Britannia coconut dance (Bacup in Lancashire), the Abbot's Bromley horn dance (Shropshire) and Helston furry (or floral) dance (Cornwall). These three dances have their own specific traditions, and are all most certainly 'exceptions to the rule', and found nowhere else.

The Britannia coconut dancers are the most striking in appearance of the three, with blackened faces and wearing their distinctive costume of white kilts over black pullovers and leggings, and with white turban-like head-dresses. They come out on Easter Saturday and, starting from the village of Britannia, high on the hill above Bacup, they dance down into the town preceded by their 'whipper in'. Originally

OPPOSITE PAGE:

*TOP: **The Britannia Coconut Dancers from Bacup, Lancashire, in their garland dance.***

*BOTTOM: **Young morris dancers dancing at a folk festival.***

his purpose was to drive away evil spirits, but nowadays he is there to clear enough space for the dancers to perform. The eight dancers carry pieces of wood, which they clatter together as they dance; these are referred to as coconuts. Apart from the coconut dance, they have a second dance in which they carry decorated half hoops (garlands). They are accompanied by a group of musicians playing brass instruments and progress in procession from one dancing place to another, the musicians leading the way, walking in single file and playing as they go.

The Helston furry dance is performed in Helston each May. A vast processional dance, it weaves a serpentine pattern through the streets of the town. Originally the procession literally danced 'in and out of the houses' – entering by the front door and leaving by the back door. On their way through the house they swept away the darkness of winter with branches of green broom. In this present day and age this is no longer considered wise, and the procession is confined to the streets, with the school-children clad in white commencing early in the morning, followed at noon by the Lord Mayor's procession wearing morning dress. To take part in this one must have been born and bred in Helston, but later in the day, all can join in – usually making a donation to local charities. The dancers move in procession with their partners, dancing a modified 4/3 morris step, periodically pausing to dance right and left hands round, or to join in sets of four to do the same. The procession is led by the local brass band, playing the famous 'floral dance' tune, and so it continues until dusk.

The Abbots Bromley horn dance is a very old tradition, but its true age and origins are lost in time. It is performed early in September, and traditionally 'the first Monday after the first Sunday after the fourth of September'. The dancers meet at 8am at the parish church, where the horns are traditionally kept, and

ABOVE: *Border morris side with handkerchiefs.*

OPPOSITE PAGE: *Molly dancers from East Anglia.*

following an early morning service, set out on their day-long tour of the surrounding countryside, stopping periodically to dance their quaint longways set. There are six dancers in the group, each carrying an enormous set of reindeer antlers on his shoulders. Three of these are painted black and three white, perhaps denoting the forces of good and evil, and indeed the forwards and backwards movements of the two lines in the longways set almost suggesting a challenge. The dancers wear a reproduction Tudor costume, their original costume having long disappeared, and they are accompanied by Robin Hood carrying a small bow, which he constantly twangs, and Maid Marian (a man–woman character), a jester, a hobby-horse, two musicians, one playing a melodeon or accordion and the other a triangle. Again, as in Helston, the ritual lasts throughout the day, until the procession arrives back in the village at dusk, and the dancers return their heavy burdens to the church and disappear into the night.

There are several other forms of morris, which are perhaps less well known as they belong to specific regions. In Derbyshire we find teams of up to sixteen dancers with set dances, which belong to the category of country dances and reels. They also dance a processional morris as they travel between dance venues. Particularly well known are the dancers of Winster and Tideswell, who dance in procession between venues, where on arrival they line up and perform their set figures. In Lincolnshire and Cheshire the morris is similar to that of Derbyshire but is much more spectacular, with lively and energetic 'stepping'. The dancers carry 'slings' made of cotton rope and the teams of ten dancers are led by a conductor. They come out at Easter, Whitsuntide and the Autumn Rush bearing. Border morris belongs to the regions that border Wales – Worcestershire, Herefordshire and Shropshire. In these groups the dancers blacken their faces and usually wear a costume covered with cloth strips of various colours. The 'molly' dancers of East Anglia also blacken their faces and their clothes are covered with strips of ribbon. The steps of their dances are taken from country dances, and they are accompanied by the 'molly', a man–woman character who takes over the role usually played by the fool. One last example, which although of recent origin should perhaps be mentioned here, is the girls' carnival morris, which has proliferated in the north-west of England. This is a highly competitive form of dance performed by teams of girls at carnivals. Based on the men's processional morris of the nineteenth century, it came into being after the First World War. At that period many of the original men's teams had completely disappeared, and new groups of young boys

124

and girls began to appear. Often taught by the older men who had formerly danced, the style gradually became more and more the prerogative of the girls, and began to evolve in a very different way that bore almost no resemblance to the original men's dance. By the 1930s the girls' teams had become an accepted fact, and have become over the years, a new and living folk art which continues to evolve in its own way. Now the carnival morris is seen at every local fête, with its highly trained youngsters in short 'majorette' type costumes performing with a professional precision. Nowadays it certainly has lost any affinity it ever had to the original source of inspiration but, known usually as the 'fluffy morris', has carved its own niche in the dance scene.

Before leaving the morris scene it would be well to clear up one of the most popular misconceptions regarding the name 'morris'. When we look at the name 'morris' today we must bear in mind that this is a comparatively new spelling and pronunciation. The name was originally 'maris', indicating that the men were 'Mary's men' and not, as popularly supposed today, 'Moorish'. In medieval times people used to utter the oath 'marry'. They were in fact swearing an oath in the name of St Mary of Egypt, who was the personification of an ancient sea-goddess named Marie. She in turn represented an even older deity, no other than Aphrodite, the love goddess who rose from the sea. This gives us a very strong argument for abandoning the theory of Moorish giving rise to morris, as the cult of St Mary of Egypt was banned by order of the Christian Roman Emperor Constantine, 400 years before the Moorish occupation of Spain, and a thousand years before we began to use the term 'morris' dancing. One more reason for the Moorish/morris confusion might be attributed to the fact that the Moors, who occupied the Iberian Peninsula for over 400 years, were a dark-skinned race and the morris dancers would blacken their faces, which gave rise to an association of ideas. In fact the black faces of the morris men were part of the magic of the early rituals. They served to disguise the dancers who on no account must be recognised, otherwise the magic would not work, and the ritual would become useless. So I think that we can safely put to rest what has become an eagerly accepted theory. Morris dancers, with all their traditions, were already of ancient lineage before John of Gaunt's fourteenth-century army began to return home from the *reconquista* of Spain with tales of 'blackamoors'.

Another very important facet of English dance is the sword dance. There are two types of sword dance: the long swords, originally found in the north, now popular with modern teams and seen countrywide; and the short swords or 'rappers', which are exclusive to Durham. In the long swords, the team consists of six or eight dancers linked together by their swords, which may be either metal or wooden. Without breaking the links they perform circling and intertwining figures, finishing with the swords locked together in a 'knot' or 'rose'. This is then held up high and displayed by the leader of the team. In the 'rapper' sword dance, there are only five men and the short swords, the 'rappers', are flexible and with a handle at each end. The dance is more lively and energetic, and between the weaving figures the dancers break into very fast and complex step dancing. In some teams a somersault by one of the dancers is included. This dance also ends with interlocked swords held high. This climax is thought to represent what originally might have been the ritual beheading of the leader. In both dances the teams are accompanied by male and female characters (the latter, of course, always a man), usually a Tommy and a Betsy. The traditional season for the sword dances has always been Christmas and the following period, and originally the dances had their own accompanying mummers' play.

Clog dancing is now a very popular part of English folk dance, and there are many classes and workshops to be had. There are several demonstration teams that tour the clog festivals, which are growing in popularity throughout the country. In earlier times, when the working people generated their own entertainment, it is reasonable to suppose that the wearing of clogs gave rise to step dancing, and certainly improvised clog dancing has long been a feature of village entertainment. The hornpipe, a simple pipe made of animal horn, was the usual accompaniment to village dancing, and a simple melodic line and easy 2/4 rhythm made it ideal for the clog dancers. Building upon a simple, and probably common, step vocabulary, the individual dancers produced their own improvisations. This introduced a competitive element, which in turn gave rise to further elaboration, so that clog dancing today can be very complex indeed. Gradually regional styles have developed, which all differ slightly, but the overall appearance of the dance remains constant, with a calm, erect carriage, no arm movements, and all the energy and complexity directed into the footwork. Possibly the greatest influence on the overall picture of English dance lies in the role of the dancing masters. Already well-established in the sixteenth century, they were in great demand at court and in the households of the nobility. With the change in the social structure, and the eagerness of the new middle class to attain the airs and graces of the upper classes, dancing masters proliferated, and every town and city had its resident teachers and assembly rooms where classes and balls took place, while travelling masters toured the rural areas setting up dance courses in villages, farms, manor houses and even barns. The system was to provide several weeks of lessons, culminating in the Dancing Master's Ball, at which the children demonstrated their proficiency, followed by general dancing for the adults. Several programmes relating to these balls still exist, and give an illuminating insight into the mixture and variety of the dances taught. The dancing masters were also accomplished fiddlers, who accompanied their own classes. A detailed picture of the dancing masters, their classes and balls may be found in the beautifully researched book *Traditional Dancing in Lakeland* by the Fletts. It gives a wealth of detail and many examples of dance programmes. So, even with this brief survey, we can rest assured that we are 'second to none' in the wealth of our indigenous dances.

England. The egg dance, researched and revived by Mrs Kathy Mitchell of Hull, and performed as a promotion for the Egg Marketing Board. Historically one of our most popular dances.

Finnish harvesters. Country girls in work dress (c.1900).

14 FINLAND

So often when dealing with the northern territories, Finland is included with Scandinavia. This is an easy mistake to make, but very wrong indeed, as Finland is an individual country in every possible way – ethnically, linguistically and culturally. When arriving in Finland and enquiring about the dancing, one is immediately asked, 'Are you looking for Swedish–Finnish, or Finnish–Finnish?'; and in fact the two are very different, as we shall see when we look at origins and development.

Finland, or in its own language, *Suomi*, is a country of lakes and forests and in spite of long years of foreign occupation, the people have retained their individuality of culture and language. That the Finns have always had their own music and dance is without doubt, and one of the earliest references to Finnish dances occurs in the Finnish national epic, the *Kalevala*, when the maiden Kyllikki is carried off by the hero Lemminkainen while dancing with the other maidens. She makes a condition of her marriage that he must never again wage war. He promises but makes his own condition:

> But thyself on oath must pledge thee
> Not to wander in the village
> Whether for the love of dancing
> Or to loiter in the pathways.

This reference to dancing dates back to at least the twelfth century, a time when girls were already singing the ballads of the Northern countries while they circled in the chain dance. Later both girls and men danced together in the chain; the next development was a dancer in the centre of the ring selecting a partner. Eventually, with outside influence, the chain in some regions breaks up into the couple dance.

Dances imported from other countries, and destined for the ballrooms of the wealthy, eventually fell out of fashion and become the property of the peasants, who adapted them to suit their own style of dancing. The names of these dances show that their countries of origin ranged from France, England, Russia and Scandinavia. In their new style they are still the folk dances of today and in popular use. Older dances, created by the country people, reflect their surroundings, so that we can see the bear's dance, the seal's jump, the fishermen's net-dragging dance and many others, to which the farmers added the reaping dance, the cowman, and others, which reflected their work. There is also a solo stick dance, danced over crossed sticks, and several dances that include comic or satirical mime.

The polka arrived in the ballrooms of Finland in the mid-nineteenth century; both the Poles and the Czechs lay claim to being the country of origin. It came into the ballroom as a couple dance and has now passed into the popular repertoire in several countries, where it forms the basis of a variety of dances. So, returning to the question of Swedish–Finnish versus Finnish–Finnish, we can see a marked difference between the two. The Swedish occupation of the western coast of Finland brought colonization with their own culture, and here today the dances are almost exact counterparts of those still danced in Sweden. The Finnish dances belong to an ancient tradition and have their own quality and style. They are on the whole lighter in quality. Very often the dancers wear the old-style Finnish birch-bark sandal, which gives a lightness to the step. Themes can overlap, of course, and in the same way that the Finns have their animal dances, the Swedes have dances with similar motifs; so we find dances attributed to seals, crows, bears and even flies. But the folk scene today presents two communities, each with their own specific dance repertoire giving a clear-cut picture of what they regard as their own tradition.

15 FRANCE

When considering the style of dancing in France, we must be aware of the very large size of the country, its complex and varied history, and the contrasting geographical regions, which go to make up the country. Having acknowledged this, before we look at the contrasts offered by the many different regions, we can already see an overall pattern emerging – a basic style that will prove valid alongside whatever each region offers. It is of neatness, sharpness, and steps and movements that do not travel very far. This exactly

mirrors the music, which has a small range of sound – neat, sharp and rhythmical.

France occupies a very large area of the European continent, from the English Channel in the north to the Mediterranean in the south, and from the Atlantic Ocean in the west to the German frontier in the east. Land boundaries are with Spain in the south-west, and from north to south in the east, with Belgium, Luxembourg, Germany, Switzerland and Italy. This large area is diverse in geography and climate, and combined with varied historical roots, and even ethnic grouping of the people, one can expect to find considerable contrast in the cultural heritage of the different regions, all of which is reflected in their music and dance. So, starting in the north, we can travel round the country and consider the contrasts offered by the different regions.

In the north-west lies Brittany, and here immediately we meet with an exception to the norm. Brittany is ethnically unrelated to any other part of France, with its own language and jealously guarded ancient Celtic culture. The people are a proud and independent race, always ready to remind you that they are Celts and not in any way French. In view of the French desire to assimilate Brittany into France, the Bretons have had to fight hard to retain their ancient culture. For example, it is only very recently that schoolchildren have been allowed to have any classes in their own language. Even a generation ago, the Breton language was banned in public and only survived within the homes of the people. Now once again free to use their own language, signs everywhere are in both Breton and French. Their music and dance reflect their Celtic origins, dances consisting of circles and chains, which have remained unchanged for centuries – many in fact identical with the early medieval Branles. In many dances the steps are tiny and very complex, and often danced at incredible

Celtic designs. The distinctive spiral pattern used in Celtic decoration is seen here in the background carved on stone at the prehistoric site at Newgrange, Ireland. The same motif is used on the Breton costumes in the foreground – a clear statement of Brittany's Celtic heritage.

speed considering the complexity of the choreography. The dancers keep a close hold in both circles and chains, often linked by little fingers, and the arm movements are sharp and staccato, working from the elbow. The dancers do not travel very far, distance being dictated by the speed at which they move. The complex circles and weaving lines reflect favourite Celtic patterns. The small Breton bagpipe, the binyou, gives a very distinctive sound to the music, and the combination of music and dance could never be mistaken for anything other than Breton.

South-east from Brittany lies Limousin. In this region there is a great interest in folk dance, and the many lively couple dances indigenous to the region are carefully preserved by the folk-dance groups. Here the people often dance in sabots, which gives a special quality to their footwork. The melodic line of the music is simple, and the accompaniment is the typical French pipe and drum.

Eastwards lies the province of Auvergne, a mountainous, heavily forested region bounded on the south by the limestone mountains of the Cevennes, the 'backbone of France'. Here the dances are simple village social dances – couples, two couples and simple circles, often with a short refrain for the dancers to sing. The dance repertoire here is very localized, often known only in the villages, and not included in the generally known popular French dances.

South-west from the Auvergne lies Les Landes, the Atlantic coastal region. Here the people have a basic repertoire of typical country dances, couples and figures, but it is the men who add a new dimension to the programme. Originally this was a region of marshy lands, where the men worked as shepherds

Stilt dancers from Les Landes, France (Atlantic coast).

herding their flocks of sheep. Walking was difficult – with each step you could be up to your knees in the marshy ground, and the height of the marsh grass and shrubs limited the vision. The men long ago solved this problem by wearing stilts. Originally a working necessity, these have become a part of their lives to the extent that nowadays one can see a group of men pacing out the figures of a dance on stilts. Not for the faint-hearted.

Coming to the foothills of the Pyrenean Mountains we find another totally different ethnic group of people. The Basques are a mysterious and very ancient race. Their origins are completely lost in the mists of antiquity, and research has never discovered where they came from. Sufficient to say that their language is totally strange, and has no linguistic connections with any other European language. Again, researchers have never been able to find linguistic roots or clues to its origin. In keeping with this exclusivity, the dances of the region are completely different from any other European folk dances. The men's dances are very athletic, with high kicks, leaps and beaten steps – the latter very similar to the *entrechats* of ballet. The men's dance style is in fact very balletic in appearance and choreography, but performed with immense strength and virility. The girls' dances are much more like the couple dances found everywhere, but here again there is a complexity in the footwork, and sharpness in quality, which belongs exclusively to this region. There are also charming 'arch dances', in which the dancers carry decorated wooden hoops and dance quite complicated figures. For the men there is also the 'seven springs', an ancient dance in which the men promenade round the dancing space, stopping seven times to show different movements. The man's solo 'reverence' is an old traditional dance performed as a formal welcome for visiting dignitaries. This is a very complex and elegant dance, and boys learning it must undergo a strict training régime, which includes barre exercises similar to those of a ballet class. The music throughout the Pyrenees usually has a pleasing and tuneful melodic line and is played exclusively on pipe and drum, both instruments played by the same musician. It is not uncommon to see the local dancing master playing pipe and drum and teaching the dances at the same time.

Crossing the Pyrenees to the south-east lies Rousillon, where the people are more closely related to their Catalan ancestry than to France. The Catalan language is commonly spoken, and the music and dance have a unique quality of their own. The music is tuneful and has a greater range of sound than is usually found in France. The instruments used are mandolins and guitars, which can produce a full range of harmony and depth of sound, and often several musicians come together to play the accompaniment, which produces a full orchestral quality. The dances have great charm and often have a theme that tells a story based on historical or social events. Carnival is especially important in the Roussillon region, and there are many dances associated with the carnival where the performers wear masks. The dance here has a flowing almost swinging quality, and there are many couple and figure dances with delightful choreographic patterns. The girls usually swing their full skirts in a style very reminiscent of Spanish dance, and the whole picture has a special distinctive quality.

The next important region is Provence, the southernmost region bordering the Mediterranean. One of the areas richest in tradition, Provence was originally settled by Greece and later by Rome. In fact the name Provence was given to what became the first Roman province in Gaul. With a long tradition of music and dance, and their own lively temperament which permeates it, we are soon aware that this is yet another exception to the rule. Here again the people claim their own identity and speak their own language. They cling with determination to their own dances and customs, and their repertoire owes nothing to the rest of France. It can be generally classified as follows:

* The indigenous folk dance of the people as performed at village fêtes – done by everyone.
* Guild dances, which once represented some particular trade or corporation.
* Dances originally confined to high society.
* Ritual dances, performed only on special occasions.

There are a number of named dances still in use today, either in local dance repertoire or preserved in the programmes of local dance groups. For example, *li tisseran* (the weavers) probably originally a trade dance. In this the dancers dance round a framework hung with ribbons, which represents a loom, and each in turn moves and mimes the weaving. *Li triho* (the vine arbour) shows the gathering of the grapes and the wine-press. This dance is found only in the vineyard areas, and is danced at the grape harvest. *Li jardinero* (the gardeners) belongs to the gardening regions while *les bergères* (the shepherdesses) comes from the alpine areas and shows the shepherds reeling the thread, while the shepherdesses spin on the distaff.

There are many similar dances that exist alongside them in a large repertoire of ordinary folk dances – the social dance of the people. A group of dances known as 'dances of high society' originally belonged exclusively to the upper classes, and the court, but following the usual pattern of dance development, they gradually filtered down into common use. A good example of this is the *rigaudon*, which rose 'through the ranks' to achieve popularity in high society, and then gradually returned to its origins, where the common people had kept it alive. It has now joined the ranks of country dances as a popular circle dance with the girls constantly changing partners, until they have danced with each man in turn.

The most famous dance from Provence is, of course, the *farandole*. As a social dance the *farandole* was popular throughout medieval Europe, where it appeared as a linked chain following a leader. The leader moved at will, choosing his own pattern around the dancing area. On meeting another chain, all released hands to allow the two chains to weave through each other, rejoining hands when the figure had been completed. Historically the *farandole* has a long history rooted in Greek mythology. (We must remember that Provence was originally a colony of ancient Greece.) Here the story is linked with that of Theseus and the Minotaur. According to mythology, in ancient times Athens was forced to pay tribute to Crete. This took the form of seven boys and seven girls sent annually to Crete, where they were sacrificed to the Minotaur, a bull-headed monster kept in a labyrinth beneath the royal palace of King Minos. Sickened by this useless cruelty, Theseus, son of the King of Athens, offered to join the victims in the hope that he could kill the monster. Fortunately for his plans, he was seen by the King's daughter, the high priestess Ariadne, and she determined to save him. She gave to him a sword with which to kill the Minotaur, and a ball of thread with which he could mark the way out of the labyrinth. The monster was killed and Theseus was

The farandole *danced in Provence.*

Child from Alsace wearing the large black head-dress of the region.

able to lead the boys and girls to safety. As they sailed home, they landed on the sacred isle of Delos where they acted out their adventure in thanks to the Gods; thus the first *farandole* was performed, a chain dance illustrating the winding paths of the labyrinth. Still in popular use, it serves to remind us as to how folk dance can preserve history and mythology over several thousand years. Nowadays the *farandole* has become a vital part of the Provençal dance scene, and throughout the region there are now many *farandole* schools, where the dance is studied along with the *pas grec*, *gavotte* and *gigue anglaise*. The dances are studied at various levels – the dancers may be training for competition work (there are *farandole* competitions at the local fêtes), as teachers of folk dance (every folk dance group has its own specialist teacher) or purely for social purposes. As in many countries, the dance is continually developing and keeping in step alongside the people's social development. The *farandole* has certainly bridged the gap of centuries to move forward into the future, keeping its traditions well and truly alive. The interest shown in the competition aspect certainly ensures continuation and possible further development, and it would seem that the *farandole* competitions, with their distinctive red and white uniform, have become an important feature in the Provençal dance scene, and are likely to remain so, certainly for the foreseeable future.

Travelling across to France's eastern frontier with Germany, we arrive in Alsace, and again find a region which has language and traditions which it fully intends to preserve. Alsace has a long and chequered history, passing between France and Germany several times. Although Alsace has drawn culturally from both countries, and both French and German are spoken, it has its own ancient language and traditions. In appearance the region has a very German atmosphere with black and white timbered buildings and a wealth of geranium-filled window boxes. The local food, with its accent on sausages, pork products and sauerkraut, seems

French dancers at the International Folk Festival in Mallorca. Group from Grenoble, Massif-Centrale.

typically German. Dance in Alsace is an integral and living part of the social life of the people, and appears on all festive occasions. It is a popular activity at all levels of society, and for all age groups. This latter fact in particular ensures its continuation, as the many young people who join in the dance are a sound insurance for its passing on to the next generation. Alsace is a land of fêtes, and dance is always an important factor on these occasions, as well as at baptisms and weddings. In this region the cherry and grape harvests are celebrated in dance; the men have a special dance, the winepress. There are dances for corn harvest and for the spring, and the cock dance is especially popular with the country people. Strangely, with regard to the dance,

there has been little merging of styles but rather two distinct forms co-exist. The circle dances, which are direct descendants of the medieval branles, proclaim their French ancestry, with their small steps and complex rhythms, while the large number of couple dances with their polkas, valse steps and gallops are very Germanic in style. Originally the pipe and drum accompanied the French dances, while the Germanic fife was used for the German music. Violin, mouth organ and accordion were played at the smaller fêtes and village celebrations, but as brass instruments came into use, the growth of the brass bands ensured a full and lively accompaniment, which in turn brings a strong Germanic flavour to the German tunes and dances. The band musicians have their own special fête, which dates back to 1390. It is very important that a full range of instruments accompanies the dance, as otherwise there is a tendency to constantly use the accordion, which although very convenient, can detract from the quality of the older tunes and tends to make everything sound alike, which results in loss of identity.

Lying in the heart of France is the province of Bourbonnais. It lies on the border line between the Langue d'Oc and the Langue d'Oil, and its mountains and forests form a beautiful setting for the valleys and hillsides covered with vineyards. Here dancing has always been held in high regard. On Sundays following mass, the young people, wearing their own special regional costumes, dance in the village square. They dance on every celebratory occasion and during the long winter evenings, when people gather together for either some specific shared task or for amusement. These dances are related to those of neighbouring provinces, but preserve a character and a restraint of their own. They reached a peak of popularity and correctness in the eighteenth and nineteenth century, but sadly now have lost their style and quality, and are gradually being forgotten. The oldest dance is the *bourrée*, which claims descent from the Gauls and has a specific binary rhythm, rather than the tertiary associated with the *bourrée* in other regions. For generations it was the favourite dance, until in the second half of the nineteenth century it gave way to the quadrille, but while going out of favour in the more sophisticated ballrooms, it became fashionable in the rural areas. There is a most interesting series of miming dances in which different animals are imitated: the leaping of goats; the *pas de loup* (wolf's dance), showing the furtive movements of the wolf; and the *moutons* (sheep), with its constantly changing chain patterns representing the confused movements in the flock of sheep. In the Bourbonnais, a rural wedding is a great occasion on which all the older dances are performed – circle dances and the medieval branle in its basic simple form – all are shown by dancers following the wedding banquet. In particular there is the dance round a fire, over which all must jump. The music is played on the vielle (hurdy gurdy) and the mosette (a bagpipe made of goat-skin). The vielle is a particularly ancient instrument, already described in tenth-century chronicles. So, the music in the Bourbonnais has a full rounded sound, and accompanied by the percussive tapping of the dancers' sabots, spells out its own lively quality.

Back in the north lies the maritime region of the Pas de Calais situated on the northern coast. The region has a wealth of contradances, which are danced with very neat and rhythmical footwork, and a keen spatial awareness. There are also many couple dances and double circles with figures very similar to those of English country dance. The music is very typically French, using a small range of notes and a sharp even rhythm.

So, although we have seen something of the contrasts and variety that can be found in such a large country, one becomes aware of a common factor dictated by the structure of the folk music. It has a very small range of notes, often less that an octave. It moves in small often repetitious phrases, and the rhythm is sharp, even and never adventurous. These factors combine to produce a similar underlying quality in the dance. The dances overall are not adventurous in the use of space, with the possible exception of the 'follow my leader' structure of the *farandole*. Rather they all have a neatness of placing and sharpness closely related to their small size, and whatever special style a region claims, this underlying very 'French' quality is never completely lost.

16 GERMANY

In looking for information regarding German dance we are fortunate in the vast amount of material available. This means that we are able to get a clear picture of dance development through the ages in Germany. Early myths refer to the creation of the world in the terms of a 'vast cosmic dance'. Primitive humans soon recognized that the two most important occasions were the summer and winter solstices, and the earliest dances were the circles when, on these occasions, they danced round a sacred tree or a fire. These early circle dances were not purely recreational, they were for a purpose – rituals to ensure the return of the sun and the continuation of the food supplies on which they were dependent. With the advent of Christianity these primitive dances did not disappear. Rather, they were so ingrained in the lives of the people that they continued, and what had originally been part of a serious life-preserving ritual gradually became part of the social scene. Dance never leaves us but always accompanies us on our way, adapting as need be. The wheels and circles, symbols of the sun and moon, became the basis of an ever-increasing repertoire of social dances, and the winding snake dance turned into figures in an endless series of dances, which ever grew more complex in keeping with human social development.

In Germany, the circles were accompanied by singing – the words often dictating the steps. There exists one early example of the song and dance ballad recorded in the year 1000. In this example, the words, music and steps are already inseparable. In the seventeenth century, instrumental music began to replace the singing and, once started, developed rapidly. There is a chronicle from 1653 detailing the instruments used – hurdy-gurdy, shawm, bagpipes, lyres, drums, scrummel pot, tambourines, pipes, cymbals and jaw's harp are all mentioned.

Bridal couple from Bavaria.

The dance likewise developed. The early couple dances were imported from France and this opened up endless possibilities for figure dances. From as early as the fourteenth century there are many descriptions of couple dances with a mime, often

ABOVE: *Young German girl wearing her distinctive black bonnet.*

RIGHT: *The Black Forest, Germany. Girls wearing bridal crowns.*

comic, and including scolding, kissing and teasing. Many of these early themes are still in existence today in German folk dance.

An important symbol that still features in German dance is the wheel, symbol of the sun from ancient times. There are records of peasants in northern Germany dancing round a burning wheel at weddings, and the wheel can be seen in many folk dances today. The most popular usage is when the boys place their feet in the middle of the circle and, supported by the girls, lie back forming the spokes of a slowly turning wheel.

There are many references to sword and hoop dances, and dancing round maypoles, while at carnival time the various trade guilds performed their own dances. Butchers, cutlers, coopers, all had their own dances, which survive today with groups of young people who dance their own version of them to earn some pocket-money during carnival. The style of peasant dancing has always been boisterous and at times sufficiently rowdy to arouse the wrath of the Church, which has imposed innumerable bans on the dance with its 'unseemly behaviour'.

For a long time, two dance forms moved along together: the slow and dignified processional of the aristocratic couple dance; and the lively turning dance of the peasants. When the new middle class began to take into its ranks people from both upper and lower classes, the dances came together, uniting both of these dance forms and creating what became known throughout Europe as the 'German dance', the 'allemande'. In this the processional dance became the 'fore dance' in duple time, while the turning dance became the 'after dance' in triple time.

At the beginning of the seventeenth century, certain dances began to carry the label of national dances, as they were closely associated with specific regions and countries. One of the most widely recognized of these was the *ländler*, a turning dance in triple time. With the introduction of the *ländler* to the French court, a dancing master's instruction book was published in 1768. In this the dance is referred to as the *allemande*, a German dance in triple time, and detailed drawings illustrate the various arm holds. In the hands of the dancing masters the dance was gracefully performed, but in Germany its licentious flirting motifs caused yet another ban to be imposed

upon dancing. For the first time, in 1748, we find reference to the dance being called the waltz (from *waltzen* to turn or roll), and in 1760 came a further ban prohibiting people from dancing these 'waltzing dances' in the streets. This time the ban was read out in the churches and even the musicians were threatened with punishment in the form of heavy fines should they be caught playing for it. The prohibition, as ever, proved ineffectual, and the fiddlers' music books of the period contain a great many waltz tunes.

Although the waltz plays such a large part in the German dance scene, it was by no means the only dance form of importance. In northern Germany there are many polkas and marches danced in a rather heavier style, while in Bavaria in the south, the triple time is again in evidence, and the popular dance is the *schühplattler* with its lively clapping and slapping based on a rhythmical 3/4 time. Here the local costume of the boys, the lederhosen (leather trousers), allows them to give full rein to their boisterous slapping, while the girls waltz quietly in the background. In eastern Germany the mazurka, imported from Poland, was very popular. So we can see a wide variety of dance in Germany, and its popularity continually grows, as more and more folk groups are formed. The style is lively, rhythmical and at times rather heavy, and often shows considerable interplay between couples. In the dances performed at folk-dance festivals, the dancers often introduce mime, which can give rather a heavy-handed humour to the performance. The interplay between couples is a very old feature of German dance; writing in 1023, the poet Ruodlieb refers to a couple dance in which the boy is wooing the girl while she 'flies away'. This theme of the boy pursuing and the girl pretending reluctance is the motif of many German and Austrian *ländlers* and can still be seen in many couple dances presented by folk-dance groups. As for the waltz, no amount of Church prohibition could quell it, either at home or abroad, where it soon invaded the ballrooms of Western Europe and scandalized polite society, until eventually it received international approval when the young Queen Victoria danced the waltz with her husband Prince Albert. The simple German folk dance had now staked its claim to recognition at every level of society and is never again likely to lose its favoured position in the dance repertoire.

17 HUNGARY

The Magyars, ancestors of the Hungarian people, were a non-European race that came out of the east and, fighting their way into Europe, settled on the vast plains of Hungary. As part of the European continental family, their development nominally would have followed much the same pattern as that of their neighbours, but at the same time retaining inborn traits of their very different origins. The Magyars were a Mongolian people, whose life on the steppes of Asia was closely bound up with a nomadic form of life in which the horse was the central feature. Not surprisingly then, this dependence on their horsemanship remained with them as an essential part of their lives, and when they finally put down roots and began to live a settled life, horse-breeding became their main activity. The *puszta*, the vast Hungarian plain, offered ideal conditions – unlimited areas of fertile ground – and so Hungary became another member of the European family of countries.

As part of this continental group, the emergence of social dance from early ritual would follow a

LEFT: Hungarian bonnets showing the elaborate work. The embroidered ribbons are usually hand-worked.

OPPOSITE PAGE: Romanian dancers in costume showing Hungarian influence.

Typical Hungarian costume showing the national love of colour and decoration. Note the elaborate pom-pom head-dress.

other western sources were becoming part of the repertoire at the court – galliard, courante, pavane, among others were a welcome addition at court balls and the houses of the nobility. It is interesting to note, however, that in line with these different ethnic origins, the contredanse, a favourite in all European ballrooms, in Hungary developed its own form. One such development was the *palotás*, the palace dance. This was a dance of great dignity and Hungarian character, in which even the clergy could take part. However, hands could not be held but instead their partner's handkerchief. It was this *palotás* that seized the imagination of those visitors who witnessed it, and eventually found its way into the character sections of the great classical ballets. It is the very distinctive musical accompaniment that inspired classical composers; for example, Brahms Hungarian Dances. Apart from the usual court dances, it was the custom to include the folk dances of the peasants in the programmes of aristocratic balls, and this in turn led to the aristocracy affecting traditional peasant costumes.

As in other countries, the Church began to take an interest in dancing and voiced its disapproval, so that the usual, sadly familiar, medieval decrees began to appear forbidding dancing. In 1038 a ban was placed on the playing of any musical instruments apart from those used in church, and in 1279 the clergy were instructed that there must be no tolerance of dancing in churches and churchyards. The Synod of the Reformed Church even forbade its officials to take part in any form of dance. Of course, dancing has always been the breath of life to people – very often their only pleasure. So, as in every other country, all these edicts fell on deaf ears, and people continued to dance.

The best known names internationally in Hungarian dance are most surely the *czardaś*, the *verbunkos* and the *hajdutang*. The *hajdutang* was probably the most popular dance in the sixteenth and seventeenth centuries and has been described many times. An English traveller, Edward Brown, physician to Charles II, witnessed it in 1609, and tells of it being danced with naked swords, 'clashing the same, turning, winding, elevating, and depressing their bodies with strong and active motions' and singing at the same time! These early descriptions

similar pattern in Hungary, but as a people who were ethnically and linguistically individual, it is easy to see that, in spite of the obvious overall development, their dance would always retain something of their ancient origins. This remains true today, as Hungarian dance most certainly has strong characteristics of its own, and is very different from that of its neighbours. The name Hungary is always synonymous with music and dance, and indeed there are early chronicles that refer to dance in Hungary. There is a very early description of Hungarian soldiers dancing 'jubilant with joy' before their leader following a battle. Later, in the fifteenth century, there is a reference to King Matthias Corvinus performing a Hungarian dance, while his bride, Beatrice of Aragon, was shown dancing 'in the Hungarian manner'.

As in every other country, dancing was two-fold – for the peasants and for the aristocracy and the court. By the seventeenth century, dances from do not make it clear whether this was a genuine hilt and point sword dance but we know that it was a peasant dance and not a guild dance, and the various movements described indicate that this must have been a true sword dance of ancient origin. It has survived to the present in the stick dance, *botos tánc*, of which there are many variations; for example, the dances of shepherds and swineherds, where sticks are replaced with axes. The dance nowadays takes the form of the dancer stepping over crossed sticks. There is also the *botolo* dance, a couple dance in which the stick signifies the man's power over the woman. This is especially danced at weddings, where the bridegroom is ceremoniously presented with a decorated stick.

The *verbunkos* is the men's recruiting dance. This grew out of the wars of the eighteenth century, when the army embarked on a tremendous recruiting campaign. The dance was first described in the 1770s and the form established was followed nationwide. A small band of hussars led by their sergeant would arrive at a village, find a suitable place, hoist their flag and form a circle. They would begin their dance, which was made up of alternating slow and quick sections. The sergeant would act as master of ceremonies, while the corporal organized the dancing and, of course, the drinking. Both these activities were favourite pastimes with the peasants, and soon the boys were tempted to enlist and join in the merrymaking. Taking the *shako* (military hat) signified the boys' enlistment, and the celebrations would continue until the recruiting was satisfactorily concluded. That it was obviously a most successful method is shown in the reference from the town of Szeged where, in one day in 1840, 1,300 young men were successfully recruited into the army. By the late eighteenth century, the *verbunkos* had developed its special characteristics, its slow and quick sections, staccato rhythm, ankle knocking, heel clicking and hand clapping. The violin accompaniment and establishment of major or minor melodies had all fallen into place as an accepted format. The more stylized version seen today developed in the 1830s with music always based on a folk-song. The nationwide acceptance of the stylized *verbunkos* came at the same time as the great revival in national aspirations,

and was soon echoed in the flowering of national literature and the emergence of Hungarian composers composing special music for it. Foreign composers, such as Haydn, Brahms, Beethoven and Berlioz, were captivated by the compelling rhythm, and it became the source of national opera and ballet. It inspired Bartok, Kodaly and Liszt, becoming the inspiration of modern symphonic music in Hungary today. The *verbunkos* is the very essence of Hungarian dance – it became the opening dance at court and aristocratic balls, and the people have continued to dance it on important occasions.

The *czardaś* has become very much the national dance of Hungary. *Czardaś* means 'inn dance' and was given this name by the aristocracy who referred to it as being danced 'by the daughters of the serfs in the lowest inns on Sundays'. In spite of this initial disdainment, it spread like fire through the ballrooms of the nobility, and typically, returned to where its popularity elevated it, to the position of 'the Hungarian national dance'. We find a good description from 1839, when an English traveller, John Paget, wrote:

> We had an opportunity this evening of seeing the Hungarian national dance very well performed. The dance becomes quicker and quicker as it goes on, 'till at last the gentleman seizes his partner in his arms, whirls her round and round, quits her, again seizes her and at last conducts her to a seat quite exhausted. To me it seems the most pantomimic of any dance I know. It is impossible not to see the courtship of the lover, the coy reserve of the maiden, the gradual yielding, and the final triumph of love.

After this effusive description he finishes by mildly remarking, 'I cannot say that it is an elegant dance, but it is full of expression, and requires no small agility to perform it well'. I can heartily endorse his reference to agility, as on attending various village dances as a spellbound spectator, the number of different variations (the dance is not set) and the speed of performance were quite breathtaking.

As in every peasant society, the wedding is the most important occasion in peoples' lives. It is a very special time for music and dance, a great deal of which owes its survival to the importance of the wedding ceremonial. The wedding has in fact been of such importance in the lives of the peasants, that in order to fulfil all the ritual requirements, particularly regarding the rules of hospitality, the peasant families have often ruined themselves. It is therefore not surprising that some years ago the government stepped in and forbade these 'over the top' celebrations. In order, however, to preserve an ancient and valuable part of their culture, each village is allowed to hold one 'proper' wedding each year, which is paid for by the state. We were fortunate in being invited to one such occasion, and the spectacle was unbelievably exciting. Everyone, from the youngest to the oldest, was in full festive folk costume, gaily decorated carriages were drawn by beautifully groomed aristocratic-looking horses, and music was played by various gypsy bands. A never-to-be-forgotten occasion. We were unable to discover who had the terrible task of choosing the lucky couple, but felt thankful that no local family was footing the bill for such a massive celebration. Amongst all the special dances and songs that are prescribed by tradition, an interesting custom is attached to one dance – the bedmaker's dance. The wedding guests catch a little boy and throw him up on to the immense pile of eiderdowns, which are part of the wedding gifts. This is a form of sympathetic magic, that the first-born child may be a son. It is then that everyone dances the bedmaker's dance. There is also a beautiful dance done at weddings in the Nógrád region, in which the women dance a pillow dance, each carrying a pillow high above their heads, while others follow carrying the eiderdown. The dance is elegant and rhythmical and very beautiful to see.

Dancing is probably the most widespread activity of the people, they dance in houses, barns, inns and outside in yards or village squares. When a new barn is built everyone joins in the dance to level the floor. At a village dance the men will begin to dance by themselves and gradually include the girls, often calling them in by name. The girls are each invited to the dance by the young men, who pay the entry fee for their guest. According to strict rules of etiquette, the boy must fetch his girl to the dance and escort her home afterwards. At carnival time, special separate 'dancing rooms' are hired for married and unmarried couples. Etiquette decrees that if a girl refuses to dance with a boy but accepts another, at the next ball the offended boy calls upon the gypsy fiddlers to play the 'marching out' tune, and the girl, followed by her weeping family, leaves the room in disgrace.

The best known music of Hungary is that of the gypsy musicians. Records of these travelling players date back to 1489, and by the nineteenth century they were regarded exclusively as the only possible true accompaniment for folk song and dance in Hungary. However, it should be remembered that gypsy musicians interpret the music in their own way – even their style of violin playing is essentially their own – and these facts have greatly influenced the indigenous music of the country. To rediscover the original Magyar inheritance in the music, composers like Bartok and Kodaly have had to literally unearth the old pentatonic sound from beneath the layers of the gypsy influence with its all-pervading ornamentation. The gypsy accompaniment is played on the violin and cimbalom, a sound now completely synonymous with Hungarian folk music. Nowadays the gypsies usually live in the villages alongside the local people. They live the normal village life, following their own particular trade, but are always called upon when music is required. So, in looking to encapsulate the Hungarian style, we find a lively and energetic movement, percussive footwork and a high degree of ornamentation, as the dance closely follows the music, separate special dances for men and women, and strong controlled but energetic turning steps when they dance together. Certainly Hungary has a unique and immediately recognizable style, both in music and dance.

18 ITALY

Italy is a large country with complex geography, bounded in the north by the Alps, Europe's highest mountain range and by the Mediterranean Sea to the south. These two factors alone suggest a wide range of climatic conditions, as the Alps are a region of heavy snowfalls and extremely cold winters, while the Mediterranean is synonymous with warmth and sunshine. It also points to the possibilities of a varied historical background and different ethnic roots for people living in such a widely spread area. Apart from a long frontier with Switzerland in the north, there are two shorter frontiers: with France in the north-west and with the former Yugoslavia in the north-east. These land frontiers have always provided points of entry over the years, so that local culture is easily open to outside influences. The remainder of the country is bounded by the sea, so that any invasions would have to come by sea. The first important one was from Greece, and the ancient Greeks established many settlements and colonized regions around the south coast of Italy. Evidence of this can be seen today in the traces of their settlements, ruined temples and perhaps most obviously in place names. Later the Romans established their vast empire, which stretched from Africa in the south to Britain in the north. Italy became the heartland of the Roman Empire and it is from this time that we begin to hear about dance officially. The Romans were fanatical recorders of history and meticulous keepers of records. One of the first records refers to the Salii of Rome, a sect dedicated to the war god, Mars. One of their rituals was the dancing in of the New Year, which took place on the old Roman new year's day, 1 March. The dancers were twelve in number and they danced carrying small oval shields named *ancilia*. The Salii were still dancing in AD382 when there is a reference to their altars

being repaired; their dance lives on today in the sword and morris dances of Europe. Their original festival gradually lost its meaning and the dance became part of the social scene associated with the annual spring holiday. A remnant of the original ceremonial was the *mamubacia*, in which a man dressed in animal skins and representing the old year, was driven out of the village.

The development of dance in Italy has followed much the same pattern as in Europe generally, but can accurately pinpoint its roots. These can be found in the circles and chains of ancient Greece, and a strong tradition of sword dancing, which certainly is a direct Roman heritage. The sword dance can claim an unbroken tradition through the centuries and there are many interesting examples that have survived the passage of time. From the Piedmont area there is a sword dance led by a harlequin. This has gradually developed into a dance-drama to include a strange assortment of characters; from the *Commedia dell 'Arte come Brighella* there are Moors, a Turk and a Senator. The dance even includes a figure from the maypole.

Italy has the *morisca*, the dance showing the fight between Christians and Moors. This appears in many regions and can be seen in Genoa, Naples, southern Italy and Sicily. There are even records that on the isle of Elba in the nineteenth century it was performed on horseback, and in seventeenth-century Venice it appeared under the name of *saracinesca*. Although all these dances with their regional variations are collectively titled sword dances, the implements used varied greatly – swords, torches, spades and hoes were used, in all probability reflecting the everyday work of the dancers, or even local availability. The *morisca* has also been adapted as an entertainment at court, and in Sienna in the sixteenth century it was presented as a drama. On this occasion the Moors and Christians were replaced by peasants and hermits fighting for the favours of a lovely damsel. From Rome in 1555 comes a reference to a hoop and sword dance. It followed strictly laid down rules and followed a leader. It was taught to adolescent boys and was practised in the eight days before Lent, with large numbers taking part. It was described as a beautiful sight – a numerous armed company going through the various required formations with accuracy and agility.

In Italy we can find all the remnants of the ritual dances connected with the growing of crops, although today they usually appear in children's games. The game 'oats, beans and barley grow' is found in identical form in Italy and several other countries. The processional dance found throughout Europe since ancient times survives today in Sicily as the *riattate*. On the second Sunday in May it is danced during the festival of the Madonna of the Myrtles. Dancing in procession, the celebrants wave branches of myrtle. It is an occasion of great joy and the dance is ecstatic. The remnants of the ancient chain dance can also be seen at Cagliari, where, on St Efisio's Day, the entire population move slowly and with great dignity round the main square.

The couple dance developed early in Italy – initially it was often shown as a dance for a boy with two girls, which gave a different dimension to the dance. However, as the normal couple dance of one boy and one girl it gradually developed, again as in many other countries, with a motif of boy wooing girl and her initial rejections. The most obvious example is, of course, the *tarantella*, a dance that has become synonymous with Italy. The influence of the Church shows here, as, in spite of the strong courtship element, there is no physical contact between the dancers. The *tarantella* is found throughout southern Italy, Sicily and Sardinia. The story is often told of the supposed connection between the dance and the tarantula spider, but old pictures of the dancers with arm positions very akin to the Spanish *jota*, and the use of castanets, points more securely to a Spanish origin; indeed, Spain occupied these regions for several centuries. The name *tarantella* has only been in use in the last four or five centuries. Previously the dance had several names, such as Lucia, *sfessania* and *villanella*,

and the interpretation varied in the different regions. For example, in Apulia the boy dances around the girl singing and playing his castanets and inviting her to dance. She dances with great modesty but eventually responds by holding the end of his proffered handkerchief, while taking care to avoid any physical contact. In Calabria the girl may take the handkerchief and wear it on her head or round her neck. At Sicilian weddings the *tarantella* is danced by all the guests in honour of the bridal couple, miming all the usual courtship actions and ending in a final kiss. In the more southerly regions, the girl maintains a very modest demeanour, but in Naples and Sorrento she dances with much more abandon, encouraging her admirers. There is a charming story regarding the origin of the Sorrento *tarantella*. According to ancient mythology, the sirens who tried to lure Ulysses by their seductive singing were very piqued when they received no response. They did not realize that Ulysses had been forewarned of their attempts to seduce him, and had plugged his ears with wax so as not to hear their songs. The sirens asked the Graces to teach them something that he could not ignore, and the Graces accordingly created for them the *sorrentina*, a dance so delightful that no-one could resist it. Unfortunately they had not allowed for the fact that with fishtails the poor sirens could not dance. So the dance waited for many centuries until the girls of Sorrento and Capri inherited this charming creation.

There are many examples of courtship dances: *della sopiro* (the sigh), *della segglio* (the chair) and *della specchio* (the mirror). All have the same basic motif of courtship, refusal and submission. The *monferrine* is a charming courtship dance in which the dance is accompanied by singing and mimes the teasing and coaxing aspects of the courtship. The *furlana* is in the same category, and is found in two forms: the *furlana ziguszaine* with mime showing flirting, courting, quarrelling and eventual reconciliation; and the *furlana* of Venetian origin – an older version. This latter version is found also in the Greek Ionian Islands, which were occupied over 400 years ago by the Venetians. At that period Venice was a great naval power and a very wealthy state. This strength showed in their dances, which in these regions are virile, agile and dynamic in performance. The *saltarello* is another courting dance from central Italy and the Alenuzzi region. It does not have set steps and figures, but shows the usual courtship theme and moves with high leaping movements. This has given rise to its name, *saltarello*, from the Latin word *saltatio*, which describes a high jumping dance. This dance was originally associated with the spring rituals – again the theme of human energy encouraging nature to be prolific.

A dance in popular use since medieval times is the *trescone*, a square dance for four couples. In it the girls dance lightly '*sur place*', while the boys dance vigorously from one girl to another competing in the brilliance of their individual performance. It is still danced at certain times in the agrarian calendar; for example, at the picking of hemp or the stripping of corn cobs. In earlier times it was popular at weddings, where four couples would dance it in the centre of a circle of singers.

There are strange tales of a dance mania sweeping through medieval Europe. In Italy in 1233 this dance mania surfaced as frenetic dancing, when people carrying burning candles followed the penitential preachers in a state of uncontrollable ecstasy. This strange phenomenon became known as the 'great hallelujah' and finds a parallel in the Pied Piper of Hamelin story, when, in Germany, over 100 children, spurred on by some irresistible urge, left their homes and set off in procession for Armstadt. Those who did not die on the way, were afflicted with palsy for the remainder of their lives. From this period come the stories of young girls who ignored warnings that with too much dancing they could be abducted by the devil. This story is certainly the origin of the story of the Red Shoes, which was first recounted in fairy tales by Hans Christian Anderson and turned into the ballet 'The Red Shoes' choreographed by Robert Helpman. In both instances the only way to prevent the girl from dancing was to cut off the feet wearing the shoes – very gruesome.

In Italy today dancing is still very much alive and a vital part of the social life. It is particularly important to the many Italian folk-dance groups. Many of these groups travel abroad to folk festivals and although often their programmes show a considerable input of present-day choreography, the basic Italian style and original themes shine through, and the dance is always lively and energetic – usually with the eternal courtship motif. Time and circumstances never succeed in changing this ancient theme.

19 THE NETHERLANDS

The Netherlands poses a rather different picture regarding folk dance than is generally found throughout Europe. We have seen strong evidence everywhere that folk dance belongs initially to the country people, the rural population that has nurtured the folklore, which almost always has its roots in the agrarian calendar of a country. In the Netherlands we have a small country with a large population and a history of early urbanization. There is also the unusual aspect of the reclaimed lands. The large area of land that has been reclaimed from the sea, of course, has no history and consequently no folklore. If we draw a line dividing the Netherlands approximately into two halves, north-west and south-east, we can begin to see how regional developments have taken place. In the north-west section, town life predominated over country life from an early period and, in this situation, social life soon replaces the festivals of the agrarian calendar of a more rural population; this is quickly reflected in the dance. The influence of town life also soon influences the surrounding countryside, and by the time that the new lands were reclaimed from the sea in the seventeenth century, the people who settled them were already urbanized and had nothing to bring to the new territory by way of the old rural folklore. They also had a Puritanical and Calvinistic attitude to life and tended to regard folk dance as the 'devil's work'. Very sadly the 'new lands' inherited very little folklore and certainly nothing of folk dance.

The south-eastern provinces, however, have much more to offer, as here lived genuine country people who were unaffected by urbanization and the constant battle with the sea, which has always dogged the coastal regions. These south-eastern areas have a long history of a settled rural population who lived by the agrarian calendar, and had a deeply rooted ancient folklore. Here the people celebrated the seasonal festivities of their life in song and dance. The Catholic Church retained its influence in these regions, so that Calvinism was unable to take over. The Catholic Church has always looked tolerantly upon the festivities of the people, and the tendency has been to absorb these rural celebrations into the Church calendar, rather than try to ban them. This has resulted in the preservation of much of the

Mother and daughter from Middelburg, wearing their 'angel's wings' bonnets.

ancient folklore through to today, and so it is to these provinces that we can look for the older dances and, indeed, the regional dances here have retained a popularity and living tradition not found anywhere else in the Netherlands. They can still be seen at weddings, fairs, and all the traditional feast days.

The dances are well known and very much 'alive', while the traditional dance tunes and songs are known by all. Here we can see both group and couple dances, and although they are now basically part of the social scene, some of them still show remnants of older rituals, and the words sung by the dancers often carry clues to their ancient origins. For example, *riepe garste* (ripe barley) shows the action of the windmill sails, and has strong harvest connections, while *de hoaksebarger* is a typically humorous peasant dance, in which the dancers walk hand in hand solemnly singing, but with a comic mime content. There is also from Gelderland the *peerdesprong* (the horse's jump). This imitates the prancing and leaping of horses. These three examples all show their close affinity with country life, harvest and animals, and interestingly, although pattern develops, they are all built on the ancient circle formation.

As in nearly all the western European countries, folk dance in the Netherlands has hovered on the brink of extinction, and it is thanks to the people's genuine love of music and dance that it has been pulled back from the brink. At the turn of the twentieth century researchers were busy seeking out remnants of dance, and initially they turned to the old people from whose memories they began to recreate the dance repertoire. This is probably the only place to look for information, but it has its problems, as the dance demonstrated to the researchers by a 90-year-old, can look very different from the style in which she danced at her wedding 70 years previously. Certainly there have been times when this has resulted in the dances thus collected appearing slow and heavy, and even now there are one or two elderly groups who accept that this is 'the way it should be done' and perform accordingly. Fortunately, with the tremendous interest in folk dance in the Netherlands today, there are many young and energetic dance groups, which have breathed new life into their heritage and restored the lively style that it must originally have had.

Mother and daughter from Groningen in working dress.

One can truthfully say that Dutch dance has suffered more from popular misconception than that of any other country, with a generally accepted picture of dancers weighed down by clogs. In actual fact, the Dutch have seldom used their clogs for dancing. Dancing is a social occasion, and people would wear their best dress and leather shoes. Clogs were left firmly in the porch. For those to whom shoes were an unaffordable luxury, the slipper-socks worn inside the clogs gave a light-footed quality to the dance. Today several folk groups include a 'clog programme' in their performance when they dance abroad, but these are usually specially choreographed and not truly traditional. Exceptions to this basic ruling may be found when dancing takes place outside, and even here the dance can display a range of hops, jumps and polkas, and the pace is

Rich merchant's wife from Groningen. Under her lace cap she wears a solid gold casque.

usually brisk and lively. In Gelderland, in the east however, clogs are still worn for most occasions; this is not affectation but a necessity of life in a region that has known poverty for generations, and clogs are the normal footwear.

Dance in the Netherlands has been influenced by the geographical position of the country, on the 'edge' of Europe, while her vast rivers and internal waterways have ensured that isolated communities would be left to develop their own cultural entities. Even with the eventual unification of the country, these early isolations show in the panorama of Dutch folklore today, when nearly every region has its own costume, dance, music and folklore, and often language – an immense diversity for such a small country. As in the rest of Europe, early dance shared the same roots. As their rôle in primitive society and ritual became irrelevant and ceased to exist in its original form, the chains and circles slipped quietly in the developing social life of the people and the Christian Church calendar. Remnants of these early dance forms still exist today. In southern Limburg, in the village of Eijsden and the small town of Ootmarsum, the ritual chain dance can still be seen, safely preserved within the celebrations of the Christian Church. This takes place a fortnight after Whitsuntide, and takes the form of a church procession followed by a fair. These celebrations culminate in the *cramignon*, a chain dance in which everyone takes part. The leader carries a bunch of flowers as his 'badge of office' and the dancers, with linked hands, follow him in a winding procession, skipping in and out of the houses and through the village. The dance gradually slows down as the dancers tire. This dance is a close relation of the Helston floral dance, both are rooted in ancient pagan spring rituals. The *cramignon* has survived its pagan origins by becoming a part of the Christian Church calendar.

The processional dance at Votmarsum is the *vloggelen*, a solemn and dignified dance. It is led by the *poaskerls*, the 'Easter men', and the dancers walk with

Group from Lochem in Gelderland, near the German frontier. The simple costume reflects the poorer farming region. The creases on the aprons are left to show that the apron has been freshly ironed and folded. Clogs are worn for work and also with this group for dancing.

measured step singing an old Easter Carol, *Christus is opgerstanden* (Christ is risen). The song is of vital importance, and to make sure that no one forgets the words, each dancer pins a copy of the words to his or her back, so that the next one following can read it.

There are many remnants of the old circles still to be found in today's dances. Several of the most popular social dances start with dancers in a circle singing the refrain. Several of these carry traces of their roots; for example, *donder in 't hooi* (thunder in the hay) is an old dance in which the dancers sing as they circle. The clapping and stamping in this dance may reflect the belief in primitive times that by imitating the sound of the summer storm, they would create the 'sympathetic magic' that would bring the rain essential for growth. In early times, the circle dance was sometimes performed round a focal point, which was a magic symbol –

a sacred tree, a special stone and even a coffin. There is a girls' song related to this custom:

> Up in Heaven there is a place,
> Allelujah,
> There all the little maidens dance,
> Benedicamus Domino,
> Allelujah, Allelujah.

The theme of their song is often found in the hymns of the Catholic Church.

Nowadays, by far the most popular and the largest proportion of dances performed are couple dances, either danced as individual couples, or as a couple in a circle or quadrille formation. The influence of neighbouring German Westphalia shows in the northern provinces of Groningen and Drenthe, where the lively polka steps and waltz turns reflect the cross-fertilization brought about by the movement of workers in search of employment. Farm workers, in particular, crossed in to the northern provinces seeking work on the prosperous Dutch farms, and like all people away from home, carried with them their own customs, music and dance. In these northern regions we can also see steps and clapping patterns, which remind us of the close proximity of Denmark and Sweden. Travelling pedlars with their back-packs were another source of music, as in selling their wares they would literally 'sing their praises', and the pedlars' songs were well known throughout the northern countries.

We find in the Netherlands several dances that are common to the north European countries. For example, 'Lott is dead', with its 'resurrection' motif, is found under different names in several countries. The theme is two-fold: one being that the dead man loved dancing so much that on hearing the music at his funeral, he leapt out of his coffin and joined in the dancing. This is the theme of the Polish version, which is named 'Matthew is dead' (*umart Maciek*). The second theme is the story of the man who wished to find out who his friends really were, so feigned death in order to see who would come to take away his possessions. This is the theme accepted in the Netherlands, where it appears as 'Robinson' – this being the name of the man in the coffin.

Every country has its own story and name, but the music remains the same and the dances are very similar. Another dance common to all these northern countries is 'seven springs', a men's dance in which the dancers circle round with a walking step, stopping to mark the end of each phrase with a different action – stamping right foot, left foot, kneeling on right knee, both knees, placing right elbow on the ground, placing left elbow on the ground, and finally placing the forehead on the ground – seven different actions. The form of the dance, the actions and the magic number seven all point to its ancient ritualistic origins.

One especially important area is Friesland in the north. Perhaps in England we know this best through its distinctive black and white cattle, which are a common sight in our own fields. The Friesian people were amongst the first to settle this northern region and they are still there today, a proud and independent

people who still speak their own language. The popular dance here is the *skotse trije*, which the Frieslanders have adopted as their own special dance, and the lively melody and dignified style go well with the aristocratic costume of the province. Sometimes the dance incorporates actions from the shoemaker's dance, which is actually a singing/action game. In this the gentleman mimes the sewing of the lady's shoe. The shoemaker's dance is particularly popular in Sweden, and its introduction into the Friesian dance reminds us of this sea-faring province's connections with Sweden.

There are many dances that are claimed by specific regions, but there are also many more that, by popular acclaim, belong to the whole country. Particularly in constant use are the *boanopstekker*, the large circle dance, which usually opens the evening's dancing; and, at the opposite end of the festivities, the *slaapmuts* (the sleeping cap), which is always the last dance, signalling time to go to sleep. Popular also are *hakke toone* (heel and toe), *kamp van siejst*, *driekusman* and *malbroek*. This last one has a very well-known tune, known in England as 'for he's a jolly good fellow'. The fellow in point being John Churchill, the first Duke of Marlborough, hero of the battle of Blenheim, whose military victories made him a popular hero of the time.

There are, of course, dances that reflect the work theme. A good example is *molendans*, which with its circles and lines is reminiscent of mill wheels. Very popular with the folk dance groups, this is likely to be of more recent origin. The influence of English country dance, which arrived in the Netherlands in the late seventeenth century, can be seen quite clearly in some of the longways set dances. A good example of this is *gort met stroop* (corn and syrup), a progressive longways set. Incidentally, its weaving pattern is very reminiscent of strip the willow, the plaiting pattern that is found in several countries. So, if we analyse Dutch dancing, what do we find? Simple steps that are performed with enthusiasm – the variety is not vast, but they are fully utilized in an immense and very varied repertoire of patterns. The dances are enjoyable and contribute to a very happy social scene, and the number and variety are considerable. So we can safely say that dance in the Netherlands is alive and well, and a vital ingredient of the people's social life.

20 POLAND

The picture of Polish dancing is very clear indeed. Poland has suffered greatly and for long periods from the occupation of her territories by her powerful and aggressive neighbours – Russia, Prussia and Austria. Unlike the effect that situation has had on many people, it served in Poland to fuel the Poles' determination to preserve their identity at all costs. Consequently every facet of their folk culture became a vital part in their campaign to survive. In many cases, when outside influence has succeeded in infiltrating the culture of a people and influencing style and even content of their music and dance, in Poland it would seem that the opposite has happened and every folk tune and dance has been preserved with a clarity that could only come from the love of a people determined to hold their own. So in Poland we find an overall folk culture supported by clearly defined regional variations – strong enough to be able to reverse the flow, Polish dance would go forth and influence others; no one would influence Polish dance. From this point then perhaps we should begin an examination of the dance.

An early reference to Polish dance comes from a book published in 1544 in which Hans Newsidler mentions 'polnisch tanz' and indicates that Polish melodies were already travelling to Sweden. Jan of Lublin, organist at Krasnik near Lublin, has left several dances with Polish connections dated 1537–48. A late-sixteenth-century version of a Polish dance bore the name 'Batory tanz', which could refer to the Polish King, Stefan Batory (1576 – 86). An alternative interpretation of the name of the dance refers to the original title 'ein pollnisher danz/pator', *pator* being the Latin word for 'opening' and reminds us that in the late sixteenth century, the Polish dance was used (as was the polonaise at a later date) as a dignified processional dance

to open a ball – from peasant wedding to court ball. In a collection of songs published in Nürnberg, there is a 'tanz Diomedes'. Diomedes Cato was born in Venice around 1570 and, as a skilled lutenist, became court musician to the King of Poland. Of the four dances in the collection, one is labelled 'tanietz', a German form of the Polish word *taniec*. The use of the Polish word for dance, and the reference to Diomedes with his strong Polish connections, point to another Polish export. These are books in the collection of the German Church in Stockholm and it is suggested that when King Sigismund Vasa of Poland was crowned King of Sweden in 1593, he took with him his Polish court choir and musicians, including Diomedes. If the books did come to Sweden at that time, they must be the earliest Polish dances exported. Polish folk music certainly arrived in Denmark during the reign of King Christian IV (1588–1648), who employed Polish court musicians.

By the eighteenth century, the polonaise and minuet were influencing folk dance in Sweden and Finland, and Swedish fiddlers' notebooks contain much evidence that the music for these dances was the mainstay of their dance-music collections. The oldest music in Finland has its roots in the Polish dances that spread throughout the Nordic countries in the seventeenth century – the same period in which the fiddle became popular in Finland. In the old manuscript books they are all labelled *polska* – a term that was generally used to denote a dance tune, and which could cover couple dances, circles or chains and pot-pourri.

The beautiful national dances of Poland are recognized world-wide, and in their own country belonged to all levels of society. Originally, predating the introduction of instrumental music, the dances were accompanied by singing, usually improvised, and some possibly based on ancient poems, which bear traces of the Vendic language. The Vends were never an oppressed race, and consequently their folklore showed pride and strength, qualities which were passed on to the dances, which the songs accompanied. The polonaise (in Polish, *polonez*) is very characteristic of the people, showing the spirited pride of an independent race. It is more of a procession than a set dance and, led by the highest ranking couple, it encompasses the entire company, all following in order of precedence. The procession can be broken up by bows and curtseys, and one of its earliest features was the custom of a gentleman giving up his partner if another claimed her. This was originally a sign that all nobles had equal rights. The one claiming the lady's hand must bow to her and clap his hands to make his claim. Originally a dance for the upper classes, it became the custom to open a ball with the polonaise, and the custom was introduced at courts throughout Europe. It was adopted by people everywhere, and in the form of a march became the opening dance at village festivals. The form in which it generally became most used was when the couples, in order of social standing, led down the centre of the ballroom, cast off alternately and when meeting up again, led down in fours. They in turn cast off to meet in eights and again in sixteens. By the time all were lined up in sixteens, the lines formed either longways sets or quadrilles, according to the next

ABOVE: *Typical Polish group carrying palm branches and baskets of Easter eggs going to church.*

LEFT: *Polish dancers performing the krakowiak.*

dance on the programme. In this form it can still be seen at some of the Danish folk dance evenings.

The mazurka (*mazur*) is very much the dance of the people in Poland. It first appeared in the first half of the nineteenth century and rapidly spread throughout Europe. It embodies the very essence of Polish dance, both musically and in steps and choreography. It has infiltrated all levels of society, and even became a part of military training, when it was taught to the regiments as part of their training in physical control and co-ordination – in the same way that the Scottish regiments include highland dance in their physical training. It fired the popular imagination to such an extent that it was taught and danced at the Tsarist court in Russia, and even found its way into the hands of ballet masters and choreographers, and can still be seen in some of the great classical ballets of the nineteenth century. It became the inspiration for classical composers – one of the best examples of this being the multitude of mazurkas written for the piano by Chopin. (The name mazurka is only used in this context outside Poland, as *Mazurka* in Polish means a young girl from the region of Mazur.)

One of the most popular dances, which is danced nationwide, is the *obertas*. The name immediately gives us some indication of the style of the dance as there are two possible translations: firstly it can mean 'turning around' and secondly, perplexity or confusion. It is in fact, lively to the point of wildness, a couple dance full of turns and with an impelling triple rhythm, in which the accent falls on the second beat in the bar.

The *krakowiak* is one of the best known Polish dances. Coming from the town of Kraków, the old capital of Poland, it has an interesting story relating to its origin. When the Tartars were at the gates of Kraków, a Polish cavalier rode out and engaged the Tartar leader in battle. He defeated his enemy and then dressed himself in the defeated man's clothes, and took his horse. Riding back into the town, everyone was terrified as they thought that the Tartar leader had won the day. When the Polish hero revealed his true identity the townspeople went wild with joy, dancing in the streets. According to legend this was the birth of the *krakowiak*. The dance incorporates several facets of ancient dance – it is a couple dance but still at times becomes a circle.

The *cwál* step (gallop) reminds us of the strong horse-riding tradition of the country, and the strong 2/4 rhythm gives rise to heel beats, which again supposedly reflect the sound of galloping hooves.

The *kujawiak* is another dance in triple time, but here the quality of movement in the valse steps is more gentle and lyrical. It is a couple dance in which the accent is on dancing together. Originally it was danced as a fertility ritual on Shrove Tuesday and was named *podkoziolek*, the goat dance. It was also an important dance at weddings, when the bride, after receiving her married woman's cap, went through a ritual dance with each guest in turn. This ritual, unlike many of these wedding occasions, also included all the female guests. The *kujawiak* is often preceded by the *chodzony*, a walking dance, a peasant version of the polonaise (processional dance). At weddings, the bride is often led around by the best man in a ritual *chodzony* before she begins her partnering of everyone in the *kujawiak*. It is a typical 'showing off' the bride dance.

The *troyak* is a dance for three, two girls and one boy. Before the dance commences, they sing a song about planting the corn. They sing that 'from one end of the field to the other we have sown the corn'. Then they celebrate by dancing. There is some mimed flirting and rivalry between the girls. The boy turns with one girl, while the other girl dances alone and appears very sulky. Partners then change over and the first girl now sulks. In the end, however, as they all spin together, the girls let go of the boy suddenly, so that he ends up on the floor. One last dance that we should mention comes from the Carpathian mountains. The people here are the *górale*, with their own linguistic and cultural background. They work as woodcutters in the forests, and their long-handled axes feature in the men's dances, either wielded by hand or laid on the floor and danced over, as in the Scottish sword dancing. The dance in this region is affected by the footwear of the dancers, which is a soft moccasin type of shoe, so that the quality of movement is much lighter than the rest of the country, where boots are very often worn. Looking at Polish dancing overall, we see strong rhythmical work danced with proud carriage and in elegant style. Lovely work, to be undertaken with great care and understanding of what has gone into creating its style.

21 PORTUGAL

Portugal has developed her own very specific dance, music and style. The overall impression is of a cheerful and relaxed people, taking great pleasure in their dancing. The dance steps are generally fairly simple (apart from those of the Algarve in the south), so that everyone can join in and enjoy the dancing. To visit one of the Portuguese folk festivals and see dances from all the different regions gives an impression of overall similarity in style and content, but Portugal is a country of enormous geographical contrasts and this is reflected in some ways in the dance.

Portugal's land boundaries in the north and down the eastern frontier are all with Spain; bounded to the west and south by the Atlantic ocean, Spain is her only near neighbour. In view of these facts, it is most surprising that when we look for influences on Portuguese dance, Spain does not feature at all. Portugal has her own firmly established dance style, which owes nothing at all to any outside influence. Comparing the lifestyle of the people, we should look at the different regions and compare their geography. The mountains to the north-east are rugged and very inhospitable, and the people, working as shepherds, have a very hard life in the harsh climate. This is a colourless country, a region of grey and brown rocks, where living conditions are spartan and the people are poor. There is a drabness in the costume of the people, a lack of colour reflecting their surroundings. The homespun fabrics are often grey and brown with natural sheepskins worn for warmth. The shepherd usually has an enormous floor-length coat of straw, which is impervious to the heavy rains, and can indeed be used as a tent in which to shelter from the harsh weather. In a region infested by wolves, the shepherd's dog wears a collar with sharp spikes, as protection from attack. Dancing here is very basic, following a simple pattern of couples in a circle, but however poor the people, dancing is still an important part of their lives, and they present their simple dances with pride when taking part in a folk festival. The accompaniment is always sung, and when musicians join in the pattern, they always follow the same lines. The musicians start to play and, during this opening music, the dancers wander into place. When the singing commences, the dancers burst into action – the two seem inseparable. This, in fact, is the general musical background to all dancing throughout the country. The song is very often a duet taking the form of 'question and answer' between a man and a woman, and it usually has a story to tell.

In the north-eastern corner of the country there is one bright spark among the otherwise universal drabness. Here we find the *palitheros*, a group of male dancers. With their dances rooted in ancient history, they are the equivalent of the English morris men, indeed with similarities in both dance and costume. They are attired in long white lacy skirts and colourful patterned shawls, and their hats are decorated with multi-coloured flowers and ribbons. They carry handkerchiefs or decorated sticks, and would certainly look quite at home on an English village green.

In the north-west lies the region of Minho. This is a prosperous and well-populated area, and this is reflected in the local costume, the brightest in Portugal, with colourful fabrics, sequins and embroidery, and the amount of gold jewellery worn. The dance here is lively and, again, usually comprises couples in a circle. Favourite colours are red, royal blue, emerald green and yellow, apart from the girl's wedding dress, which is of black silk with as many gold necklaces as possible, as these form the basis of her dowry. Elsewhere, the general poverty has inhibited the development of elaborate dress. Although Portugal has for centuries owned wealthy colonies and more or less held the valuable spice

*ABOVE: **Group of villagers from Almeira.***

*RIGHT: **Dress worn by harvesters.***

trade firmly in her hands, the vast revenue went into the estates of a very few extremely wealthy families, and the majority of the population lived a very poor feudal-style life. This probably accounts for the fact that the overall impression of costume is of working clothes and using whatever materials were easily available. The one exception is the bright floral patterned shawls worn by many women. Apart from this, the costume is plain, except for the occasional wedding or special festival dress, and the dance follows the same pattern.

The Ribatejo region lies further south, to the south of Lisbon, and this is the region of the Portuguese cowboys. Here the black bulls are raised, and the herdsmen on horseback round up their cattle. The clatter of the horses' hoof beats is reflected in the quick beaten steps and galops of the dance. Again the dances are made up of couples in a circle, but here figures are developed within the circle. The dances are

A wealthy merchant.

generally danced at great speed, and the backless mules worn by the girls are often lost in the liveliness of the attack with which the steps are performed. A very typical dance from this region is the *verde gaio valseado*. The dance takes its name from the green caps worn by the boys. *Verde gaio* means green jay, and the boys' caps are very similar in shape to the cockaded head of the bird.

Moving south we come to the Algarve, the region skirting the Atlantic, and here the dance has a style of its own, with couples turning together at a furious speed. The usual form is for the dance leader to call a couple onto the floor, where they show off their virtuosity in a series of turning steps performed at incredible speed. The girls here wear little ankle boots, unlike the footwear of the rest of the country, which varies from wooden-soled shoes worn by the peasants in the north, through to the cork-soled sandals of the forested areas. Cork, harvested from the bark of the cork oak trees is an important export, and most of the western world's wine bottles are sealed with Portuguese corks.

One especially important dance in Portugal is the fandango. This is a dance in the form of a competition for two men who seek to outdo each other in inventing complex beaten steps. Number 1 man dances his improvisation while number 2 prowls watchfully up and down. As number 1 runs out of ideas, number 2 takes over and gives rein to his own special inventions while number 1 'waits in the wings'. And so it continues until one competitor retires. Occasionally the fandango may be seen performed by a man and a woman, but this is very likely to be a special arrangement for presentation in a folk festival or show.

Two names synonymous with Portuguese dancing are the *tirana* and the *vira*. These dances are performed throughout the country, each region having its own variation and usually giving its name to its own version of the dance. *Tirana* is made up of typically Portuguese *pas de basques* in many forms, while the *vira* is a turning dance. Both are lively and danced with attack.

During the general revival of folk dance in Western Europe at the beginning of the twentieth century, many countries formed their own organization to promote research and to ensure its preservation. That such an organization is firmly established in

Portugal is obvious from the care with which the folk-dance groups present their programmes. Simplicity and authenticity are the basic rules, and there is no place for choreographed interpretation. This is seen clearly at the Portuguese dance festivals, and is very evident in the performance of groups travelling abroad. The work is clear and uncluttered by any attempt at theatrical effect. A most interesting point here is that, despite the simple approach, Portuguese groups have won first place at so many international festivals – festivals of repute, in which groups from so many different countries take place. So often on these occasions incredible works are presented, costume-wise, and they are choreographically of a very professional quality, but inevitably the simplicity and integrity of the Portuguese groups inspire the adjudicators to reward unspoilt tradition. So it is comparatively easy to identify an overall Portuguese style: varying from relaxed and easy-going to lively and energetic in quality, the steps throughout are basically the same. *Pas de basque* appears in every possible form and speed, and there is a clear repertoire of beaten steps, which again can vary considerably in performance. The beaten steps in Portugal are always '*bater*', beating the ground. The overall impression is of enjoyment. Apart from the fast-moving dances in the Algarve, the dances offer ample opportunity for everyone to dance. It is a simple social scene, uninhibited by any drama.

ABOVE: A milk-maid carrying her can and measures.

RIGHT: The parasol is a very important accessory for the girl. The blue tiled wall in the background is very typical and can be seen throughout the country both as internal and external decoration.

22 Russia

With the disintegration of the Soviet Union, many of the states that were a part of the Union claimed their independence and reverted to their original status. We should remember that these regions were in fact countries, mostly with their own languages and certainly with their own culture stemming from their very different ethnic roots. So when we refer to European 'Russia' today, we are looking at the territory (now several countries) that stretches from the Polish frontier in the west to the Ural mountains in the east, the mountain range that forms a natural barrier between Europe and Asia. For the people of these regions music and dance have always been a vital force, in fact in the case of the serfs, the enslaved peasants, it was possibly the only light relief in their life of slavery.

Dance is well documented in Russia, and there are references dating back to the eleventh century that tell us something of its development. There are three main categories of dance: the *khorovod* (choral dance); the *plyaska* (improvised dances); and dances with defined figures.

OPPOSITE PAGE:
Dancers from Georgia showing the lovely line of the girls' dresses and the elegant carriage of the wearers. Georgia was formerly a part of the Soviet Union, but is now an independent country.

THIS PAGE:
RIGHT: *Georgian village girl.*

BELOW: *Georgian couple. The short country dress allows freedom of movement to the girl in contrast to the slow stately dance usually associated with the region.*

Georgian sword dancers in action. Note the small shields.

THE CHORAL DANCES (*KHOROVODY*)

These are very old and vary considerably in character and content. The chief characteristic is the large number of dancers taking part and the sung accompaniment. The song usually had a theme, and the theme would be acted out during the dance. Themes could vary a great deal, but always reflected some aspect of everyday life. They could be based on work done in the fields, such as ploughing, sowing and so on, or they could tell the story of the relationship between a boy and girl, their joys and sorrows, quarrels and reconciliations. Sometimes they would detail the choosing of a wife or husband, and could range from sadness to humour. They could poke fun at drunken husbands, snobbish wives or idle folk. Normally the *khorovod* was danced in a closed circle with the dancers holding hands or joined by hand-

kerchiefs, but very occasionally the dancers could be unlinked. The theme of the song would be acted out by a group standing in the centre round which the rest moved in a closed circle clockwise while singing the narrative – telling the story. In another version, a leader would begin singing, while the rest of the group followed, taking their cue from the leader and acting out the words as they circled round.

Another form of choral dance took the form of two lines facing each other and taking turns in a 'question and answer' song theme. The strength of choral singing in Russia owes much to its long history and gradual development, and in its present form with sensitive phrasing and in-depth harmony, brings a very special quality to the music, and in turn to the dance movements. The birth of choral singing came about when Tsar Peter the Great in the seventeenth century tried to westernize his country and in doing so forbade the use of all traditional musical instruments, such as the balalaika and the bandura. In any other circumstances this might have spelled the end of folk dance, but to the Russians singing was second nature, and singing became the standard accompaniment to the dance. The structure of Russian folk melodies and the instinctive musicality of the people soon led to the deeply moving harmony that is the hallmark of Russian choirs today.

There are some choral dances that do not have actions, and this of course enabled the dance to develop beyond the circle and acting, so that more complex figures, chains, figures of eight and so on, could be included. The dances would be performed on feast days with the whole village joining in. Sometimes they would be introduced by the village girls singing a special 'gathering song' as they went through the village calling everyone to come and join in the *khorovod*, which would open the festivities. In the same way there would be a similar farewell ceremony with a special 'dispersal' song. Choral dances have been preserved in various regions of the former Soviet Union, and each has its own characteristics. Travelling north, the dance is quiet and rather staid in appearance, so that the dancers seem to move a little stiffly and the overall style is of less movement. Further north still, and the girl must not make eye contact with her partner during the dance – only at the very end may their eyes meet. During the dance she moves quietly – the movement has been likened to that of the peahen. In the central regions round Moscow the dance is much livelier and has more variety of movement.

THE *PLYASKA*

The *plyaska* has a wide repertoire of steps, which are common to both girls and boys. It has no set form but is entirely improvised, making use of the wide variety and number of steps available. In all probability it grew out of the circle dance, when individual dancers moved into the centre to show off their virtuosity, but the *plyaska* has now become an important dance in its own right. It is an opportunity for both boys and girls to show off their own special skills in an improvised dance. The musical accompaniment is instrumental, which gives the dancers greater freedom to move as they wish.

In the category of *plyaska* we find the *perepliass*, a competitive dance in which the dancers take turns to show off their improvised steps. The name comes from the Russian verb *pereplyas*, which means to dance too much – a good description of some of the amazing improvisations shown. It is this type of dance, performed to perfection by the professional Russian folk-dance groups that visit Western theatres and festivals, that is a statement of all that we have learned to expect of Russian dance – bravura performance, acrobatic tricks and so on. Yet when we met the head of Moscow's ethnic dance research, and *perestroyka* had guaranteed her freedom of speech, she was adamant that this type of dance was in fact 'cabaret'. She affirmed the fact that it owed nothing to

Georgian dancers. Swords are used in some of their dances. Note the large fur hat worn by the man in the background. The Musician is carrying his stringed instrument.

LEFT: *Couple from Belarus, originally part of the Soviet Union, now an independent country.*

Head-dress detail.

traditional Russian dance, but was an entirely fictional creation designed to earn hard currency for the Soviet Government. It was choreographed especially for the theatre, and the 'folk dancers' were in fact professional dancers trained in the State Ballet Schools. She said that she could still show us in Russia the true traditional dance of the people, but it would never be used in performance as it is based on simple basic movements – inward looking, in fact folk dance for the people and certainly not for an audience.

DANCES WITH DEFINED FIGURES

In every country when the social structure is clearly defined and headed by court and aristocracy, dance develops according to the requirements of that social order, and the requirements of its different sectors. So figure and couple dances proliferate in the ballrooms of the rich people, and dances are imported as fashion dictates. In the fashionable ballrooms of the wealthy we find stylized versions of the mazurka

164

Head-dress detail.

and the polonaise, imported from Poland. The emergence of a strong middle class and its tremendous influence on all aspects of the social scene never happened in Russia. Outside Moscow and St Petersburg, the bourgeoisie never flourished, and so the dance scene remained as it had been for centuries, belonging to either the top or bottom of the social scale. In the ballrooms of the rich the dance followed the fashionable dictates of the day, while elsewhere the dance of the peasants remained unchanged, and in doing so preserved its 'Russianess'. Certainly Russian dancing shows the best possible evidence of the truth that music dictates style, as the breadth of movement and fluent quality of the dance exactly mirrors the musical accompaniment. Whether vocal or instrumental, Russian music has a soaring melodic line, moving in sweeping phrases and depth of harmony, which span the heights and depths of emotion and proclaim its country of origin loud and clear.

23 SCANDINAVIA: DENMARK/SWEDEN/NORWAY

T he northern countries known collectively as Scandinavia have a great deal in common but in each case retain many individual characteristics. Linguistically there are strong connections and although the written languages may look different, the people can generally understand each other. Geographically the differences are much more obvious.

Denmark presents a very gentle and 'comfortable' aspect to the eye. The countryside is gently undulating with well-spaced out farms, picturesque sleepy villages and small towns. The few hills are hardly noticeable and never disrupt the landscape. The people may refer to their 'forests' but to the observer they appear as friendly shadowy regions where the sun can usually find a way in. The forest animals have not been hunted to distraction, so that hares, badgers and foxes can afford to ignore the occasional human intruder. On three sides the country is bounded by rolling sand-dunes, endless long sandy beaches and white-capped waves. In a country that has not been exposed to endless chemical treatment, spring and summer throw a veil of wild flowers over fields and hedgerows and all is calm and quiet.

In Sweden the land is a little wilder, forests are deeper and more impenetrable, and the large number of lakes offer a wonderful unspoilt habitat for birds and animals. Sweden stretches up to the Arctic circle, offering a home to the Laplanders and their vast reindeer herds. Swedish Lapland is a land of cold bleak winters where the sun never appears for several months each year, and heavy snow makes life a continual struggle for survival for the hardy native population. Off-shore, Sweden is bounded by endless small islands – some thickly wooded

and habitable, while others are barren, uninhabited rocks, occupied only by visiting birds.

The geography of Norway is by far the most dramatic. The mountains are high and barren, sweeping down to drop sheer into the sea, which penetrates the long narrow fjords. Here in the coastal regions the easiest, and often only, method of transport is by the local ferries, which link up the occasional small towns and settlements. The passengers are usually a mixture of schoolchildren, travelling between school and home, and tourists visiting this land of the midnight sun, and in the case of many Americans, looking for the land of their ancestors. In Norway forests are forests in the true and awe-inspiring meaning – dark, impenetrable and enchanted. Between the mountain ranges lie deep isolated valleys, completely cut off from the rest of the country in winter when the steep mountain roads become impassable. Norway also extends into the Arctic circle regions and suffers months of winter darkness, but these northern regions also benefit from the midnight sun during the summer months when the sun never sets. At this time of the year everyone makes full use of every minute of both day and night, and picnicking and dancing throughout the night is commonplace.

Dance follows the same pattern of similarities and contrasts. The three countries share a common pool of steps, figures and styles, but there are some very marked individual characteristics.

In Denmark the music is usually arranged for violin, viola, clarinet and bass, which gives to it an almost 'chamber music' quality of sound. This is reflected in the quality of movement overall, so that dances have a gentle easy style of movement, producing an easy-going social approach, which

ABOVE: *Danish costumes. Men: left to right, from Møn and Randers. Ladies: left to right, from Møn and Amager.*

RIGHT: *Norway. Girls from Setesdal.*

encourages everyone to join in and dance for pleasure. Dance in Denmark has had a long and peaceful development, so that the social aspect predominates, and couple and figure dances have proliferated. The number of recorded dances is incredible, with some 2,000 dances published in regional collections.

In Sweden, dance music is usually played on a violin – often by a large number of violins playing in unison; in the same way that people gather together to join in the dancing, so the musicians will happily join in the music. This playing in unison by a number of instruments gives a tremendous 'lift' to the quality of the dancing. The first written record of dance in Sweden describes the wedding of King Valdemas in the thirteenth century and refers to dancing as being part of the festivities. Weddings are important occasions and the inclusion of many ancient dances in every wedding ceremony has ensured their preservation. Dance in Sweden can take many forms: circles (large and small), quadrilles, longways sets and innumerable couple dances. One of the oldest dances is the polska, a strange compelling rhythmical dance with leisurely walks alternating with rapid turning steps. It takes its name from Poland, Sweden's neighbour with whom there has always been close ties. Certainly the most popular dance today in Sweden is the hambo, a lively dance in quick triple time. It first became popular in the mid nineteenth century and has remained in constant use ever since.

Norwegian music has its own special instrument – the Hardanger fiddle. This has an extra set of 'sympathetic' strings, which produce a very special resonance that gives great depth to the music and to the quality of the dance movements. In Norway the ancient dances still exist. They have strange compelling rhythms, which are closely followed by strong rhythmical movements. The couples dance separately, the woman moving quietly round the dancing space, continually turning, while the man follows, improvising as he wishes and showing off his agility and acrobatic skills. There is also a very special man's dance, the *halling*. In this the girl sets his hat on a pole, which she holds high above her head. The man dances, showing off his athletic prowess and culminating by a high leap to kick the hat off the pole. All the ancient dances are part of the living dance tradition and can still be seen today. Apart from these ancient traditional dances, Norway has similar social dances to those of Sweden and Denmark, which are danced on most social occasions today. Norway has, however, another rather strange dance tradition. At the turn of the century, and at the height of the great European folk-dance revival, a Norwegian woman, Hulde Garborg attempted to re-create the old song-ballades, which had always been a common heritage in the Scandinavian countries. Unfortunately she had no idea what these song-dances were really like, so she modelled her choreographic creations on the chain dances that she had seen in the Faeroe Isles. In her new creations the people move in a linked circle, singing and carrying out various actions. The words

OPPOSITE PAGE:

TOP LEFT: **Norway, Hardanger. Usually a white linen head-dress is worn with this costume.**

TOP RIGHT: **Norwegian boy wearing special garters made for him by his fiancée. Normally the garters are tucked out of sight, but if she has made them especially, they are allowed to hang down.**

BOTTOM: **Norway. A bridal crown.**

to the songs inevitably had a strong nationalist element, and amongst a population that had endured several centuries of occupation, they quickly caught the public's imagination. Despite the fact that it was soon shown that the new choreographies did not in the least resemble the old ballades, they were popularly accepted and have become a feature of Norwegian folk dance today.

In mentioning the Faeroe Isles, we should look at the genuine ballades that have persisted through the centuries and can still be seen today. They consist of a linked chain following the song leader and joining in with him, singing the stories of ancient times. In a time when people could not read or write, this was a reliable method of ensuring that important stories, both historical and mythological, were not forgotten, and as a vital part of their culture, the ballades remain unchanged today. It is, however, said that amongst the tales of gods and ancient heroes, the leader has been known to slip in a little local scandal, which he feels should be drawn to public attention!

Midsummer is still an important date on the Scandinavian calendar and the midsummer bonfire is seen everywhere. In Denmark, every town and village has its bonfire, and the beaches in particular show a ring of fire around the coast. Everyone gathers round the fire, and ancient songs and poems are sung and recited. Very often a new song or poem is composed to mark the occasion in each locality and they carry out their custom of baking bread. Special dough is attached to a stick and the children sit round the fire toasting the bread. Often half-cooked and thoroughly blackened, it can hardly prove appetizing, but it is toasted and demolished avidly. In Sweden, midsummer is the time for raising the maypole. The

Denmark. Costumes from Amager, an island near Copenhagen where in the sixteenth century farmers settled by invitation of King Christian II who employed them to grow vegetables for his Dutch Queen. The baggy trousers worn by the man are very reminiscent of the Dutch origins of the costume.

pole is decorated by the entire community – there must be nine specially prescribed varieties of leaves and the pole is carried round the village for all to see. It is then ceremonially raised and everyone joins in circling round it with the ancient songs and dances. A memory of the primitive summer solstice ceremonial, it is still a very important event in Swedish life today. The summer bonfire is equally important in Norway, where records show people in medieval times singing and dancing round their fires.

Folk dance continues to be a vital factor in the social life of Scandinavia today. In every town and village folk dance proliferates, and the folk dance evening is an important social event. The evening commences with dancing for everyone. This is directed by the dance leader who calls out the steps and figures to be done, and teaches new steps and dances. These dance leaders have all been trained by the official folk dance organization in each country, so that the work is consistent in every detail and changes do not creep in. When the session ends, baskets of cookies and cakes appear, along with huge thermos jugs of coffee. When everyone has been fed, the song books appear and for the remainder of the evening folk songs are sung by all. These evenings first started when people lived in isolated farms and settlements, and were a way of neighbours keeping in contact. Nowadays they are recognized as being an important part of social life in the community. Throughout Scandinavia today, folk-dance groups have proliferated. Dance is encouraged and everything possible done to preserve each country's dance heritage. Now one can usually see Scandinavian groups at the international folk festivals and the pride of the people in their own particular dances can clearly illustrate for us their individuality in the overall scene.

24 SPAIN

To think of Spain is surely to think of dance – the two are synonymous. Usually when we think of a country, many pictures come to mind – scenery, architecture, literature, music and possibly dance, but in picturing Spain I think that everyone will immediately conjure up the excitement of Spanish dance, with its rhythm of beating feet, the strident voices and the compelling rhythm of the castanets. Dance is as much a part of the country as the white houses, burnt brown landscape, orange groves and vineyards. It not only belongs to the people, but is a part of them, as natural as breathing. Cervantes wrote, 'There ne'er was born a Spanish woman yet, but she was born to dance'. To the foreign observer, the overall picture of Spanish dance can be awe-inspiring in its content, and overwhelming in its demands for the would-be student. Unlike the situation in many countries, where one can comfortably join in the dance without looking too foolish, Spain presents a very different

Spanish group from Asturia.

situation, and the challenge initially seems almost impossible. However, perhaps if we begin a basic analysis, we may open a few windows on different aspects of the scene. It is never going to be easy and any student of Spanish dance is facing a challenge, but at least we may identify some possibilities if we can begin to recognize what we are aiming at. Basically we can divide Spanish dance into three categories, and each is a very specific study in itself: first, there is the folk dance; second, classical dance; and third, flamenco.

Folk dance is a vital category, as this is the root from which all else has sprung. It is danced by the country people, and as their natural social dance, it differs from one region to another, sometimes in detail and sometimes in complete style, as Spain is a very large country and this immediately opens the door to many regional differences. Bounded by the cold Atlantic in the north and the warm Mediterranean in the south, the geography offers many variations with ethnically a Celtic people speaking their own language in the north-western regions, while to the south-east the Catalan preserve their own language and culture and owe more to Roussillon and Provence then to central Spain. The dances overall are generally lively and energetic but basically simple as they are danced for recreation and certainly not for exhibition. They belong to village life, enjoyed by family and friends, and danced on family occasions and as a part of

Northern Spain. Girls from Zamora in their elaborately embroidered festival dress.

local festivities. Having said this, they would still offer a challenge and they are not easy to pick up. Very often these family gatherings and local dance evenings start with improvisation – one dancer will come forward and with four claps will claim the dancing space as his or her own. On their retiring amidst shouts of approval from the onlookers, another will come forward to take their place. This lively introduction sets the atmosphere for the folk dancing to follow.

On thinking of folk dance, the name *jota* immediately proclaims itself loud and clear, and with its easy recognition internationally, could be named the national dance of Spain. Originating in the region of Aragon, the dance has now spread throughout the country, and one comes upon *jota* competitions in villages everywhere. It is a lively couple dance in triple time, and although there are many regional variations in performance, there is a definite and very large vocabulary of steps, in every case commencing with the same basic *jota* step, followed by any of the others at will. The basic *jota* step is as follows:

1–2 Hop on L, pointing R toe to L toe, hold;
3 Hop on L, extend R to side at knee level;
4 Step on R behind L;
5 Step sideways on L;
6 Step on R in front of L;
Repeat alternate legs; 4–5 are performed like a *pas de bourrée*.

The dance today has a vocabulary of at least forty steps from which the man makes a selection, followed by the woman. There are so many variations, that it would be almost impossible to see it twice alike. The style can vary from an almost aggressive presentation found in Aragon, with sharp rhythmical clapping, and the incredible noise of the *taconeado* (heel beats), to the softer and graceful style of the *jota* Valenciana (the *jota* from Valencia). Here, in the *jota del carrer* (the *jota* of the street), the man leads his partner into the street, lays down his striped blanket to claim dancing space and the couple begin their dance, with an almost delicate quality. In the Balearic Islands also, the *jota* has a different quality. In Mallorca it moves quickly and gracefully, with a lovely flow of movement.

Detail of embroidered collar on the costume from Zamora.

Although the *jota* claims pride of place in the folkdance repertoire, there are of course many other dances equally popular with the people, for example:

Seguidillas. For one couple or a group of couples using castanets. The dance is made up of a series of *coplas* (couplets) separated by an *estrabillo* (chorus). Very often 3/4 but this can vary regionally.

Allegrias. 3/4 or 6/8. With or without castanets. A woman's solo. *Taconeado* (heel tapping) is an important part of the dance. The dress is often a long frilled skirt with a train, and deft and rapid twirls of the train made by the foot are a special feature.

Fandango. 3/4 or 6/8. Especially rapid footwork. With or without castanets. A very old dance, it has been suggested that the *fandango* was the origin of the *jota*.

Back view of the Galician costume. The black over-shirts are heavily embroidered with jet. The colour of the under-skirt can vary from red to yellow or emerald green.

Tango. Quick 2/4 rhythm. Both a folk dance and now also a stage dance, originally from Cordova. It has no connection with the popular Argentinian couple dance of the same name. Very rapid and complex heel and toe work.

Charradas. From the Salamanca region. The peasants in this region are the *charros* and their dances are *charradas*. There is a tremendous contrast between the performance of the men, who dance with high leaps, and that of the women, whose movement is so minimal as to appear almost static.

These are just a very few of the several hundred folk dances still in the popular repertoire. There are three special regions that have their own distinctive culture and where the people are ethnically and linguistically different, and consequently this affects their music and dance. In the north-west regions, Galicia proudly claims a Celtic heritage, and the people emphatically tell you that they are Celts and not Spaniards. Certainly with a different cultural history and language, their music and dance also mirror their Celtic heritage and differ from that of the rest of Spain. The musical instrument that takes pride of place is the gaita, the bagpipe, with its especial sound – at once shrill and plaintive. Nowadays it is joined by a guitar, imported from the south, and the tambourine is in popular use and is usually played by the girls. The music reflects its northerly roots, in its easy melodic lines and clearcut rhythms, and the dance offers more opportunities for 'joining in'. There are many simple dances that do not make technical demands on the dancer. The favourite dance is the *muiñeira*, a lively couple dance in 6/8 time. Its flowing movement takes pride of place at every fiesta, either for individual couples or as a set dance for three couples.

Crossing to the north-east we come to the Pyrenees, the massive mountain range that separates Spain and France in the north. Here the Basque people are of a different ethnic background, one which in fact no one has been able to trace back to antiquity. Sufficient to say that, settled here over the centuries, they have become neither Spanish nor French but they have retained their own identity and they have a very singular language, which is totally unrelated to any other known language. Their dances are

LEFT: Couple from the Basque country, Pyrenees.

ABOVE: Basque costumes. The most popular and easily recognized style.

very much their own, and have resisted outside influence. The high leaping and beaten steps of the special men's dances are almost balletic in appearance, while for the girls there are 'arch' dances in which they carry decorated half-hoops, and dances in which they partner the men in lively social dances. The music is very melodic, and rhythms are strong and simple. Music is usually played on pipe and drum, both instruments being played by one musician. In the folk dances, the every-day social dances, the steps are basically simple – skips, gallops, skip-change step – and the patterns interesting. Music and step go hand-in-hand, simple and rhythmical.

The third region with claims to its own individuality is the Catalan region of the south-east, bordering southern France. Here again the ethnic background and language are their own, and in fact, as already noted, owe more to Roussillon and Provence that to the rest of Spain. Here the music literally sweeps the dancers along in a lively flow of movement. It is played on guitars and mandolins, often with large groups of musicians, so that it has both lift and depth. There is a large variety of dances in this region, from quadrilles to couples, and several with interesting themes and motifs, and the dancing is lively, tremendously rhythmical and with some very agile work.

LEFT: *Spanish couple. The girl is wearing a strange 'back to front' bonnet. The legend is that when the first of these fashionable bonnets arrived from France, no-one was quite sure how to wear them and in making a guess wore them the wrong way round, and so created their own fashion.*

ABOVE: *Front view of the 'back to front' bonnet.*

The second category of Spanish dance is the classical Spanish, the dance of the dancing school, and as seen in the theatre. It was originally based on the folk dance, and came into being when teachers and dancers, inspired by the great nineteenth-century ballerinas, saw the possibilities of incorporating the indigenous folk dance into a theatrical performance. This category of dance takes a great deal of study, on a par with classical ballet training. Teachers usually compose their own dances based upon both flamenco and folk dance, both of which in this context have become stylized beyond recognition of the original dances. This is the style of Spanish dance usually seen in theatres abroad. It is very much what the non-specialist onlooker recognizes as 'Spanish dancing'.

The third and certainly most well-known category is the flamenco, beloved by the tourists and generally (but wrongly) associated with gypsy culture. Nowadays, the gypsies have made it very much their own and provide a great deal of entertainment for the tourist trade, but there are just as many Spaniards dancing flamenco as there are gypsies. If we look back over the centuries we can find the roots from which the flamenco has grown.

For thousands of years traders have visited the southern shores of Spain. Attracted by the abundance of rich ores, Phoenicians, Greeks and

Carthaginians had all established colonies long before the Iberian peninsula was absorbed into the Roman Empire. By this time the region was populated by a lively cosmopolitan community made up of people from all over the eastern and southern Mediterranean. Their culture was made up of a mixture of these many cultures, including their music and dance. By the time that the Romans settled there, the musicians and dancers of Tartessus were recognized and highly prized as entertainers. So much so in fact, that when the Romans expelled all foreigners, the musicians and dancers were allowed to stay. Thus, long before the Moors and the gypsies arrived in Spain, exotic eastern dancing was one of the popular entertainments. It was on this foundation that the unique style of Andalucia was based, and from these roots flamenco grew, undoubtedly influenced by the Arab culture of the Moors, during their occupation of the peninsula. This would strengthen the eastern influence, as the Moorish culture drew on the same eastern exotica that had so enraptured the Romans.

So it is in Persia, Egypt and Arabia that the true origins of flamenco are to be found, and the nomadic gypsies when they eventually settled in Spain were only too ready to adopt this vivid style, which was so well suited to their temperament and performance. The dance has developed into an intricate combination of the four elements: singing, dancing, guitar-playing and *jaleo* (the complex rhythmic hand-clapping and shouts of encouragement). The singing has two contrasting elements: the *cante jondo*, sad and serious singing, which can include *solea*, singing of unrequited love; and, in sharp contrast, the *cante chic*, which is gay, light-hearted and often includes a humorous element. Flamenco gives unlimited scope for virtuosity and unrestrained bravura. It combines the virtuosity of singers, musicians and dancers, with fiery uninhibited rhythms, the stamping, foot tapping like drum rolls and the finger snapping or castanet playing in an exhilarating and breathtaking performance.

Before leaving Spain, we must mention the incredible heritage of ritual dance. Sword and stick

Spanish jota *dancers.*

dances are found everywhere. These men's ritual dances appear in great variety, with the dancers carrying either swords or sticks or as in Aragon, a sword in one hand and a stick in the other. An interesting development is seen in Santiago de Compostela, the great pilgrimage centre in Galicia, where the dancers have now adopted the staves carried by the pilgrims in place of their swords. In Galicia the dances are mostly performed by sailors and fishermen, and the most important celebration takes place on St James' Day, 25 July. On this occasion the local fraternity of fishermen arrive at the church marching in three files of five dancers, linked by their swords and by red cords hung with metal rings. The statue of St James is brought out of the church and three swords are placed on the ground in front of it. A complex ritual dance is then performed over the swords.

Andalusia is synonymous with flamenco but here also there is a sword-dance tradition of hilt and point dancers going from house to house and being rewarded with sweets and drinks. This dance comes from the mining area of Rio Tinto. These mines were being worked as long ago as 2000BC, when they provided the silver for Solomon's temple. World famous for its steel industry, Toledo has its sword dance tradition in which the symbolic beheading of the leader takes place. In Burgos, in the north, the men dance with swords and metal shields, which are clashed as the dancers perform steps very similar to the English morris. This is followed by the usual figures of the hilt and point before making the lock on which the leader is hoisted above their heads. There are innumerable references throughout the country to sword dancing – even in literature; for example, when Don Quixote attended a village wedding he was informed that there would be dangerous dancing with swords and little bells.

Maypole dances are a well-known feature in Spain, especially in the south-east, in Catalonia. The pole is usually carried around the village with each dancer holding the end of a ribbon, forming patterns as they go, and reciting topical verses. There is an interesting girls' maypole from the north, where the girls make only a half circle with very complex patterning and plaiting. Bonfires feature at carnival time and at midsummer, and dancing

Dancer from Galicia, north-west, Spain, carrying a loaf of bread.

goes on throughout the night along with special rituals as, for example, in Valencia when life-sized figures are set alight. The wealth of dance in Spain is enormous, and we have only given the briefest outline of these ancient survivals, but hopefully it can remind us to open our minds to 'Spanish dance' and not think too readily of flamenco or castanets.

25 SWITZERLAND

Swiss dancing has a gentle rhythmical quality, with a comparatively small vocabulary of steps, some pleasing holds and a predominance of couple dances. Switzerland's geographical situation and the ethnological grouping of its people most certainly has moulded the character and culture of their small country. Despite its size, Switzerland is inhabited by four different races, each speaking their own language. In the west, on the lakes of Geneva and Neuchatel, is a French-speaking population; on the south side of the Alps, in Ticino, Italian is used; and in the central and eastern regions, German is the main language; while in the south-east of the country, in the Grisons, the language is Romansch, an ancient language, which is a derivative of Latin. Each of these ethnic groups have their own cultural heritage, which shows in their music and dance but, as one might expect in such a comparatively small area, the overlapping of the people brings about a certain amount of interchange. Thus, in Schaffhausen on the German frontier, the indigenous German-speaking people dance the *française*, typically French as its name indicates; while in Geneva on the French border, the French-speaking population can be seen dancing a Bavarian polka. However, in spite of this interchange, within the four regions, each has its own recognizable style. Each ethnic group has its special characteristics, and these are reflected in its folk tunes, which in turn dictate the quality and style of the dance.

So, looking to the French region, we find the music light and lively and very much reflecting the temperament of the people. It is usually written in either 2/4 or 6/8 time, which gives 'lift' to the tunes and again, fits well with the spoken language – light, quick and expressive. In contrast, in the German-speaking region, the music is more commonly in 3/4 or 4/4 time, and like the language is rather slower, a little heavier, and often more emphatic. The Italian-speaking population of the south have a lively and often sharply accentuated and dramatic approach to their folk songs, while in the Romansch-speaking region, the folk music has a quiet serenity, and is much more harmonious. The music has a gentle quality reminiscent of Christmas carols. Throughout the country, the major key is favoured, regardless of region, and the use of the minor mode is very rare in Switzerland. Everywhere the couple dance dominates the social dance scene and the overall impression is of gentle enjoyment rather than drama and excitement. The step vocabulary is fairly limited – steps tend to be used in their basic constant form, rather than over-decorated, but the use of the arms in the many interesting holds offers a very pleasing picture, with some complex patterning.

Switzerland is scenically very beautiful, and the calendar of the year brings with it a series of beautiful pictures. In the spring, the glorious display of spring flowers and blossoming fruit trees can be breathtaking, while summer brings a wealth of herbs and flowers to the high alpine pastures, where the dairy maids spend the summer months with their herds. Autumn brings to the forests a dazzling array of colour, and as winter approaches, a snowy mantle envelopes the country. Always there is the blue of the lakes, the dark green of the forests and a backdrop of snow-covered mountains, many of which never lose their sparkling white coats. Small wonder that in such pleasant surroundings, the music and dance reflect the overall gentle ambience of the country. The *ländler* is one of the most popular dances and its even rhythmical valse has found favour in all regions. In the Alpine areas it has gradually taken on the character of a country dance and, particularly in the German-speaking central and eastern regions, it has developed its own mimetic style, with the boy taking the lead with a display of stamping, leaping and clapping. In those regions it is extremely lively and full of excitement.

The cowherds make full use of their wooden clogs, the *holzboden*, which they use to emphasize the rhythm of their dances, and which offer them possibilities of development and improvisation. Another very popular dance is the *kreuz polka* (cross polka). This is especially favoured in German-speaking regions, while in the French areas a very similar dance appears as the polka *piquée*. Some square dances can still be found in French-Switzerland, probably the remnants of the once very fashionable quadrille, with either two or four couples placed in square formation. They are named *monferrine*, and the basic motif in each dance is usually the continual changing places of the couples within the set. The *monferrine* is known also in the Italian-speaking Ticino region. Change of places between couples can also develop into change of partners, which brings a lively excitement to the dance. The use of the longways formation is very rare indeed, and only two have been collected, one from Valais and the other from Schaffhausen, probably both imported.

In many of the simple couple dances an element of mime has crept in, reflecting the country folks' love of acting out little scenes of love or comedy. In Appenzell this is carried to some lengths, so that little mime interludes are interpolated between sections of waltzes or polkas. In French-Switzerland we can still find the *picoulet*, often used by children as a singing game, but still also danced by adults. The dancers skip round in a circle holding hands and singing. The leader then moves into the centre and acts out various gestures, with fingers, hand, fist, elbow, foot and head, all of which must be imitated by the circle. Between each action, a skip round in the circle is interpolated. It is now regarded as a 'fun' dance, but its construction is very similar to the ancient 'seven springs' danced for generations by the men of Germany, Holland and the Basque country. Seven again reflects an ancient magic.

Several chain dances can be found in the more remote areas, where they survive under the name of *coraule*, a direct derivative of the carole of medieval times. The *allemande* can be found in both German- and French-Switzerland. The main theme in this dance is the dignified walk of the couples in a large circle. This most certainly reflects its origins in the ancient German promenade dances, which found their way into the ballrooms of Europe and into the music of Beethoven, Bach and Purcell. In its present form in Switzerland, the promenade is followed by a chain, turning steps and usually finishing with a gallop for everyone.

The maypole dance appears in several forms. In Basle it is represented by a young fir tree, while in the Ticino (Italian region) it is a birch tree. In Valais a plaited ribbon dance is danced round the May tree by sixteen boys and girls each holding a ribbon. The mill wheel is preserved in German-Switzerland. It is danced by eight men in a circle. Four of them then lie down and press their feet together in the centre and the other four hold them by their arms and slowly turn them like a mill wheel. The fact that this is an all-male dance indicates its age and possible roots in ritual. The sun wheel is an important motif amongst the pastoral communities of the Alpine regions, and the symbol is often used to decorate the wooden houses and utensils of the farmers and herdsmen, with either paintings or carvings.

At carnival time masked dancers appear. They wear leafy clothes and masks and carry bells and brooms. Accompanied by drummers they dance all day from one inn to another with a strange leaping dance. In the region of Schwyz they are called *nusslers*. A similar ritual is carried out in Appenzell on New Year's Eve. Here they wear fantastic costumes with huge decorated head-dresses and carry giant-size cow bells. Again, the all-male leaping dance denotes its age and origins in ancient ritual. In the Rhine Valley (Canton St Gall) there is a Shrovetide ritual where the dancers wear elaborate head-dresses, masks and bells, and carry small syringes full of water, which they use to sprinkle the crowd, particularly any unmarried girls. Their dance is a solemn polonaise in which they are marshalled by their leader, the king of the maskers. The musical accompaniment varies from region to region, but the old combinations of instruments are gradually being lost since the introduction of the accordion.

So, while we find variety as one would expect in a multi-racial society, there is an overall quality that is very definitely Swiss.

Denmark

Pigernes Aftersang (Girl's Evening Song)

A couple dance. Music 2/4 time.

Formation

Couples in a double circle with boys backing centre and ballroom hold throughout.

Dance Description

Music A

1 Polka counter-clockwise (in big circle).

1 Polka clockwise.

4 Hopsa steps turning – boy commences left foot (LF), girl on right foot (RF) – making two full turns clockwise, while travelling counter-clockwise round the room.

(Hopsa is a small *pas de basque*.)

Music A

Repeat all.

Music B.

Gallop counter-clockwise (16 gallops).

Music B

Repeat gallops clockwise.

APPENDIX II
SWITZERLAND

Montferrine for Four

have their partners on their right.

Dance Description
Music A
6/8 Time.
Commencing on LF, 7 walks clockwise.
On eighth count close R to L, without weight.
8 Gallops to right.

Music B
2/4 Time.
Facing centre, 4 small *pas de basques* to L–R–L–R on the spot, making a bow with the head on each – to centre, to R to L to R. R hand star, 7 walks clockwise. Closing R to L without weight on eighth count.

Music B
Repeat.
Facing centre, 3 walks forward – R–L–R, closing L without weight.
Repeat.
Backwards L–R–L–R, face partner, step to R and point L, in front, step to L and point R, in front.
Turn on the spot to R with 3 walks, R–L–R, and close L to R without weight.

MONTFERRINE FOR FOUR

Formation
Four dancers in a circle with hands joined. Men

Appendix III
NETHERLANDS

BOERENPLOF

A couple dance. Music 2/4 time.

Formation
Couples joined with a peasant hold.*
Boy on the inside.

Dance Description
1 Polka sideways to centre. Boy commence L, girl R.
1 Polka sideways away from centre.
Repeat all (lean into the movement).
Dance 8 step hops turning clockwise and moving counter-clockwise round the room.
Repeat ad lib.

* Peasant hold – boy places hands on girl's waist, while girl places hands on boy's shoulders. The first beat of the first polka and the first step hop are marked with a stamp. In the step hop the raised leg is kept low.

Boerenplof

Appendix IV
Sweden

KLAPPDANS

A couple dance. Music 2/4 time.

Formation
Partners in a double circle with inside hands joined. Boys on inside.

Dance Description:
Music A
Repeat.
Both commence outside foot.
1 Polka forward swinging joined hands backward.
1 Polka forward swinging jointed hands forward.
Repeat the 2 polkas 7 more times.

Music B
Repeat.

Face partner. Girls curtsey placing RF behind and holding skirt. Boys bow (arms at side).
Repeat the curtsey and bow.
Shake R forefinger at partner (count 1 and 2).
Repeat with L.
Turn on spot to L with 4 walks, clapping R hand with partner on first step.
Repeat this section for repeat of music B.

Music A
Repeat.
With a ballroom hold, dance 16 polkas turning travelling counter-clockwise round the room.

Music B
Repeat as before.

Appendix V
Portugal

Passo Largo

𝅘𝅥 = 136

PLAY BARS 9 - 16
AS INTRODUCTION

LAST TIME

186

Passo Largo

Couples in a circle. Music 2/4 time. The steps are well beaten out with an accent on '2'.
Special steps required – change step.
& hop on L 1 small step forward on the RF
& close LF to RF on the ball of foot, 2 small step forward on the RF.
Can be done with either foot – like a hop step ball change.

Formation

Couples side by side facing counter-clockwise.
Boy on inside has R arm round girl's waist.
Girl L hand on boy's R shoulder. R hand on her waist, boy's L hand holds his shirt front.

Dance Description

Boy LF, girl RF, 2 skips forward.
1 Change step turning sharply to face other way.
2 Skips forward travelling clockwise.
1 Change step to face partner.
With a Ballroom hold travel counter-clockwise with 6 polka steps – boy travelling forward, girl backwards.
Turning steps (turning on ball of feet, 2 steps, to 1 bar of music making a half turn on each step (like a *chaîné* turn in ballet). Repeat 2 steps.
2 Polkas turning.
Turning steps. As before.
Repeat ad lib. The last time in place of turning steps, the girl does 4 turns under the boy's raised R arm.

APPENDIX VI
RUSSIA

U Rekje

Moderato

Steps Required
3 Step – 3 steps forward. Pause on 4 but allow the flow of movement to continue. Pivot step.

Formation
Dancers in a circle facing centre, with hands joined low V.

Dance Description
Facing centre. 2 × 3 steps forward. Arms raising to W. Commence R.
Repeat backwards, lowering arms to V.
Step side close side to R.
Repeat to L.
Close feet together and bow.
8 × 3 steps in L.O.D. to R.
Repeat of music 8 pivot steps sideways to R. Close L to R on last one.
Repeat pivots and close to L, bringing arms forward and hands on to hips on last four.
4 Pivots turning to R.
4 Pivots turning to L.

U REKJE

A circle dance. Music 4/4 time.

Close feet together, lowering arms.
Russian bow – R hand to L shoulder, raise above head, bow lowering arm, palm facing forward.

BIBLIOGRAPHY

GENERAL

Baines, A. *Catalogue of Musical Instruments*, Vol 2. Victoria and Albert Museum. HMSO, London 1978.

Coon Carleton Stevens. *The Races of Europe*. The Macmillan Co., Harvard University 1939.

Crosliffe, Barry. *The Celtic World*.

Frazer, Sir James George. *The Golden Bough* (abridged edition 1922). Wordsworth.

Geipel, John. *The Europeans*. Longmans 1969.

Graves, Robert. *The White Goddess*. Faber and Faber, London 1960.

Simpson, Jacqueline. *European Mythology*. Hamlyn, Twickenham 1987.

Simpson, Jacqueline and Roud Steye. *A Dictionary of English Folklore*. Oxford University Press 2000.

COSTUME

Aerni-Von Erlach, Felicitas. *Swiss National Costumes*. Éditions Générales 1970.

Andersen, Ellen. *Folk Costumes in Denmark*. Hassing, Copenhagen 1952.

Aubert Octave Louis. *Les Costumes Bretons Leurs Histoire, Leurs Evolutions*. St Brieuc Aubert 1936.

Baur-Heinhold, Margarete. *Deutsche Trachten Königstein*. Langewiesche 1958.

Benaki Museum, Athens. *Hellenic National Costume* (2 vols). Athens 1948–1954.

Bogatyrev, Peter. *The Function of Folk Costume in Moravian Slovakia*. Mouton, The Hague 1971.

Bruhne, W. and Tilke, M. *A Pictorial History of Costume*. Zwemmer, London 1955.

Fochler, Rudolf. *Traghten. Aus Österreich*. Wels and Munich Welsermühl 1965.

Gáborján, A. *Hungarian Peasant Costumes Budapest*. Corvina, London Clematis 1969.

Gallois, Emile. *Costumes Espagnols*. Laurens, Paris 1939.

Gallois, Emile. *Le Costume en Espagne et au Portugal*. Laurens, Paris 1954.

Gibert, John. *National Costumes of the World*. Hamlyn, London 1972.

Hammerstein, Hans Von. *Trachten Der Alpenländer*. Reichner, Vienna 1933.

Harrold, Robert (Illus. Phyllida Legg). *Folk Costumes of the World*. Blandford Press Ltd, Poole 1978.

Hulkemb, Riet. *National Costumes in Holland*. Meulenhoff, Amsterdam 1951.

Huxley, Francis. *Peoples of the World in Colour*. Blandford, London 1964.

Lepage-Medvey, E. *French Costumes*. [Preface by André Varagnac.] Hyperion, Paris 1939.

Mann, Kathleen. *Peasant Costume in Europe* (Books I & II). Adam and Charles Black, London 1938.

Markov, J. *The Slovak National Dress through the Centuries*. Artia, Prague 1956.

Metropolitan Museum of Art, New York. *History of Russian Costume*. By L. Elfimovia and others. New York 1977.

National Museum, Finland. *Folk Costumes and Textiles*.

Noorlander, H. *Wooden Shoes. Their Makers and their Wearers*. Armhem–Zutphen 1978.

Palotay, G. and Konecsmi, C. *Hungarian Folk Costumes*. Officinia, Budapest 1938.

Primmer, Kathleen. *Scandinavian Peasant Costume*. Black, London 1939.

Šmikous, Karel and Šotkova, Blažena. *National Costumes of Czechoslovakia*. Artia, Prague 1956.

Snowden, James. *The Folk Dress of Europe*. Mills and Boon Ltd, London 1979.

Stryjenska, Zofia. *Polish Peasant Costumes*. Szwedzicki, Nice 1939.

Tilke, M. *Costume Patterns and Designs*. Zwemmer, London 1956.

Valeva, Maria G. and Lepartsova, Eugenia. *Bulgarian Folk Costumes* (2 vols). Bulgarian Academy of Sciences, Sofia 1961–74.

VICTORIA AND ALBERT MUSEUM, LONDON

A list of works on costume in the National Art Library, London.
Eyre and Spottiswoode, 1881.

DANCE

Alford, Violet. *The Hobby Horse and Other Animal Masks*. The Merlin Press, London 1978.

– *Sword Dance and Drama*. The Merlin Press, London 1935.

– and Gallop, Rodney. *The Traditional Dance*. Methuen and Co., London 1935.

Allenby-Jaffé, Nigel. *Folk Dance of Europe*. Folk Dance Enterprises, Skipton 1990.

Allenby-Jaffé, Nigel and Margaret. *European Folk Dance Series. The Netherlands*. Folk Dance Enterprise, Skipton 1982.

– *Denmark*. Folk Dance Enterprises, Skipton 1987.

Armstrong, Lucile. *Dances of Spain. South Centre and N.W.* Parrish and Co., London 1950.

– *N.E &. East*. Parrish and Co., London 1950.

Bragaglia, Anton Giulio. *Dance Populare Italiane*.

Breathnach, Breandan. *Folk Music and Dance of Ireland*. The Mercier Press, Dublin 1971.

Budey, George. *Dances of Hungary*. Max Parrish and Co., London 1950.

Crosfield, Domini. *Dances of Greece*. Max Parrish and Co., London 1948.

Collan, Anni and Ynguar, Heikel. *Dances of Finland*. Max Parrish and Co., London 1948.

Flett, J.P. and J.M. *Traditional Step Dancing in Lakeland*. The English Folk Dance and Song Society 1979.

– *Traditional Dancing in Scotland*. Routledge and Kegan Paul, London 1964.

Grindea, Miron and Carola. *Dances of Romania*. Max Parrish and Co., London 1952.

Harrold, Robert, Wingrave, Helen and Del Campo, Conchita. *Spanish Dancing*. Parapress, Tunbridge Wells 1950.

Rippon, Hugh. *Discovering English Folk Dance*. Shire Publications Ltd., Aylesbury 1981.

Katsarova, Reina. *Dances of Bulgaria*. Max Parrish and Co., London 1951.

Martin, György. *Hungarian Folk Dance*. Corvina Press, Budapest 1974.

Nordiske Museet, Stockholm. *Swedish Folk Dances*. Stockholm 1939.

O'Rafferty, Peador and Gerald. *Dances of Ireland*. Parrish and Co., London 1953.

Petrides, Ted. *Greek Dances*. Lycabettus Press, Athens 1975.

Sach, Curt. *World History of Dance*. George Allen and Unwin Ltd, London 1938.

Salvén, Erik. *Dances of Sweden*. Max Parrish, London 1949.

Sharp, Cecil J. *Sword Dances of Northern England*. Novello and Co, Ltd, London 1951.

Ven-Ten Bensel, Elise Van Der and Ven, D.J. Van Der. *De Volksdans in Nederland*. A. Rutgers, Naarden 1942.

Williams, Huw. *Welsh Clog/Step Dancing*.

Witzig, Louise. *Dances of Switzerland*. Max Parrish, London 1949.

Zeromska, Olga. *Tance – Polskie Narodowe i Regionalne*. (Poland). Almps Book Co., London 1963.

INDEX